AMERICANS

WARNED OF JESUITISM,

OR

THE JESUITS UNVEILED

BY

JOHN CLAUDIUS PITRAT,

A MEMBER OF THE UNIVERSITY OF FRANCE; FOUNDER AND EX-EDITOR OF THE JOURNAL "LA PRESSE DU PEUPLE" IN PARIS; AND FORMERLY A ROMISH PRIEST.

JESUITISM is a monstrous machine of destruction, which, its spring being in Rome, its wheels everywhere, moves the world.

NEW YORK:

J. S. REDFIELD, CLINTON HALL,

CORNER OF NASSAU AND BEEKMAN STREETS.

1851.

TABLE OF CONTENTS.

CONTENTS.

CHAPTER VI.

SUMMARY OF THE DOCTRINES WHICH THE JESUITS HAVE HELD AND STILL HOLD, HAVE TAUGHT AND STILL TEACH.

CHAPTER VII.

SUMMARY OF THE HISTORY OF THE JESUITS.

NOTICE OF THE AUTHOR.

AMERICANS, I am a stranger among you; then allow me to introduce myself to you. All that I shall say respecting myself I can prove by authentic testimony and official letters.

I was born near Lyons, France. My father and mother were Roman Catholics, and brought me up in that belief. My father died when I was seven years of age. After my first studies, my mother sent me to colleges directed by Romish priests, where, witnessing the scandalous lives of the clergymen, I became an infidel. Having completed my studies—I was then seventeen years of age—I came again to the maternal house. My mother, who saw my indifference to religious practices, even for prayer, questioned me about it.

I answered that I had no longer a religious belief; that the Bible was a tissue of tales; that Christ had been merely a philosopher; that the gospel did not contain the true teaching of Christ; that our souls are not immortal; that the doctrine of the future life is a kingly and sacerdotal invention to lead and oppress more surely the people: in short, I answered that religion is mere quackery, and that the priests are either mountebanks, abusing the public credulity, or ignorant men. I added that I doubted even of the existence of God.

My mother appeared deeply afflicted; still she listened to me with attention and without uttering a single word. When I stopped, she raised her eyes to heaven and exclaimed: "What a misfortune for a poor mother! I have sent to the priests my son who was a Christian, and they send him again to me an infidel!" She wept bitterly.

My mother, who had remarked that since my arrival I was constantly silent and thoughtful, asked me what was the cause of my anxiety. I refused to answer: but she shed tears so abundantly, spoke to me so tenderly, and used other maternal means which were so irresistible, that I yielded, and averred that I had resolved to kill myself; for not believing in a future life, and considering the present as a burden rather than a gift, I thought that it was a reasonable act to cast it away, and to imitate one of my friends, who, partaking of my principles and applying their consequences, had shot himself.

I cannot paint what my mother felt on account of my answer. . . Her affliction moved me so much, that I resolved, for her sake, to bear life.

But how could I live without religious principles to settle my mind and rule my behavior? I could not. When I looked for them, thirsting for truth, God rewarded my sincerity. I became a Christian—but, alas! I was to be a victim to the prejudices of my education and instruction, of my imagination, of my youth, and chiefly of my ignorance of the priests.

Knowing what they had taught me and nothing else, I thought that Romanism was the true and exclusively true religion. I espoused it so blindly and so ardently, that, against the will of my mother, and in spite of her entreaties, her tears, her anger, and threats, I resolved to be a priest, and went to the Ecclesiastical School of Brou (Département de l'Ain), where I studied Theology during four years, was ordained priest, and started out in the world so furious an Aristocrat, so strong a believer in Popery, and so devoted an adherent, that I would have killed a Protestant, even a Democrat, as readily as I would have killed a fly, at the order of my Ecclesiastical Superiors. Of course, I was a fanatic, but a true Romish priest (I mean a clergyman faithful to his sacerdotal obligations) cannot be otherwise.

I had so cruelly broken the hopes of my mother, and I had been, with my obstinacy, so displeasing to her, that she married again, after many years of widowhood, without informing me of it.

God alone knows all that we have both suffered since that time in living far from each other, for I am her only son, and she could give me a comfortable living!

Here begins my sacerdotal life. Americans, perhaps it would be interesting for you to know what I have learned about the Ecclesiastical Administrations, and about the political relations between Governments and Romish leaders: perhaps you would be pleased if I should anatomize before your eyes the gigantic body of Popery, and explain to you the physiological functions of all its systems, of all its members and organs; but I cannot, for it would require many volumes. Likewise, you perhaps would be glad to know several political affairs in which I have been mingled in the mysterious closets of the castles of the nobility; at first to cast down Louis Philippe, and crown in his stead the Duke of Bordeaux, and after a while (when we had despaired of success) to make firm the throne of Louis Philippe against the attacks of the Liberals: but I should be obliged to point out the names of many of my actual enemies to whom I will never do an injury.

I exercised the ministry several years in Lagnieux and Thoissey, towns of my native diocess in the neighborhood of Lyons; whilst I studied medicine for the purpose of being useful to the poor. Thence, on the invitation of the Archbishop of Bordeaux, I went to that city, where I fought strongly against the Protestants, trying by all means to convert them to Romanism.

I owe to the last circumstance my intellectual, moral, and religious emancipation; for, though studying Protestantism with prejudices and hostile views, I began to suspect that my intolerance was anti-Christian; that my zeal for Catholicism was a black hatred against Protestantism; that religion ought not to be a political lever, but ought to be quite distinct from the civil government; that the Pope and the Bishops trample on the reason and the gospel in imposing upon the priests and the people a blind belief and obedience; that Catholicism as it was, and as it is, is not fitted for the present and future generations, and that the aristocratical principles which Popery generates are mostly injurious to society.

In order to have more leisure to study these vital questions —the solution of which was to change entirely the direction of my life—I asked and obtained the care of a small congregation in the neighborhood of Bordeaux. There, after mature investigations and meditations, my doubts were changed into certainty: I remained a Roman Catholic, but I considered my church as a monstrous compound in which the human elements stifled the Divine institution, exactly as in a tree the useless branches absorb the fruit of those which are fruitful: in one word, I wished an entire reformation in regard to the points which were not fundamental principles. As to the liberal and democratic principles, I admitted them fully; I became a Republican.

As soon as my new religious and political opinions were known, the nobles, the aristocrats, and the priests, denounced me to the Archbishop as a man dangerous to society and to the church. The Archbishop was alarmed, and tried to win me by promises and kindness. But I did not yield. Then he used another way: knowing that among my friends I had many distinguished men who were Liberals and Republicans, he obliged me not to see them, chiefly the celebrated writer and orator Mr. Bac, whom the great Lamartine styled (in his Journal "Le Bien Publique") "Le Vergniaud de la Revolution," namely, "the first orator of the Revolution of 1848." For that purpose he appointed me pastor of a parish very distant from Bordeaux. I did not accept it, and left the diocess to go to Paris, intending to write against the abuses of the church, and against the absolutism, tyranny, and anti-Chistian behavior of the Bishops.

Now, Americans, I place before you the following letters to inform you about my standing in the diocess of Bordeaux, both as a man and as a priest. I translate them from French into English.

ARCHBISHOPRIC
OF
BORDEAUX.

BORDEAUX, May 7, 1849.

For a long while, my dear M. Pitrat, I have been without news from you. Do you believe that I forget you? Please write to me as soon as possible, or rather come to see me.

Your very devoted,

† FERDINAND, Archbishop of Bordeaux.

The Archbishop addressed me the following letter when he intended to send me to another parish.

ARCHBISHOPRIC
OF
BORDEAUX.

BORDEAUX, September 19, 1847.

MY DEAR M. PITRAT: I desire ardently that you go in a short time to Pleigne-selve, your new parish. My affection for you is now what it was when you understood it so well. I shall always be happy to give you proofs of it in every circumstance. Do not inform your congregation about the contents of your letter. Yours in N. S.

† FERDINAND, Archbishop of Bordeaux.

When I left the diocess, the Archbishop gave me the following official letter, which I translate from the Latin.

We, Ferdinand Francis August Donnet . . . . Archbishop of Bordeaux, declare and make known, that our beloved John Claudius Pitrat is a pious and honest priest; that he is not tied by ecclesiastical censures and sentences, hindering him from exercising the ministry in whatever diocess he shall visit (still with the consent of his Superiors).

Moreover, we declare and make known, that he deserves to be treated everywhere as a priest who has obtained from us the permission to leave our diocess.

Delivered in Bordeaux, under our seal, with our signature and that of our General Secretary, the 4th of October, 1847.

† FERDINAND.

By the order of the Illustrious and Reverend Lord–Lord–Archbishop of Bordeaux.

MONTARIOL,
Can. Hon. Secretary.

Before going to Paris, I visited my mother in the neighborhood of Lyons, where the Bishop of Belley, who had ordained me, wrote to me the following letter:

BISHOPRIC
OF
BELLEY.

MY DEAR PRIEST,

I would be pleased to know what you are doing now, for I retain my affection towards you. I still suppose that your actual position enables you to be useful to the church. If I am not mistaken, you were a little scrupulous when you exercised the ministry in Thoissey. The practice of the ministry makes us bold, but we must ayoid the other extreme, and keep the middle track.

Give me a part in your prayers and good works. I renew to you the assurance of my sincere affection. † A. R. EV.

In Paris I did not take employment in the ecclesiastical administration. I united with many clergymen who partook of my principles, and we wrôte in several newspapers which opened to us their columns. Soon after I became one of the founders, editors, and publishers of the daily journal, "La Presse du Peuple," "The Press of the People." I sent an address to the priests of France, to invite them to claim their rights against the Bishops. In October, 1848, the Government sent one to our colonies, of the sea of Antilles, to found a National College, which the Provisory Government had decreed after having emancipated the slaves.

I went to Guadaloupe with Mr. Chauvel, General Inspector of Public Instruction, and while we waited for the funds necessary for that costly undertaking, I was appointed Intimate Secretary of the Director of the Interior, and attached to the administration of personal worship and public instruction. I accompanied the Director of the Interior in a tour through the colony, we found the greatest part of the plantations abandoned, the buildings wasted, the lands uncultivated, and even the sugar canes not harvested for want of hands. The population was divided into two camps. The one, that of the few whites, who having not been allowed to leave the country, were struggling against poverty and despondency, and had to fear even for their lives. The other, of the colored people, who had fled from the plantations, burned many of them—did not work, stole from the whites, food, clothes, and money, and plotted (at least their leaders), to renew the drama of Hayti, to kill the whites remaining in the island. The Government of the colony had to pacify the country by conciliating the parties, but it was a difficult tȧsk. A plot for a massacre had been unveiled. The Governor of Dominie (an English possession) had informed Mr. Fiéron, Governor of Guadaloupe, that the colored people had purchased from

English merchants, ammunition. A goelëtte loaded with guns and powder had been seized. On these the Governor having employed energetic and coercive means, he had become the object of the hatred and attacks of the blacks, who through their representatives slandered him in Paris. As my political friends, being deceived and misled, supported them in the National Assembly, I sent to them an exact statement of the situation of affairs in Guadaloupe. At the same time, I wrote to show to the people how wise, conservative, and truly Republican, though firm, were the political measures taken by the Government to preserve the country from the most threatening calamities. I undertook for that purpose, the publication of a series of articles, but for reasons of the highest importance, I was not allowed to complete my task.

This is a letter which the editor of "L'avernir" newspaper, which has contributed powerfully to the safety of the colony, wrote to me about it:—

Pointe a Petre, March 5, 1849.

My Dear Sir: Those who said to you, that in continuing the series of your articles, you would be more noxious than useful to the country, are false prophets; you have faithfully represented what was the situation of the country under the last administration. Now, you would have merely to support the actual administration which is devoted to the country, and to control its acts, in order to oblige it to keep the middle track. You will not be responsible, but the newspaper alone. If you write you will save the administration and be useful to the country. Now the iron is hot, the fresh bomb has burst; you must continue the fire. If you will not, I am compelled to do that in your stead. The position of the Governor and of the Director of the Interior is at stake, and depend on it, if wrongly informed I do not succeed, and the hostile camp overcome, the consequences will be imputable to you. Then reflect, and consult about it the Director of the Interior. I salute you heartily,

DE GONDRECOURT.

Under these circumstances I became acquainted with the Ecclesiastical Superior of the colony, who won my esteem and confidence. He approved of my ideas of reformation of our Church, engaged me to enter again in the ecclesiastical administration; and assured me that the organization of the Church would suit me better in the United States, than in any other country. I yielded to his counsel and sacrificed my temporal prospects in a political career to the triumph of my ideas. He gave me letters of introduction to the Bishop of New Orleans, Mr. Rousselon, his grand vicar, and to Mr. Percher, editor of the newspaper "La Propagateur Catholique," and I took passage on board of a goelëtte, sailing to St. Thomas (a Danish colony), to go from that place to New Orleans. I spent a certain while in that island, waiting for a ship, but commerce having been cast down there by the emancipation of the slaves, not one was coming. Then I was compelled to avail myself of the opportunity of the brig Glencoe, destined to New York, to go from that city to New Orleans.

After three days sailing I fell dangerously sick, and remained unconscious till I arrived at the hospital at quarantine in New York. I met with Irish and Germans, without understanding a single word of what they or the servants uttered to me, being dangerously sick, having only three shillings, and being without an acquaintance.

Thanks to the good care of the Director of the hospital, I was cured in three weeks, of suffering, and in one month I was entirely well. This gentleman had been kind to me so far as to call for me the Romish priest who attended the hospital, but this clergyman believing that he had fulfilled his sacerdotal duty in conversing with me four or five minutes, did not visit me again. I went to the city. But what was I to do, not knowing English, being without money and without acquaintances? I wandered several hours in the streets, feeling exhausted with fatigue, till I reached a mean inn kept by a Frenchwoman, who accepted me as a boarder. A few days after, I visited Bishop Hughes, who received me with exquisite politeness, but who, as soon as I mentioned my name and profession, said to me with a Jesuitical smile and fair words, that he "felt sorry to have to attend to some important business; that in two hours he would be at my service." I was faithful to the appointment, but what I had foreseen happened; he did not come, and sent me a certain priest with manners as attractive as the door of a dungeon, and with a voice as soft as that of a hangman. He treated me so impolitely and so harshly, that after a moment of conversation I took my hat and went out, still with politeness.

The Rev. Mr. Lafont, a French priest, by a polite and kind reception, made a compensation for the mean proceedings of the Bishop, and of the roughness of the priest. Presuming that my travelling expenses, etc., had left me without money, he offered me twenty dollars, which I accepted as a loan. I paid my board, and my passage in the ship Rajaz, starting for New Orleans, and with two dollars which I had saved, I purchased some bread, etc. I embarked, but the voyage lasted forty days; and after fifteen days I was without food. God alone knows what I have suffered with hunger, being too proud to ask for anything or to show my wants. Two Spaniards, who suspected my position, had pity on me and compelled me to accept some of their biscuits, etc.; but while I was eating, several sailors barked at me, to intimate that I was like a dog, begging from his master what was left of his dinner; a strange position for me, when I recollected the former luxury of my life! However, I kept up my spirits, for I was an apostle in my belief; and I knew that apostleship is martyrdom.

As soon as we landed at New Orleans, it was in September of last year; I went to the Bishop, the Right Reverend Mr. Blanc, who received me heartily, and has since that time lavished upon me the most delicate attentions. Certainly, had my conscience allowed me to exercise the ministry I would not have left his Diocess. For, though I do not partake of his religious principles, I confidently believe that he is both sincere in his belief and a true Christian. He is the first Romish Bishop I have met with, though I know many in Europe, who is not either immoral, avaricious, tyrannical and hypocritical, or a mountebank.

He gave me money to say masses, and sent me for the purpose of studying English, to the Right Reverend Chanche, Bishop of Natchez, whose kindness I shall never forget. I spent three months in Natchez, and from that place was sent to Milliken's Bend, to take charge of a small congregation. I have never met a more tolerant and truly Christian people than these Catholics. I feel happy in recollecting their kindness towards me, chiefly that of Mr. Minnis, Mr. and Mrs. Maher, whose names I mention because they are objects of the greatest regard throughout that country.

I took charge of the congregation for three months, but no longer believing several fundamental articles of the Romish creed, I sent my resignation to the Bishop of New Orleans, and came to Louisville.

Americans, I produce the three following letters, as proof that I have left the Romish Clergy voluntarily. This first was written to me by the Bishop of New Orleans, while I lived in Milliken's Bend. (It is written in English.)

New Orleans, March 7, 1850.

My Dear Mr. Pitrat:—I received, at last, your long-desired letter, of the 18th of February. It gives me great pleasure to hear that you are pleased with the welcome you received from the gentlemen to whom I had recommended you, and that their kind attention to you continues the same. I rejoice, above all things, that you have improved in English so far as to be able to preach every Sunday. This is, undoubtedly, the most efficient means of improving still more, at the same time that you render your ministry quite profitable to the people. I see that the congregation of Milliken's Bend is yet small; but it will progress in time. Perseverance in zeal and good example, will bring many into the fold, in proportion as they will receive instruction. I desire very much that the Catholics of Milliken's Bend, should appreciate the benefit of your ministry among them; because, I am at this moment in great want of priests. Indeed, I do not know how we will do this next summer, unless we receive some aid from other quarters. If you were not sufficiently appreciated there, and profitably occupied for the salvation of souls, I would not feel justifiable in leaving you there, while we have other places in which your ministry would be more profitable to religion. I will try, however, to spare you as long as I can for their spiritual benefit—if I find you succeed with them. Religion suffers a great deal in our city. * * * * *

Mr. Rousselon is well, and sends you his best compliments.

Adieu, believe me most affectionately, dear Mr. Pitrat,

Yours in Christ,

† ANT, Bishop of New Orleans.

The Very Reverend Mr. Rousselon, Grand Vicar of the Bishop at New Orleans, wrote to me the following letter, after my resignation: [I translate it from the French.]

VERY DEAR SIR:—As my Lord is absent for a few days, I have opened your letter, which has thrown me into the deepest affliction. I cannot believe what you say to him. Is it possible that you have taken so lamentable a resolution, which will afflict the heart of our Bishop, who intended to call you near him and inform you about it? Please be not too hasty in such a design. Reflect, pray to God to enlighten you. As to me, I will pray, and will order prayers for you. The proof of confidence which you have given me, allow me to entreat you to communicate to me your future projects. You know my affection towards you, and in order to give you another proof of it, I had begged and obtained from the Bishop, that you live with us in the Bishopric—you would have come to the city in May. Then appreciate the greatness of disappointment and affliction. I repeat it, "reflect" on so important a business.

I wait with impatience for your answer, and entreat you to believe I am your very devoted friend.

E. ROUSSELON, V. G.

New Orleans, April 2, 1850.

The Bishop of New Orleans wrote to me the following letter which I translate from the French:

NEW ORLEANS, April, 1850.

MY DEAR MR. PITRAT:—I have just returned from a pastoral visit. I cannot express to you what I have felt in reading your letter of resignation. What! is it possible, my dear priest, that after the temporal advantages which you have sacrificed to enter again into your ecclesiastical calling, you renounce it! . . . and when in my arrangements I had resolved to offer you a share in my living! . . . O! please, my dear priest, reflect; your eternal salvation is at stake, . . . I think that my kindness towards you deserves your confidence, . . . pray, unveil to me your heart about the motives of so dreadful a resolution! I will not abuse it; you can trust in my word. Do not hasten the execution of your design till you get an answer from me. If you prefer, go to Natchez to ask counsel. Pray God with all your heart, for you are about to sacrifice your future prospects and your eternity. I am starting for the Red River, . . . but it matters not, write to me in New Orleans, I shall receive your letter.

I will not forget you in my prayers. This morning I have said the mass for you. Farewell again.

Your devoted and affectionate servant,

† ANT, Bishop of New Orleans.

In reading these two letters I felt so moved, that I shed abundant tears. I was so sorry to leave men so deserving of my esteem, affection, and gratitude, that had I been permitted to practise with my conscience, I would have devoted myself to their friendship; but I could not. All I can do is, to preserve feelings of gratitude towards them, which will never die in my heart.

Americans, such has been my past life. Judge for yourselves whether or not my standing, both as a man and as a priest has been honorable; whether or not I deserve your trust and good will.

AMERICANS WARNED OF JESUITISM,

OR

THE JESUITS UNVEILED.

CHAPTER I.

INTRODUCTION.

AMERICANS, whatever you may be—in politics, "Whigs" or "Democrats"—in religion, "Catholics" or "Protestants"—I respectfully address this writing to you, hoping that it will be useful to you. It shall not be a book of controversy, but rather a moral and political one. What I shall write shall be so astonishing, so frightful, that I beg you to scrutinize its truthfulness by the strictest and most minute inquiry. I, withal, should entreat you to be indulgent to my style, for I am a Frenchman, and began one year ago the alphabet of your language.

I foresee all that is reserved for me, all the storms which ignorance, fanaticism, and, above all, hypocrisy, will heap upon my head, but I fear not. I owe myself to truth, to freedom, to your Republic: in spite of my reluctance, I write.

CHAPTER II.

AIM OF THE JESUITS IN THE UNITED STATES.

Americans, your Republic is the polar star of the apostles of liberty, who wander on the ocean of systems, at least at at present, inapplicable. She is the sun that enlightens the nations, the hope of the oppressed, and the terror of tyrants. The goddess of freedom, with exuberant breasts, having been her mother, and a soul of unknown power, a supernatural perfection having been bestowed upon her, her first breath in the political life, was the breath of a giant. She, still in her cradle, shook off the yoke of England, the colossus of the civilized and uncivilized world, who tried to stifle her. Since that time, so wonderful has been her growth, that the enlightened of all countries, the victims of all tyrannies, and the lovers of freedom, seeing on her forehead a kind of divine seal, flock together under her sheltering arms.

Undoubtedly your Republic rests upon the granite, but I come from below the ground; there I have seen miners—I want to warn you. Their hammers, forged in the hatred of political and religious freedom, in the fire of fanaticism and superstition, are harder, more durable than diamond: the point is sharp, piercing, irresistible. I saw the granite falling in large and heavy blocks, as fast as they sap. Of course they must work a long while, before they reach the surface, and blow up your Republic—but these miners never die, soon or late they will succeed.

Do not believe they do not work because the strokes of their hammers are without echo. I warn you, for I know them—I have seen them—even, I was ready to sap with them, when, yielding to the voice of my conscience, loving liberty, loving your welfare, your Republic, I threw away my hammer and fled.

"Who are these miners?" ask you.

They are many Societies, of which the most formidable is that of the Jesuits. They hate each other, and war incessantly for sharing the spoils of the Catholic believers and unbelievers, but in darkness—as robbers contending about their booty in the forest—lest the thread of their trade be discovered. However, though they hate one another, they heartily agree to attack your institutions, your freedom; in one word, to undermine your Republic.

"The Jesuits and other Romish Religious Societies," reply you, "are less dangerous in our Republic than you believe."

Take history and read. You will see that the fame of the misdeeds of several of them, a long while, filled the world; that they spread ruin through all nations, darkened the pages of history, and shed the blood of the apostles of the gospel and of democracy. Since the sun of improvement, in his rising, has enlightened the world, they, like birds of darkness, whose eyes have been burnt, have artfully slided out of the governmental life, or rather, being too cowardly to fight openly, they, as moles, break through to light only when they can surely stir up nations against nations, provinces against provinces, citizens against citizens, kindred against kindred—as lately in Switzerland—but everywhere and silently, they loose the ties of society, and, hiding their mischievous hands, endeavor to deceive their looks. They borrow among you a false skin, proclaim that they love your freedom, worship your Republic . . . . But, beware . . .Now, as always, it is truly said:

Timeo Danäos et dona ferentes. "I fear the Greeks, even when they bring gifts."

"Since you believe," reply you, "that the Jesuits and other Romish Religious Societies hate and sap our freedom, our institutions, and our Republic, unveil to us their principles, what they are. Then we will draw the consequences."

Americans, read attentively what I shall write, and reflect about it. Afterward you will judge for yourselves.

I shall unveil only the Jesuits, for all the other Societies which I denounce as dangerous to your Republic are educated and taught nearly the same way in the noviciate, hold almost the same principles, and have pretty much the same spirit, and the same views. The Female Romish Religious Societies, indeed, are not initiated in all mysteries of their Orders, but, they are bound to the blindest obedience to the priests, their absolute leaders; consequently, are as dangerous as they, even, in one sense more dangerous, because, uniting to the charms of their sex the sincerity of their corporal, intellectual, and moral slavery, they are most influential on Catholic and Protestant families.

CHAPTER III.

ORGANIZATION AND ADMINISTRATION OF THE ORDER OF THE JESUITS.

SECTION I.—*Organization of the Order of the Jesuits.*

AMERICANS, the Jesuits, who fill the Roman Catholic Churches, invade your colleges, and educate your children, who are scattered every where in the richest cities of the United States, who are in Oregon, in California, wherever money is made, whom you meet aboard of the steamboats and the railroads with a studied smile, eyes cast down, very modestly dressed, and with the most reserved posture—looking so humbly—are those men whose *organization and administration, education in their houses of noviciate, doctrines and teaching, past and cotemporary history,* I shall summarily expose to you.

The Order of the Jesuits is divided into seven classes or categories:

I. Jesuits of the short gown.
II. The Novices.
III. The Approved Scholars.
IV. The Temporal Coadjutors or Lay Friars.
V. The Spiritual Coadjutors.
VI. The Professed.
VII. The General.

The Jesuits of the short gown are those Roman Catholics who do not take the same vows as the Jesuits, but who feign piety, confess, take the sacrament in hypocrisy, or, at least, practise the external ceremonies of Catholicism, neglecting the spirit and moral of the gospel; in short, who veil their selfishness, impiety, improbity, and immorality, under the appearance of religion. In Europe they are numberless, everywhere, and stand on all the steps of the social scale.

The Novices are the beginners, the children of the jesuitical life, whom the Reverend Fathers raise and prepare in their houses of noviciate, to become worthy members of their adopted family. After a certain time of retreat and probation, they undergo an examination, take communion, and then submitted to a second trial (Examen, ch. i. 59; Instit. Societ. 1, page 317). Two years having expired, they take vows and advance another grade in the hierarchy of the Order.

The Approved Scholars are those who, after two years of noviciate and several less important examinations, have vowed poverty, chastity, and obedience. They are generally admitted to the higher course of Theology, where they are taught the principles which shall be exposed farther on.

The Temporal Coadjutors are those who have charge of the subaltern management of the material business.

The Spiritual Coadjutors are those who, after long trials and being priests, confess, preach, go to the Missions, teach, direct, fill some inferior employments in the Society, and are sometimes Rectors of Colleges. They are, properly speaking, the blind and material body of the jesuitical army.

The Professed are those who, having been novices two years, Approved Scholars and Spiritual coadjutors, take the four solemn vows of poverty, chastity, obedience to the Superiors of the Order, and of obedience to the Pope. A critical examination on their jesuitical learning and behavior, on their devotedness to the Order, has, ten years before, decided their irrevocable incorporation; but, being destined to be initiated to many secrets of the Order, lest, their conscience being not entirely dead, they should betray, they do not know this decision during all this time, and are submitted to other trials. The Professed constitute the general officers of the army of the Jesuits.

The General of the Order is elected for life, by the great congregation. This great congregation is composed of all the Provincial officers, and two Professed of each Province, sent to Rome by all the Professed, and moreover, of certain Superiors.

(The Reverend Father Jesuit De Ravignan. De l'Existence et de l'Custit ut des Jesuits, pp. 53, 54.)

Thus all Jesuits, not initiated into the secrets of the Order, have not a deliberative vote in the vital election of the General.

SECTION II.—*Administration of the Order of the Jesuits.*

The administration of the Order of the Jesuits is divided into Assistances, the Assistances into Provinces, the Provinces into Houses.

The General is the centre—the head of all this immense and complicated administration. His power is absolute and without control. He is so omnipotent that he has the right of deciding and directing, without one exception, all the material, political, spiritual, and religious interests, not only of all the Order, but of all individuals, who are bound to reveal to him their deepest thoughts, feelings, all they know, even their sins.

He has, in his seven palaces of Rome, and keeps registered, all the christian and family names of the Jesuits, their age, country, the appreciation of their past life, both in their families and in the world, their temperament, capacity, character, learning, qualities, vices, employments, residences: all about their parents and kindred, viz., their profession and social condition, the number of their children, the amount of their fortune, the presumed patrimonial allowance and family's inheritance which each Jesuit, at the death of his father, mother, and kindred, shall get and bring to the Order.

Moreover, the General has and keeps registered the exact amount of ali money which each Jesuit receives in his convent, in preaching sermons, in replacing, for the mass and ceremonies of Sunday, the Curates and Vicars who take trips for their health or business, or go to the springs, or take other sorts of pleasure; all that he receives in saying masses for devotees and other Catholics, or in administering the sacraments; all that he receives by gifts and donations: the whole amount of expenses and receipts of each convent.

Again, the General has and keeps registered the number of all Colleges of the Order, that of the scholars of each of them, the character, qualities, defects, and vices, of those who belong to the richest families, their less or more favorable disposition towards the Order; all programmes of these colleges, the amount of all receipts and expenses, and exact statement of their standing, property, and of all means used to get scholars. The General has and keeps registered the number, fortune, acquaintance, friends, kindred, and children, of all respectable and influential families among merchants, capitalists, bankers, proprietors, officers of governments, in both the civil and military departments, of all Catholic, even Protestant countries; the number, fortune, and disposition, of the rich ladies and gentlemen whom the Reverend Fathers confess, chiefly of the old and rich maids, whose inheritance, by a prudent confession and artful direction, they will obtain.

He has, too, and keeps registered, an exact information of the learning and influence of the various Faculties of medicine, laws, sciences; the number of all universitary colleges, of their presidents, directors, teachers, and scholars, notes about their favorable or hostile dispositions towards the Order; the number of individuals in all religious Orders, Corporations, and Nunneries, of their receipts and expenses, all documents about their means and proceedings to eclipse or to prejudice the Jesuits, either by more celebrated preachers, or by a greater consideration and influence among the people, or by a higher ability and artfulness in obtaining the favor, gifts, and protection, of the richest and most powerful families.

He has and keeps registered secret notices of the private life, of the political, administrative, and religious views of all Catholic Bishops, of all their Great-Vicars, Canons, Chaplains of Nunneries, influential priests, and generally of the secular clergy, even of the talented and distinguished Protestant ministers.

Lastly, the General has and keeps registered the most intimate notes of the private life and diplomacy of all Governors of Provinces, Ministers, Kings, Emperors, and Presidents of Republics. In what manner does the General get these documents? For what purpose?—In what manner? By spies, namely, by the Jesuits with the short gown, who are in all classes of society, and who, to earn the favors and protection of the Reverend Fathers, are incessantly upon the watch for news to communicate them to their dear and powerful leaders. The General gets these documents chiefly by the confessional. Witness the past and present social events: the ladies are potent on the human mind and heart; they are acquainted with all secrets; they very often lead the political and religious leaders, rule families, and sometimes nations. Fearing to assume the responsibility of their influence, and still wishing to keep it, they hasten to find a security in going to confess. Believing that the confessor, being bound to the sacramental silence, will be faithful to this sacred duty—knowing full well, too, that the Jesuits are the most tolerant among the priests in matter of sins and intrigues, they choose as directors of their consciences these Reverend Fathers, and inform them about everything. But, as according to many theologians, the sacramental silence obliges only to keep unknown the penitents, and as the Jesuits are bound in conscience to unveil to their superiors all their thoughts, feelings, and all they know, they reveal all these events to the Superiors of the convents, who transmit them to the Provincials, and the Provincials to the General, in Rome. It is written in the second volume of the Constitution of the Jesuits—Article, "Formula scribendi," viz., "Formula of writing:"

"Rectores et superiores domorum scribant ad Provinciales singulis hebdomadis, in Europâ. Ex missionibus pariter Provinciales scribant singulis mensibus superioribus domorum. In Europâ, Provinciales scribant ad Generalem quolibet mense."

[TRANSLATION.]

"The Rectors and Superiors of the houses are compelled to write to the Provincials every week, in Europe. From the Missions, similarly; the Provincials must write every month to the Superiors of the house. In Europe, the Provincials must write to the General every month."

For what purpose does the General require these documents? It is from his seat at Rome, to direct all the Order, as a single man, as a machinist, who by his own will imposes upon his machine an arbitrary motion. It is to govern, conjointly with the Pope, the Roman kingdom, viz., by appointing military, civil, and religious officers, only their own creatures and friends—those slavish and despotic men, who are devoted to their absolute, anti-Christian, and tyrannical principles.

Again, for what purpose does the General of the Jesuits require these documents? To rule, conjointly with the Pope, the Roman Catholic church, viz., by imposing, in the name of God, absurd, arbitrary, despotical, and cruel beliefs, ordinances, bulls, and laws, upon the minds and consciences of the Catholics, by choosing the Bishops and other ecclesiastical dignitaries among the clergymen, who are devoted body and soul to aristocratical principles. It is to influence the internal administration and foreign politics of all Governments, by directing the Provincials in their proceedings and intrigues. And what is the end of these proceedings and intrigues? To favor the promotion to employments and dignities of candidates who partake of their principles, views, and plans. And at what does the General aim? To keep to the Pope his autocracy in his temporal kingdom, his divine power in his spiritual kingdom or property—the Roman Catholic church—and to obtain for him the greatest power possible, in all Realms, Empires, and Republics.

Lest the Provincials may be traitors, or not zealous enough to fulfil scrupulously their instructions, they are surrounded with spies appointed by the General, under the name of Procurors, Ministers, Monitors, or Inquisitors, which officers are bound to correct and denounce them, and to inform the General about all particularities of their behavior.

Behold the organization and administration of the Jesuits! They are a kind of wheel, of which the General is the nave, the simple members the spokes, and the dignitaries the felloes. They are united, and support so strongly, so indissolubly, each other, that their "plurality" constitutes a perfect "unity," a whole, indestructible, except from an outward external cause.

But, to appreciate better the boundless authority, or rather omnipotence, of the General among the Jesuits, chiefly to infer more exact consequences, let us open the second volume of the Constitution of the Jesuits. We read at the article "Obedience to the Superiors:"

"You shall see always Jesus Christ in the General.

"You shall obey him in everything. Your obedience shall be boundless in the execution, in the will, and understanding. You shall persuade yourselves that God speaks with his mouth; that, when he orders, God himself orders. You shall execute his command immediately, with joy and with steadiness.

"You shall penetrate yourselves with the thought, that all which he will order shall be right. You shall sacrifice your own will with a blind obedience.

"You shall be bound, at his request, to be ready to unveil your conscience to him.

"You shall be, in his hands, a dead body, which he will govern, move, place, displace, according to his will.

"You shall resemble the stick upon which rests an old man."

Americans, these articles of the Constitution must be read

twice, weighed and seriously reflected on, to understand the doctrines, teaching, and history, which shall be exposed in this book, particularly to draw right and useful conclusions.

Thus, the General of the Jesuits is omnipotent, a kind of god among them. They must think, feel, believe, will, speak, act, preach, teach, write, do wrong, right, evil, good, according to his wishes and caprices, obey the Pope under his direction, worship God by his command and conformably to his instructions. But, as the General considers the Pope (by heart and vow) as his God in this world, he thinks, feels, believes, wills, acts, orders, in one word, identifies himself with the Pope, exactly in the same manner as the Jesuits do towards him. And what is Papacy? Witness history: it is the greatest foe of Christ, of his religion, of God, and of mankind.

Then, the Jesuits are tools, living instruments in the hands of the Pope; and as they are scattered and powerful through all the world, they are the strongest support and pillar of his anti-Christian, anti-social, and anti-human tyranny. Pius IV. told an ambassador of Portugal that "the Jesuits were his soldiers;" Benedict XIV. called them "Janissaries of the Holy See."

Before exposing the doctrine, teaching, and history, of the Jesuits, we shall examine, previously, in what manner they are raised in their houses of noviciate, and, at first how they get novices.

CHAPTER IV.

HOW THE JESUITS GET NOVICES.

In what manner do the Jesuits recruit themselves? There are in Europe a great many noble but poor families, who, still ignorant, blind, and superstitious, keep faithfully this device: "Nobility"—"Royalty"—"Papacy." The Jesuits, who for several centuries have dreamed and secretly endeavored to get for the Pope the "universal monarchy," hate kings and constitutional governments. However, they feign to agree with these families, because they know full well that democracy is the tomb of their criminal projects, and aristocracy a step to reach their aim.

This apparent identity in political and religious views being a card of introduction, they take a mask, invade the parlors, smile, counterfeit amiability, learning, humility, piety, and charity. They, according to the circumstances, extol their Order to the skies, expose emphatically their power, their influence on society, and the calmness of the religious life, carefully hiding their true principles, what they are; in short, playing with the most artfulness their hypocritical, deceitful part.

The fathers of such families, seduced by this quackery, believe their children will be happier and more considered in the Order of the Jesuits than in the world; where, in living poor and far from dignities, they might be unknown, and fall from their imaginary social rank. Then they commit to the hands and charge of the Jesuits their sons, whom these Reverend Fathers attract with caresses, flatteries, with every kind of seducing means, to throw them after a while into the mould of their doctrines, and send to the aristocratic countries as an ornament to the Order, from the nobility still preserved in their family name.

Where, again, do the Jesuits recruit themselves? In the lower classes of society. Among the peasants, in Catholic countries, the children are directly and inevitably under the influence and authority of the priesthood; and it is highly prized to have a priest or a Jesuit in one's family. Then, they harvest largely in this field, for they want a great many novices, to increase and even to maintain their army, which is scattered all over the world: and which, if it is not a numberless one, at least is so numerous and so formidable, that they carefully hide its number, lest society should be awakened and frightened.

How, again, do the Jesuits get novices? In preaching in the Parishes, Novena, Retreats, and Missions. From the pulpit they fire youth with fanatical sermons; and in the confessional, where they are without witness, they inflame them in the most dreadful manner—painting society as the dominion of Satan, where damnation is almost inevitable; and their Order as the abode of God, where salvation is easily and securely gotten; assuring them, in the name of God, as his lieutenants in the church, that they are called to the religious life, and very often imposing upon them this pretended vocation as a necessity in order to eternal salvation.

Have not the Jesuits one other way to get novices? Yes—and it is the best—their colleges; for not only do they aim in raising youth to make money, to rule families, nations, governments, but to recruit themselves.

Have they looked upon one of their pupils and resolved to seduce him, either because he will be a useful tool in their hands, or because he will be rich by his patrimony—for it may here, by the way, be observed, that the Jesuits in renouncing their parents, in hating father and mother, according to their rules, do not renounce their patrimony and other temporal rights—if, say I, they have looked upon a child and resolved to seduce him, they aim at first to gain his confidence and affection, and for that purpose grant him opportunely some favors and privileges; then use a thousand invisible but infallible means to catch and snare him, as a bird in a net.

Lest his parents suspect something, they repeat to them incessantly that he improves in the sciences, will be their glory in the world, the support of the family; and, with the most flattering words, congratulate them in having gotten from Heaven a son of so great hopes, of so brilliant prospects.

Whilst they move and inflame his imagination by mystical readings and meditations, vocal prayers of all forms, all styles, all inventions, addressed less or more fervently to all classes of Angels and Saints of Paradise, as they are less or more in credit with God, they dull his understanding chiefly in counting beads over the celebrated prayer which they repeat one hundred and fifty-three times to the mother of Christ:

"Hail Mary, full of Grace, the Lord is with thee; blessed art thou among women, and blessed is the fruit of thy womb, Jesus. Holy Mary, mother of God, pray for us sinners, now and at the hour of our death. Amen."

They inflame, above all, his imagination, in incorporating him in the Societies of Good Death, Propagating of the Faith, Saint Francis of Gonzaga, Saint Stanislas of Kostka, Guardian-Angels, Nine-Choirs of Angels, Scapala, Rosary, Sacred Heart, Holy Sacrament, and so on; by Novena, Retreats, mystical conversations, private examinations, conferences, instructions, sermons; by frequent confessions, directions, communions; in relating to him absurd stories of visions and miracles, a great many fables of monks, who, having been informed by God that they could not work out their eternal salvation in remaining in society, in their families, left them and fled to the convent, where they sanctified themselves, and deserved the everlasting glory.

Thus wrought upon a long while and so incessantly, inexperienced, confident, ardent, impetuous, seeing heaven open over his head if he embraces the Order, and hell open under his feet if he remains in society, in his family, the innocent victim of the hypocrisy of the Jesuits resolves to enter into their Company, and declares to them his intentions. Then they look astonished, feign to dissuade him; for, able politicians, they have been very careful in concealing their aim, fearing to be blamed by the families and by public opinion, but chiefly afraid of losing their pupils.

The parents, seeing a change in their son, become suspicious and question him. At first he does not dare confess his design. They insist—he disguises. They urge—at length he avers his resolutions. Grieved, they now go to the Jesuits, and ask them for an explanation, expressing how deep is their affliction. Then these Reverend Fathers, with a face cast down, a dolorous sighing, with tears share their sorrow, utter very eloquent words of consolation, and assure them that they have never excited their son to enter into religion; that they, on the contrary, have dissuaded him from his design.

The parents, believing they are sincere, and knowing their influence on the mind of their son, trust in them for yet dissuading him; but they indirectly kindle more and more his imagination. Then these unfortunate parents recall him to the paternal roof. He comes, but with reluctancy, and declares positively his immovable resolution to espouse the Order of the Jesuits. They do not consent; entreat him by the family's paternal and maternal love—he stands insensible. They order and forbid by filial duty: he denies this bond. They hold out: he stands inflexible. His kindred, brothers and sisters, are afflicted: his father despairs; his mother is bathed in tears: he compassionates their blindness, their false tenderness; and believing, without a doubt, that he is a good-hearted son, that he is enlightened by God, elected by him as a vessel of honor, as a light which He intends to place on the candlestick to shine to the people and evangelize the world, answers, with a dreadful coldness, that above all, he is resolved to save his soul; to imitate, in flying from society and his family, the just Lot flying from Sodom to escape the flames. Then, without a feeling but of pity for the blindness of his family, who in his view are evidently destined to an eternal damnation, he goes, heartily, joyfully, triumphantly, to espouse the Order of the Jesuits.

Americans, what I say, I know. I have seen it (with my own eyes seen, with my own ears heard): in exercising my ministry, chiefly in confessing, I have contributed, in my blindness, believing it to be right, to send inexperienced and too-confiding young men to the houses of noviciate of the Jesuits. It shall be to me, all my life, a matter of grief, of undying regret.

Now, let us follow these victims of the artfulness and deception of the Jesuits to the house of the noviciate, to this spot of sacrifice, or, more properly speaking, this novel and monstrous butchery, where the Jesuits immolate, not animals, not human bodies, but souls created in the image of God! We will see them moving the piston of their pneumatic machine, and extracting, one after another, all the faculties of their souls. We will see, with our hearts grieved, all these victims going forth and walking through the world with living bodies, but without souls—having left them at the disposal of their Superiors, being a tool in their hands, and the blind executors of their arbitrary, capricious, and criminal orders.

Foreseeing they will deny what I write—for it is not in vain that in the dictionaries the word "Jesuit" is synonymous with hypocrite and liar, so worthy they are of these titles of nobility—foreseeing, say I, their denial, I will unveil them only by themselves, in extracting all the quotations of the following chapter from their classical books, such especially which daily and hourly they read and study, about which they meditate and converse, and in which they are taught.

CHAPTER V.

EDUCATION OF THE JESUITS IN THEIR HOUSES OF NOVICIATE.

SECTION I.—*Mystical Science and Purgation of the Soul in Thirty Lessons and Exercises.*

THE Jesuits (I do not mean those with the short gown) begin their noviciate by a seclusion of thirty days. During all this time they must keep the deepest silence, and meditate on the "Exercitia Spiritualia" of Saint Ignatius Loyola, founder of the Order of the Jesuits.

"By spiritual exercises," writes Saint Ignatius, "we mean the method of examining our conscience, meditating, contemplating, praying mentally and vocally, in short, of directing all spiritual operations. For the same reason that to step, to walk, and to run, are corporal exercises, thus we call 'spiritual exercises,' to prepare and dispose the soul to cast off its inordinate propensities. Four weeks, corresponding to those exercises, are required to complete them.

"In the first week, we must examine our conscience; in the second, consider the life of Jesus Christ until his entrance into Jerusalem, on Palm Sunday; in the third, contemplate his suffering; in the fourth, meditate on his Resurrection and Ascension. Previously to these operations, we must know exactly the history of meditation and contemplation; and, after these spiritual exercises, use the three modes of praying.

"These four weeks ought not to be considered as absolutely composed of seven or eight days, for many are slow in completing the spiritual exercises, though they are commonly completed in thirty days."

(Exercitia Spiritualia Saint Ignatius Loyola, pp. 22, 23, 24.)

SECTION II.—*Method of Praying.*

"There are three ways of praying. The first is drawn up from the consideration of the precepts of God, from the seven mortal sins, from the three powers of the soul, and the five senses.

"We must, previously, either sit down or take a walk in thinking of the scenes on which our imaginative powers will operate.

"The second way of praying consists in weighing the meaning of each word of prayer. We are allowed either to sit down or to kneel, according to the disposition of our body or devotion of our soul. Our eyes may be open, or shut, or fixed on a spot, but without rolling to and fro. We must stop at every word, and meditate upon it, scrutinize all its meanings and similarities to other words, and bind ourselves to the pious emotions which it, generally, stirs up in our soul.

"The third consists in making the words pronounced equal to the number of our breaths. At each time we breathe, we must think of the signification of the word pronounced, and reflect about it."

(Exercitia Spiritualia S. P. Ignatii Loyola—p. 130, etc.)

Saint Ignatius Loyola explains more extensively these doctrines in two other books entitled, the one, "Directorium," the other, "Industriæ."

I ask you, Americans, if Saint Ignatius Loyola manufacturing a soul in such manner, is not a carpenter squaring a trunk, a teacher of gymnastical exercises, or, rather, a Vaucanson making his automata? I ask you if he is not a profanator, in working the image of God as a material body, in fashioning it with the chisel of an engraver?

SECTION III.—*Mystical Conversation.*

Considering that the book entitled "Pratique de la perfection Chrétienne et Religieuse," by the Reverend Father

Jesuit Alphonsius Rodriguez, has been since 1614 and still is now regarded, after the "Exercitia Spiritualia," the "Directorium" and "Industriæ" of Saint Ignatius Loyola, as the most classical book of the novices: considering that this book is the usual matter of their readings and meditations—that it is explained to them daily and many times a day by the masters of the novices—that it is considered by them as the mystical summary from which all their other mystical books are extracted, we will take from it (edition octavo) all our quotations relative to the moulding of the novices.

"We must be always serious, always abounding in mystical conversations, above all, never jest."

(The Reverend Father Jesuit Alphonse Rodriguez, Perfection Chrétienne et Religieuse. 2d vol., p. 143.)

Divine Confirmation of this Doctrine.

"Saint Ignatius, martyr, uttered often, in his sufferings, the name of Jesus Christ. The assistants asked him why he did so. 'Because,' answered the Saint, 'The name of Jesus Christ is engraved on my heart.' After his death his heart was opened, and the name of Jesus Christ found, written in golden letters on both sides.

"He who likes to jest has not the name of Jesus Christ engraved on his heart, but the name of this world with its follies, which fall incessantly from his lips."

(Idem—vol. 2d, p. 144.)

"On a certain day the monks of Saint Francis were talking on a pious subject. Jesus Christ came among them under the form of a child, and blessed them, showing by this favor how much he likes this sort of conversation."

(Idem—vol. 2d, p. 147.)

"We read in the life of Saint Hugues, Abbot of Cluney, that the Lord Durand, Archbishop of Toulouse, who had been his monk, was fond of jesting, in spite of the corrections of the Saint, who informed him he should be severely punished on account of it in Purgatory. The Archbishop, a short time after, died and appeared to a holy monk, named Séguin, with a swelled and ulcerous mouth, charging him to entreat Hugues to intercede with God in his favor—for he was cruelly tortured in Purgatory on account of his jests. Séguin reported this vision to his Abbot, who ordered seven monks to be silent, seven days, in order to satisfy for this fault. One of these monks having broken the silence, the Archbishop appeared anew to Séguin complaining of this monk, whose disobedience caused the delay of his deliverance.

"On the new report of Séguin, Hugues, at the first verified the failure of the monk, and then imposed upon another a silence of seven days, after which, the Archbishop appeared a third time to Séguin, dressed with his Episcopal ornaments, his mouth cured, and his face serene. Having prayed him to thank the holy Abbot and his monks, he instantly disappeared."

(Idem—vol. 2d, p. 145.)

Evidently this doctrine is fanatical, and the proofs of its divine confirmation absurd and profane fables. But the Jesuits do not care about that, aiming only to kindle fanaticism in the minds of their novices, and, to impose upon them an absurd belief, and a blind obedience.

Section IV.—*To be Without Eyes.*

"We ought to imitate Saint Bernard, who saw in seeing not, heard in hearing not. After one year of noviciate, he did not know what was the matter with his room's ceiling, and had seen only one window in the convent's church, though there were three. On a certain day he had walked from the morning until the evening along the shore of a lake;

the monks, his fellows, talking about it at their arrival, he asked them where was this lake—for he had not seen it.

"We must imitate, too, the Abbot Palladius, who, keeping the same cell twenty years, had never looked at the ceiling."

(Idem—vol. 2d, p. 105.)

How is it possible not to term fanaticism and folly such lessons and examples!

Section V.—*Fashion of Speaking.*

"We ought to speak low and modestly, being careful to give to our voice a peculiar inflection, and to our features a religious expression."

(Idem—vol. 2d, p. 126—Reg. 28, Commun.)

Every body knows how faithfully and successfully the Jesuits practise this article of their rules, how easy it is to recognise them every where, by their studied smile and false looks, by their affected posture and their hypocritical language.

Section VI.—*The Jesuits Commissioned by God to Cast Down Protestantism.*

"It has been by a peculiar dispensation of his Providence, that God sent our Company in that deplorable epoch in which the Church wanted so many powerful and devoted defenders. Ecclesiastical writers remark, that when Pelagius was born in England, Saint Augustine was born in Africa—God opposing, in this manner, a remedy to the evil, in order that when one would scatter the darkness of heresy over the world, the other could disperse it by the light of his doctrine, and cast down error by his learning.

"Father Ribadeneira, author of the Life of Saint Ignatius, remarks also, that when Luther began hostilities against the Church and truth, God caused Saint Ignatius to be wounded in Pampluna, to attract him to his service, and to appoint him

General of the new army, which he intended to organize for the support of his Church. He adds, too, that God commissioned our Company, which professes a particular obedience to the Pope—even by a vow—to oppose the heresy of Luther, which casts down the obedience owed to the Pope."

(Idem—vol. 3d, pp. 4, 5.)

"And you, Company of Jesus, who are now the smallest among all, cheer up; it pleased your Heavenly Father to give you power over the souls and hearts of others! I will favor you in Rome, said Jesus Christ, in appearing to our Holy founder going there. It was on account of this miraculous apparition that our Order termed itself Company of Jesus."

(Idem—vol. 2d, p. 177.)

O Jesuits, must we not admire your modesty and humility!

SECTION VII.—*The Rules of the Jesuits are Perfect.*

"The worst friendship among us is a combination of those who unite with one another to modify the Constitutions of the Order, and change its rules sacredly established and ordered. . . . . Saint Basilius writes severely against it.

"If several," says this saint, "unite and form particular societies in the Company to which they belong, they are condemnable, seditious, and rebellious; since, under the pretext of reformation, or under the shadow of a benefit to the Society, they aim only to alter the rules, and to change the Order from its original basis. For this reason, he wills that they may be, at the first, privately advised, afterwards corrected publicly, and then, considered as heathens and publicans."

(Idem—vol. 3d, p. 554.)

SECTION VIII.—*The Order of the Jesuits is a Divine One.*

"Religious Societies are not human institutions, but were established by a view of the Divine Providence, so well that all which were fixed, whether for their preservation or their advancement, ought to be considered, neither as human inventions nor projects of some private individuals, but as divine projects and creations. When God elected Saint Francis, Saint Dominic, Saint Ignatius, and other Saints, to found their various Orders, he inspired them with the means by which they should establish them.

"Moreover, the works of God alone are perfect. [Deuteronomy xxxii. 4.] Then, these institutions would have been imperfect, if these Saints had used only their human ability. But God revealed to them all that was necessary to the preservation and spiritual progress of their Companies. Also, we read in 'The Life of Saint Ignatius,' that he, deciding about a fundamental question of our Order, gave exactly the same solution as the Father James Laynez, though having not advised together. It is a great proof that in the most essential principles and bases upon which rests our Order, God, who is its first author, has revealed or inspired all things to him whom he chose to be its chief, and after him, its founder.

"Again, the manner of composing the Constitutions, which Saint Ignatius bequeathed us by writing, demonstrates this truth. How many thoughts and how many tears must each word have cost him, since, only for determining whether it was opportune or not, that our Professed Houses might be owners of some revenues, annexed to the Fabric—lands of their churches, we read, that consecutively during forty days, he offered to God the sacrifice of mass and prayed more fervently than customary. Then it is easily understood, that the Constitutions have been deeply reflected on, well concerted with God, and that he was very clearly enlightened by him, to choose and resolve what should be the more pleasing to the Divine Majesty.

"But, though what we have said may be sufficient to prove

our proposition, we have a potent testimony to demonstrate the divine institution of the Religious Order.

"The rule of Saint Francis having been but verbally approved by Innocent III., and this great Saint, willing to present it written to the Pope, in order to obtain a bull of confirmation, went with two of his fellows on a mountain, near Reate. There, fasting with bread and water during forty days, and persevering day and night in prayer, he composed his rule according to the inspiration of God. Afterwards, he brought it from the mountain, and committed it to the hands and charge of Elie, his Great Vicar, a man wise and able in the judgment of the world. Elie believing that it required a too strict and universal abandonment of all things, a too extreme humility and poverty, lost it voluntarily, in order that this rule being not confirmed, one other more suitable might be composed.

"Saint Francis, who resolved to obey the will of God rather than that of men, and who did not give way to the opinions of the wisest of the world, went again to the same mountain, fasted, prayed a second time, and obtained from God a heavenly inspiration to compose another rule. Brother Elie knowing his intention, proposed to withdraw it; and having, for this purpose, assembled several of the most skilful and influential members of the Order, announced to them that the Saint intended to make so narrow and strict a rule that not one could be able to observe it. Thereupon, they entreated him, in his capacity of Great Vicar to the Saint, to report to him that if the rule was too austere, they did not intend to observe it.

"Brother Elie refusing to fulfil alone such a mission, they went all together to the mountain, where arriving, they found the Saint praying.

"Brother Elie called him. The Saint who recognised him at his voice, went out of his cell, and, seeing so many monks assembled, asked them what was the cause of their extraordinary visit. 'These monks,' answered brother Elie, 'are the principal members of the Order. Knowing that you are composing another rule, and fearing that it may be too severe, they come to protest and to declare that it will be for you alone, because they will not accept it.'

"The Saint hearing these words fell on his knees and raising his eyes towards heaven: 'Lord,' exclaimed he, 'had I not told you that these fellows would not believe me.' Instantly a voice from heaven was heard, saying: 'Francis, nothing is of your own in the rule. All its articles are from me, and I will that it may be observed — word by word — word by word — without gloss — without gloss. I know human frailty, and I know what help I can and will bestow upon them. Let those who will not observe the rule leave the Order, and let the others observe it.'

"Then Saint Francis turning towards the monks: 'Have you heard?' said he to them, 'have you heard? Are you willing that these words may be repeated to you?'

"Thereupon brother Elie and his fellows, all trembling, out of countenance, and confused on account of their fault, went back without replying.

"The Saint having composed a rule, which was exactly the same as the first which God had revealed to him, left the mountain, and went to the Pope Honorius III., who told him that it was too severe. 'Holy Father,' answered the Saint, 'I have not written in this rule a single word of my own: Jesus Christ himself composed it. Thus the rule being his own work, He alone knowing what is necessary to the salvation of the soul, to the benefit of the monks, and the preservation of this Order, foreseeing alone all the future, both of the Church in general and of this Order in particular, then, I cannot change what He himself has established.'

"The Pope, being moved by a particular heavenly inspiration, confirmed the rule of the Saint and granted him a bull of confirmation.

"We must infer that God himself prescribes to the founders of Religious Orders all what they insert in their rules. Thus he prescribed it to Saint Ignatius, and we have even a more authentic proof of it than the aforesaid, namely, two apostolical bulls of Gregory III., which mention it particularly. He says expressly: 'Therefore, the same Ignatius, by a Divine inspiration, has judged that it was best to divide the Company into members, orders, and degrees.' Could we say more clearly that our rule was inspired by God himself."

(Idem—vol. 3d, pp. 554, 555, 556.)

SECTION IX.—*To Deny that the Order of the Jesuits is Divinely perfect is a Heresy.*

"Heresy is undoubtedly the greatest crime in the Church of God; for the heretic must be proud above all expression, to esteem their own views sublime enough as to prefer the errors of their imagination to the decisions of the Roman Catholic Church, approved by so many councils, followed by so many Saints, cemented by so many thousand martyrs, and confirmed by so many miracles. What greater folly, what more insupportable pride, and more strange blindness, can be conceived, than to prefer to all these one's own dreams, or those of Luther, and to believe an apostate, and immoral, a corrupted, a concubinary, and sacrilegious man!

"We do pretty much the same when we prefer our own judgment to that of a man chosen by God to be the chief and founder of a great Company, and persuade ourselves that our dreamed way is better than this, which God himself inspired and revealed to Saint Ignatius. Such presumption is diabolical.

"What! Would God have concealed from Saint Ignatius,

elected by Him chief and founder of this Company, what he would have revealed to you?"

(Idem—vol. 3d. pp. 557, 558.)

SECTION X.—*Demonstration of this Doctrine.*

First Testimony.—"Marcel Cervin, Cardinal of the Holy Cross, who afterwards was Pope, under the name of Marcel II., wished to change an article of our Rules, but being told by the Father Olave, that it was sufficient for us to know that this article had been established by our Founder in order that we must keep it, the Cardinal answered: 'I give up, now. I confess that you are right; for Saint Ignatius having been elected by God to establish in the Church an order as yours, we ought to presume, and even it cannot be otherwise, that God himself revealed to him all about it.'"

(Idem—vol. 3d, pp. 559, 560.)

Second Testimony.—"Gregory XIV. in his Bull, 'Ecclesiæ Catholicæ,' says: 'We in renewing the Constitution of Gregory XIII., our predecessor, and all penalties contained in it, do by the present letters patent, in virtue of the holy obedience, forbid every body, of whatever position or condition he may be—all clergymen and laymen, all monks, and even those of the Company of Jesus—and that under the penalties of Excommunication—'Latea Sententiæ'—of exclusion from all offices and ecclesiastial dignities, of the deprivation of the active and passive vote (the power to absolve, from which we reserve to ourselves) to attack or contradict directly, or indirectly, even a single article of the Institute, or of the Constitutions and Decrees of the Company, under the pretence of good or zeal, of whatever color it may be.'

"Gregory XIV. adds a very essential article prohibiting the same; even to propose and give a memorial on this subject, in order that something may be added or suppressed, except to him, or to the General Superior, or to the great assembly of the Company.

"Paul V. in a Bull issued in 1606, to confirm the Institution and the privileges of the Company, relates the Bulls of Gregory XIV., approving and authorizing their contents."

(Idem—vol. 3d, pp. 561, 562.)

Americans, the Jesuits teach their novices that God inspired and revealed to Saint Ignatius their rules. You will see farther how blasphemous is their falsehood. Jesus Christ says: "By their fruits you shall know them. Do men gather grapes of thorns, or figs of thistles? Even so every good tree yieldeth good fruit, and the bad tree yieldeth bad fruit. A good tree cannot yield bad fruit; neither can a bad tree yield good fruit. Every tree that yieldeth not good fruit, shall be cut down and shall be cast into the fire. Wherefore, by their fruits you shall know them." Saint Matthew vii. 16, 17, 18, 19, 20.* But the Jesuits have held and taught, still hold and teach, all bad doctrines, have committed all crimes, as it shall be exposed, even demonstrated. Then, in supposing their Institute and rules inspired and revealed by God, we must admit that Jesus Christ was a liar, which is a dreadful and monstrous proposition.

Shrinking horrified at the conclusion, we logically must conclude that the Institute and rules of the Jesuits shall be cast into the fire, since they have yielded and still yield so bitter and deadly fruits to Christianity and society.

Again we must infer that the Order and rules of the Jesuits are as sacred, as divine, as the Bible, or Christ's institutions—for the Popes forbid clergymen, laymen, etc. . . . to contradict them, under the greatest penalty, that of "Excommunication major;" which Ecclesiastical censure binds the faithful not to converse, deal, correspond, keep friendship or other relations with the excommunicated, and the excommu-

* I have used for the Scriptural quotations a Romish translation of the Bible.

5*

nicated to live alone, abandoned by their fathers, mothers, sons, daughters, kindred, friends, acquaintances, and fellow-citizens. Every body knows that the servants purified in the flames the dishes and plates of the silly Robert, King of France, who had been excommunicated by the Pope, and was considered by the French people as accursed, both of men and God.

Again, if the Order and rules of the Jesuits have been revealed and inspired, they must admit that Clement XIV., suppressing both their Institute and their rules, was so much an enemy of God, so sacrilegious a destroyer of His works, that he solemnly declared that God mistook in inspiring and revealing their Institute and rules. But can we reconcile this consequence with their belief and teaching about the papal holiness, wisdom, and infallibility?

Then we ought to term "quackery," the teaching of the Jesuits about the Divine inspiration and revelation of their Institute, rules, etc. . . and "impiety," the Bulls of the Popes confirming such absurdities.

Finally—as the consequences are very injurious to their confident and inexperienced novices, whom they blind and enslave; very injurious, chiefly to society, which they disturb and dissolve; as this infernal marriage between the Popes and the Jesuits to support one another in relating, in the name of God, for his glory, false and sacrilegious tales, annihilates the human reason and dignity, the social and individual freedom; leads and chains Christendom and all the world to ignorance, superstition, fanaticism, death of mind, and popish slavery—we ought to term their blasphemous falsehood and odious designs "a crime of high-treason against mankind, against the gospel, and against God."

Section X.—*Observance of the Rules of the Order.*

"We must scrupulously observe the smallest articles of our rules, etc. . . . ."—(Idem, vol. 3d, p. 374.)

Divine Confirmation of this Doctrine.

"A monk holding bread-crumbs, forgot to put them in his plate during the dinner. Willing to atone for his failure, he confessed it to his Superior, who rebuked him harshly, and asked where were these bread-crumbs. He, answering that he held them, opened his hands, and it happened that these crumbs were changed into very fine pearls. God did this miracle to reward the obedience of this monk to the holy rules of his Order."

(Idem—vol. 3d, p. 374.)

"Surius says that God granted the same miracle to Saint Eudes to reward him in a like circumstance."

(Idem—vol. 3d, p. 374.)

"When Saint Dominic lived at Bologna, the devil caught suddenly a Lay Friar, and tortured him so cruelly, that the monks who were sleeping awoke and flocked together to help him. The Saint ordered them to carry him to the church, which ten monks did, but with difficulty. On entering into the church he blew out with a single breath all the lamps. The monks being in darkness went out, and the devil tortured and thrashed him anew. Then the Saint ordered him by Christ to confess why he possessed the body of this Friar, and why he tortured him so cruelly. ''T is,' answered the devil, 'because he drank, on the evening before, without permission and without making the sign of the cross according to the rules and practice of the Order.' Suddenly matins began to ring. 'I cannot remain a longer while,' continued the devil, 'for the monks are coming to sing the praises of God'—and he fled.

"This poor Lay Friar was so broken and beaten, that during two days he was motionless."

(Idem—vol. 3d, p. 376.)

"Saint Gregory relates another circumstance of a nun,

who, having eaten lettuce, forgetting the sign of the cross, was instantly seized by the devil."

(Idem—vol. 3d, p. 376.)

"A monk, under the pretext of being a physician, was very often out of the convent, and went there only when great solemnities occurred. On a certain feast of Mary, he was assisting at the morning prayers. Suddenly he saw the mother of God entering, her whole person shining. In turning round the choir, she poured into the mouth of each monk a celestial liquor which strengthened them to sing the praises of God. But when she paused before him, she went away without stopping, and without imparting to him this liquor, telling him that the refreshments of the Paradise were not granted to those who like terrestrial enjoyments.

"He felt so sorry, that, reflecting with himself, he was converted. He amended, and practised mortification, keeping strictly his cell, and leaving it only by the permission of his Superiors. Also, at the next feast of Mary, he was happy enough to see her again turning round the choir, and telling him, 'Since you are amended, and prefer the celestial to the terrestrial reliefs, you will partake of the refreshments of your fellows.'

"A clergyman, who was fond of delicate meals forbidden by the rule, saw Jesus Christ in an ecstasy, who offered him a piece of the bread of the community. He answered that he could not eat this black bread. Then Jesus Christ soaked it in the wound of his side, and invited him to taste it. He found it very good."

(Idem—vol. 3d, p. 347.)

Americans, what kind of men can such teachers be, imposing upon the minds of their scholars the belief of so absurd and blasphemous tales? Aiming at what? To sanction by a Divine intervention a fanatical doctrine, bending their souls to their will and caprices. They will tell that they aim to reach the highest piety, in observing the smallest rules scrupulously. As to us who know them, we answer them by these words of Christ: "Wo to you, Scribes and Pharisees, hypocrites! who pay tithe of mint, and anise, and cummin, and have let alone the weightier things of the law, judgment, and mercy, and faith. These things you ought to have done, and not to leave those others undone. Blind guides, who strain at a gnat and swallow a camel! Wo to you, Scribes and Pharisees, hypocrites! because you make clean the outside of the cup and of the dish: but within, you are full of extortion and uncleanness. Thou blind Pharisee, first make clean the inside of the cup and of the dish, that the outside may become clean. Wo to you, Scribes and Pharisees, hypocrites! because you are like to whited sepulchres, which outwardly appear to men beautiful, but within are full of dead men's bones, and of all filthiness. So you also outwardly indeed appear to men just: but within you are full of hypocrisy and iniquity." Saint Matthew xxiii. 23, 24, 25, 26, 27, 28.

Americans, you will see farther that they are Scribes and Pharisees; that they deserve all these maledictions of Christ.

Section XI.—*We are Manure, Shell-Snails, and Hogs.*

"What have we been? An impure seed. What are we? A vessel of filth. What shall we be? The food of the worms. Here is a deep matter of meditation. The Pope Innocent exclaims: 'O, miserable and shameful condition of human nature! Let us consider herbs and plants: they bear flowers and fruits, but our bodies only obscenities * * * they yield oil, wine, balm, smell delightfully, but our bodies are a sink of excrements and stench!'

(Idem—vol. 2d, p. 180.)

"We are a deal of mud and filth . . . . . Our body is a

hog, which feels satisfied only in rolling continually in the mud; a shell-snail, living only within excrements."

(Idem— vol. 3d, p. 239.)

If the Jesuits lower down so ignominiously their body, we are proud of ours; respectful towards it, and grateful to God who granted it to us as the sanctuary of our soul—his living image. We believe that our body is higher in the scale of creation than manure, shell-snails, and hogs. We believe that the propensities and faculties of our body have been wisely destined by God to the preservation and reproduction of our kind, to live again in our children when we depart from this world to another.

SECTION XII.—*Humility.*

"To be humble we ought to practise the external mortifications used among us, to kiss the feet of our brethren, to eat below the table, or kneeling, to lay down at the door of the refectory, and so on."

(Idem—vol. 2d, p. 257.)

"We must imitate Saint Francis Borgia, who, traveling with the Father Bustamant, was necessitated to lodge in a mean inn, where they found only two straw trusses to sleep on, and in a narrow and dirty corner of the house. The Father Bustamant, who was very old and had gotten an inflammation of the lungs, coughed and spat all the night. At several times, he, thinking he was spitting against the wall, spat on the face of the Saint, who, nevertheless, said nothing, and did not turn his face away. When, in the morning, the Father Bustamant saw the face of the Saint, he felt so ashamed and sorry that he was inconsolable; but the Saint, who was pleased as much as his fellow felt shame and sorrow, told him 'be quiet, Father Bustamant, for I assure you that nothing in the room was more worthy your spittle than I.'"

(Idem—vol. 2d, p. 255.)

This is one of the degrading doctrines of the Jesuits. Can a man, prizing and respecting his dignity, kiss the feet of his fellow-creatures? May a man knowing that he is a son of God, a brother of Christ, either fraternize with the dogs in eating below the table, or kneel before Superiors, or lay down on the threshold of the door of a refectory, identifying himself with dust and mud? Can we look but pitifully at the degradation of Saint Francis Borgia, who would not turn away his face, and was intoxicated with delight under the spittle of the catarrhous Father Bustamant? Can we believe with the Pope and the Jesuits, that such fanaticism and insult to God was a title to canonization, to the credit and power of Saint Francis with God? Certainly not. Such belief would be injurious to God.

SECTION XIII.—*Revelation of One's Thoughts and Feelings.*

"We must neither step, nor drink a drop of water, without the permission of our Superiors. In a very holy convent, Saint John Cilmacus found monks who carried a copy-book hanging upon their girdle, in which, every day, they registered all their thoughts to communicate them to their Superiors.

"We are bound by our Constitutions to do the same; and this obligation is so important that Saint Ignatius says, 'that he reflected on it a long while in presence of God.'"

(Idem—vol. 3d, p. 392.)

"Let the monks," adds Ignatius, "keep open not only their rooms and trunks, but their conscience. [4. p. Constit., c. x.; 35.] They must conceal nothing from the Superiors, neither their outward nor their inward acts." [6 p. Constit., c. i.; sec. 2.]

"He considers this obligation so essential a one, that he insists on it in season and out of season.

"In the fifth general assembly of our Company, our ancestors declare that the observance of this bond was vital to the Order." [In Congregatione quintâ generale, Can. 17.]

Divine Confirmation of this Doctrine.

"God rewards the revealing of one's thoughts and feelings, etc. The Abbot Serapio being a glutton, stole often some rolls to eat in his cell. On a certain day, the Saint Abbot Theonas talking about gluttony with several hermits who visited him, Serapio felt moved and confessed his thefts. Suddenly a kind of flamed vapor, bursting out from his breast, filled the cell with an insupportable smell. 'You see, my son,' said Theonas, 'that God rewards the merit of your confession. Fear not the devil will ever tempt you more by gluttony.' This prophecy was realized."

(Idem—vol. 3d, p. 409.)

Americans, let us draw some conclusions from the doctrine which this miracle would establish.

When a man believes to be bound in conscience to reveal his thoughts, feelings, etc. . . . to others, his soul is half dead, He will be shortly the prey and blind tool of his seducers and tyrants, doing right or wrong according to their will. But the seducers and tyrants, viz., the leaders among the Jesuits, having been and still being the most deadly foes of mankind and God (we shall prove that farther), all members of the Order shall be, in their hands, tools of crime and destruction.

Unfortunate novices, in what hands did you fall!

SECTION XIV.—*Friendship is Sinful.*

"If any one among us, for whatever cause it may be, seems to like one more than another, we must castigate him as violating the common charity, for he injures all the community. Knowing that God is so sensitive to our offences against a single individual, that, according to his word, we hurt the sight of his eyes, how much more shall he be sensitive to our injury against a whole community!"

(Idem—vol. 3d, p. 545.)

We must infer from this principle the blasphemous consequences, that God was wrong in putting in our heart the love of friends, and that Jesus Christ sinned in choosing Saint John for his friend among his apostles.

O, Jesuits, how unnatural, inhuman, anti-Christian, and hostile to God, is your teaching!

SECTION XV.—*To Denounce Each Other is a Sacred Obligation.*

"The ninth Rule of the summary of our Constitutions expresses that we ought to be very glad, for our humiliation and spiritual benefit, if our failures or imperfections, or whatever we may have acted, and being known out of the confession, are denounced to our Superiors. [Constit. 4, Examen. 58.]

The sixth chapter of the tract of the fraternal correction is entitled: "On the rule which binds us to denounce immediately to the Superiors the failures of our brethren."

Fifteen pages octavo are filled with absurd explanations of this dreadful doctrine. But not to be too long and tedious, we will not produce them. See the author—vol. 3d, p. 457, etc.

Americans, let us not forget the title of the classical and doctrinal code from which we extract the teaching of the Jesuits, namely: "Tract of the Christian and Religious Perfection." Since the Jesuits consider denunciation as a Christian perfection, they will carry out this doctrine wherever they will prevail. Then what will happen?

A system of denunciation will be organized in society. Friends shall betray and denounce their friends, sons their fathers, daughters their mothers, wives their husbands, husbands their wives. Hatred, vengeance, and intestine war, will be stirred up. Society and families will present a wide field of contention and strife. Witness the past and present history of Europe.

O, Jesuits, what enemies of mankind you are?

SECT. XVI. — *To Die to One's Family is a Sacred Obligation.*

"If, at the imitation of Jesus Christ, you are dead to your natural parents, why will you," says Saint Basilius, "keep correspondence with them? If you wish to reëstablish in your heart their love, which you threw off for the sake of Jesus Christ, are you not prevaricators? Do not, for their love, leave your divine calling; for less or more you will forsake the spirit of your profession. The blessed Mary and Saint Joseph did not find Jesus Christ among his kindred or those of his acquaintance. Saint Luke, xi. 44."

(Idem — vol. 2d, p. 406.)

Confirmation of this Doctrine by Examples of Saints.

"Saint Francis Xavier, in going to the Indies, passed at twelve miles distance only from his paternal home. Notwithstanding, he refused, in spite of all solicitations and entreaties, to go from his road to visit his kindred and mother, though he knew full well that, not availing himself of this opportunity, never more should he see them.

"Father Lefèvre did the same in passing at fifteen miles from the paternal home.

"Saint Ignatius being necessitated to go to Loyola, refused to visit his brother and lodged in the hospital."

(Idem — vol. 2d, p. 406.)

"A holy hermit, named Syriacus, hearing a knock at the door of his cell, and knowing it was kindred who visited him, asked God to prevent them from seeing him; then he opened the door, went out unseen, and fled far into the wilderness, coming back only after their departure.

"The sister of Saint Pacŏme came to see him and get some of his news; he ordered the porter of the convent to tell her that he was well, and that she go back in peace."

(Idem—vol. 2, p. 408.)

"A hermit getting a big pack of letters from his native country, which he had left fifteen years ago, threw it into the fire, exclaiming: 'Vain thoughts of tenderness for my country and family, burn with these letters so that you never can seduce me.' Not only had he not read one of them, but not even seen their address, lest the sight of them should trouble his inward peace and quietness."

(Idem—vol. 2d, p. 409.)

Divine Confirmation of the same Doctrine.

"The Father Ribadeneira relates a pleasant fact which happened to one of our monks, who, loving tenderly his mother, visited her at Messina. On a certain day, he entered in a church where a bedlamite was exorcised before a large congregation. He began to aid the priest in conjuring and threatening the devil in the name of God. The only answer the devil returned him was to counterfeit the voice of a child calling his mother. All the assistants who knew this monk, and the cause of his visit, understood immediately the meaning of this answer, and laughed. He remained ashamed and without countenance."

(Idem—vol. 2d, p. 412.)

SECTION XVII.—*To Hate One's Family is a Sacred Obligation.*

"All, says Saint Ignatius, who enter into the Company of Jesus are bound not only to profess that they renounce their father, mother, kindred, friends, and all that they possess in the world, but to believe that these words of Christ relate to them: 'He that hates not his father, mother, even his own soul, cannot be my disciple.' Saint Luke xiv., 26. Then they must apply themselves to reduce all feelings inspired by flesh and blood towards their parents, to the bonds of Christian charity. They must consider themselves as dead to the world and its love; as living exclusively for Jesus Christ, and to whom Christ is father, mother, and all things.

"Not only our bodies, but our hearts, must leave the world. . . . It is very important for a monk to avoid the correspondence and visits of his kindred, because we are not only useless to them, but they disturb the tranquillity and economy of our life, and tempt us to sin. They entertain us with private business, lawsuits, losses, and all their troubles, so much so that we come back loaded with all their griefs. But worst of all, we are very much endangered, because the revolution of our former secular life can, by striking our imagination, open afresh past wounds, which with difficulty close up again. The sole view of a person, even of a familiar spot, can call anew certain ideas almost entirely blotted out by time and distance.

"By frequenting our kindred, we take their bad habits and propensities; our souls get filled with secular thoughts, and become cold to celestial things; we lose fervor and firmness in our resolutions; in short, we become secular again, according to these words of David: 'They have mingled among the heathens and learned their works. They worshipped their idols and it caused their loss.' Ps. cvi. 35, 36. You will easily retain their language, hypocrisy, and behavior. You already love their idols, which are vanity and self-love. You already are proud, and you will still look for your own satisfaction and glory. Are not these symptoms a proof that they have imbued you with the spirit of the world? . . . .

"Again, we ought to avoid communications with our kindred, because the natural tenderness which we feel towards them draws us too much to their interests. We cannot visit them often without naturally being glad of their success, sorry for their misfortunes, anxious about their welfare, and ensnared by a thousand cares. We continually are asking, do they want something? Will they be successful in getting such an office? Will they reach their aim? Will they honorably get off from their business? All these thoughts, all these anxieties, enfeeble so much the spiritual man that the slightest temptation casts us down.

"Then," says Saint Basilius, "we are monks only by the dress. We have neither the spirit nor the virtue of our profession."

(Idem—vol. 2d, p. 412.)

Confirmation of this Doctrine by the Example of Saints.

"A brother of the Abbot Apollo was, on a certain night, knocking at the door of his cell, entreating him to aid him to draw up from a marsh one of his cattle, from which he was unable to pull him. The holy Abbot asked him why he did not beg this service of his brother living in the world. 'Because he has been dead fifteen years ago,' answered he. 'And I,' replied the Saint, 'have been dead and buried in my cell for twenty years: then I cannot leave it to help you.'

"Every monk must imitate this holy Abbot."

(Idem—vol. 2d, p. 413.)

"The Tribune of the province of Egypt having imprisoned the son of the sister of the Abbot Pæmen, had promised his deliverance if the Abbot would intercede. The mother went to the brother's, knocked at his cell, and entreated him to free her son. Pæmen neither unlocked his door, nor gave an answer. 'Cruel, barbarous, inexorable, bad-hearted uncle and brother,' exclaimed she in her anger. Then the holy man, turning to his disciple, 'Go,' said he, 'tell this woman from me, that Pæmen never got children, and thus does not know the sadness of their loss.' Without any other answer, he sent her back, her heart full of sorrow."

(Idem—vol. 2d, p. 415.)

"The Abbot Pastor did the same. He believed that it was so dangerous to mingle in the business of flesh and blood, that he would not, in spite of all solicitations, intercede for one of his nephews condemned to death."

(Idem—vol. 2d, p. 416.)

"God commands us to hate our kindred as well as ourselves. Then as we are our greatest enemies, we ought, for the same reason, to hate in a holy manner our families. Also the brother Giles told a layman, willing to embrace the religious life, the service of God, 'Go and kill your parents.' Surprised at the answer, he wept and entreated Giles not to oblige him to commit so dreadful a crime. 'I do not bind you,' replied he, 'to murder effectually your parents, but merely in your heart, in breaking the chains of love which bind you to them.'"

(Idem—vol. 2d, p. 419.)

Divine Confirmation of the same Doctrine.

"A Sorbonne doctor had espoused the religious life in a monastery of Saint Francis. His mother who spent all that she possessed in supporting him whilst he studied, and was now extremely needy, went to the convent deeply afflicted. She wept, lamented, showed her breast, entreated him by the bowels which had carried him, and by all that she had suffered in raising him, not to cast her off in such poverty. At the first he resisted, but at length felt moved and resolved to leave the convent on the next day. Yet, after the departure of his mother, he knelt before a crucifix, his heart disturbed and full of sorrow: 'Lord,' said he, 'I will not leave you, and do not permit that it may happen. I only intend to relieve my mother in her distress. In praying so, he saw blood trickling from the crucifix, and heard a voice telling him, 'You cost me more than you have cost your mother, for I have redeemed you with my own blood. Should you leave me for her?'

"This monk being greatly moved by this vision, preferred Jesus Christ to the natural tenderness and commiseration which he felt towards his mother. Then he continued to serve God in his Order, and persevered in his resolution until his death."

(Idem—vol. 2d, p. 424.)

SECTION XVIII.—*Remedies against the Disease of the Love of our Kindred, Family . . . . Father, and Mother.*

"Remain like a dove in your solitude without chains tying you to the world. Even forget your country, the house of your family, and the king will be ravished with your beauty. Ps. of David xxxiv. 12."

(Idem—vol. 3d, p. 424.)

"Nothing can take out of our hearts the love of our families, except not seeing them, and breaking every kind of communication with them. We must be separated from them really and in fact, if we would rid our hearts of their love. . . . . It is on account of it, that our Constitutions expressly forbid all members of our Society to visit their parents. Let us be careful to spare our Superiors the importunity of our kindred. For instance, if they desire from us a compliance not according to the spirit of our community, let us not send them to the Superiors, lest they may be obliged either to break with them or to bestow what they ask. Let us be prudent as the serpent, who, to defend his head upon which he depends, hides it with all the folds of his body. Also Christ says, 'Be ye therefore cautious as serpents.' St. Matthew x. 16."

(Idem—vol. 2d, p. 425.)

Demonstration of the Efficacy of these Remedies by Examples of Saints.

"Surius relates that the mother of Saint Theodorus the Abbot, being protected by several Bishops, had been allowed by Saint Pacomius, the Superior of the convent, to see her son. Knowing this, the young Theodorus went to the Saint and told him—'My father, if you will that I see my mother, make it certain to me first, that in the day of judgment, God will not judge me on account of this visit.' 'You alone will be responsible,' answered the holy abbot. Theodorus refused to see his mother. History is filled with instances of monks lost by visiting their families."

(Idem—vol. 2d, p. 405.)

Divine Demonstration of the Efficacy of the same Remedies.

"Severus Sulpitius relates this dreadful anecdote: 'A Governor of Egypt, very rich and honorable, had been converted by the abbot John. He felt so moved by the grace of God, that he left his wife and children and came to the convent. Four years after he visited them, intending to convert them, but scarcely was he out of the convent, before the devil caught and possessed him and so violently, that he tore himself cruelly, and his mouth foamed. In spite of the prayers of the monks, he remained in this dreadful manner during two years. Having gotten rid of the devil, he went to the convent for ever cured of love for his family.'"

(Idem—vol. 2d, p. 411.)

These are the principles which the Jesuits teach their novices respecting friends, kindred, brothers, sisters, fathers, and mothers; principles which break all the most sacred ties of nature, and trample under foot one of the most sacred laws of God; principles which they wickedly assert to rest on the Scripture and the gospel, which they declare to have been many times divinely confirmed; in short, principles which, drying up and burning the heart, annihilate the most sacred duties, the noblest and most generous feelings; which attack, condemn, and destroy the most precious gifts granted by God to our souls; shake the strongest and most powerful pillars of society, and cast down all the social order.

SECTION XIX.—*Excellence of the Vows of the Jesuits.*

"Our vows rid us of all cares of the world—that of poverty, of the care of riches—that of chastity, of the care of governing a family and raising children—that of obedience, of the care of disposing of ourselves, in lying without will in the hands of our superiors.

"These vows lead surely to perfection. Christ appearing once to Saint Francis, ordered him to make him three offerings. 'You know, Lord,' answered he, 'that I have offered all myself to you, that I am yours and possess only this dress and cord, which are yours. What then can I offer to you? I would desire for such a purpose, to have one other heart and one other soul; but as I possess nothing which I have not offered to you, bestow me some new thing that I may offer you, and thus obey you!'

"Then Jesus Christ bade him to look in his breast and offer him what he should find. The Saint obeyed, and drew out a large gold piece, which he immediately offered Jesus Christ. The Saviour ordered him twice to do the same, and he finding each time a new and similar gold piece, which he immediately offered him. Jesus Christ declared to him that the three gold pieces signified 'obedience,' 'poverty,' and 'chastity.'

(Idem—vol. 3d, pp. 112, 113.)

SECTION XX.— *The Vows of Religion are so Valuable that they Remit Sins without previous Confession and Absolution.*

"The vows of Religion are so valuable and meritorious before God, that Saint Jeromius, Saint Cyprianus, and Saint Bernard, term them 'a second baptism,' and that the theologians teach that these vows remit all sins so efficaciously, that if we died soon after having taken them, we should not be purified by the flames of Purgatory, but should go straight to heaven in the same manner as those who die immediately after their baptism.

"This doctrine must not be understood of the effect of the indulgences attached to the profession of the vows, for a 'plenary indulgence' is bestowed upon the novices when they take the religious habit. It is to be understood of the proper merit of the vows themselves, which is so great, so excellent, that without the help of indulgences, it is sufficient to satisfy the justice of God for the pain due to our sins. This opinion, which is solidly based in itself, is still confirmed by the following report of Saint Athanasius, extracted from the life of Saint Anthony."

Divine Confirmation of this Doctrine.

"This great Saint had on a certain time a vision, in which he thought he was carried by angels into Paradise. The devils were opposed to it, accusing him of some sins which he had committed in his worldly life. But the angels answered the devil—'If you have to accuse him of some sins committed after his religious profession, you may bring opposition, otherwise you may not, for all his former sins are forgiven. He has satisfied entirely this debt in professing religion.'"

(Idem—vol. 3d, p. 118.)

The Jesuits maintain that they are the chief Catholics, the main soldiers of the Roman Church, consequently the strictest believers of this Church. However, it is an article of faith, that the sins committed after baptism are remitted only by confession and absolution; and in the case of perfect contrition, by the desire of confessing them. Then the Jesuits are not Roman Catholics, they ought to be termed "heretics." They still from the pulpit preach the Roman Catholic doctrine about the remission of sins. How can we explain this inconsistency?

Americans, when further you will read the summary of their doctrines and of their history, you will discover their motives and their aim. You will see that they believe or do not believe, act or act not, according to the circumstances, and always according to their interests. If they teach their novices such doctrines, it is only because they know that in exaggerating the merit and reward of the religious vows, they will succeed more surely to kindle their *imagination.*

SECTION XXI.—*Laymen Swim in Mud and Filth, but the Jesuits Dwell in a Terrestrial Paradise.*

We regret to be not allowed to produce many chapters in which the Reverend Father Alphonsius Rodriguez, proves and explains the advantages and value of the religious vows, in assuring that they give perfection, freedom, . . . that they rid the soul of the abomination and servitude of Egypt, and of the rivers of Babylon, which drown laymen. Rodriguez confirms all these pretended demonstrations by the following example:

"Saint Auselme having been on a certain day granted an ecstasy, saw a great river where ran all filth and obscenities of the earth. Its waters were dirty and stinking above all expression, and its stream was so rapid, so impetuous, that it carried away all which it met—men, women, rich and poor; sinking them at every moment to its bottom, and rolling them on without discontinuance.

"The Saint, surprised at this sight, and astonished in seeing these unfortunates rolled on in this manner, and nevertheless living, asked how they breathed, and what was their food. It was answered to him, that they fed themselves with the muddy waters and obscenities in which they swam, and where they were sunk; and that notwithstanding, they were satisfied with such aliment. It was added to him that this rapid river is the world; and where men sunk in vice, and drowned by their passions, live in so strange blindness, that though their continual agitation hinders them from finding some rest, they fancy they are happy.

"Afterwards the Saint was carried in spirit into a spacious park, whose walls were covered with silver plating and were bright. There was in the middle a meadow, where the grass was gilt, but so soft and fresh that it bended easily to our lying down, and never faded. The air breathed there was pure and delightful. Every thing, in a word, was there so smiling and pleasing that this spot was a terrestrial paradise, and made one supremely happy. This park and this meadow are the true image of the religious perfection."

(Idem—vol. 2d, p. 132.)

We feel pitiful when the Jesuits affirm that we swim and are sunk in mud and obscenities, but we feel very sorry in thinking that they deceive so many inexperienced novices, whom they mislead and tyrannize over, in imposing upon them such false doctrines, so absurd fables; we feel irritated for their requesting God so blasphemously, to be witness of their quackery, lies and deceitful designs.

SECTION XXII.—*Vow of Poverty while Swimming in Wealth.*

"In order that you may not think your reward will be bestowed upon you only in the future life, and that a credit will be required from you, though you pay cash, I say that the poor of spirit will be rewarded not only in the other world, but here below, and even most generously. Every body is interested, and the present things move us so much, that we seem to lose courage as soon as we are not excited by some actual advantage. Therefore, the Son of God knowing our weakness, would not that those who renounce all things to love him, be not indemnified, even in this life. He says:

"'Every one that hath left house, or brethren, or sister, or father, or mother, or wife, or children, or lands, for my name's sake, shall receive a hundred-fold, and shall possess life everlasting.' St. Matthew, xix. 29. But this hundred-fold must be understood of the present life, for Christ declares it: 'We shall receive a hundred times as much now in this time, and in the world to come, life everlasting.' St. Mark, x. 30."

I.—*Hundred Fold relatively to the Family.*

"Really, that is literally true. You have left for Jesus Christ a house, and now you possess many of them, which God grants to you for one which you have sacrificed. You have left a father and mother; and God grants to you, for indemnification, many other fathers, who love you much more, who are more careful towards you, and watch more attentively over your interests than your former father. You have left your brothers, and you find here plenty of them, who love you more than the former, since they love you only for the sake of God and without selfishness; but in the world, your brothers would love you only for their own benefit, and whilst they would have need of you. You have left in the world several servants; or perhaps you had none; and you find here plenty of them, who all the time are attentive to serve you. One of them is your procurer, another your porter, another your cook, another overseer in the infirmary. And, moreover, go to Spain, to France, to Italy, to Germany, to India, and to whatever part of the world it may be—you shall find your house all ready, and with the same number of persons employed to serve you, which a prince of the world has not. Is not this the hundred fold in this life, even more than the hundred fold?"

(Idem—vol. 3d, p. 153.)

II.—*Hundred Fold relatively to Wealth.*

"What shall we say now about what you have left? I mean wealth. Are you not richer in religion than you were in the world? In religion you are much more master of all wealth of the world than those who are its owners, for they are rather its slaves than its proprietors. Also the Scripture terms them 'men of wealth,' Psalms lxxv. 6—meaning that wealth does not belong to them, but they to wealth. They continually struggle to acquire, increase and keep it. The more they heap, the more trouble and anxiety they have, and even their plenty, as says the wise man, hinders them from sleeping. Eccls. v. 2. The monks, on the other hand, want nothing; do not care whether the goods are dear or cheap, whether the seasons are good or bad, and they live (I borrow the words of the apostle) as having nothing and possessing all things. II Cor. vi. 10. As for rest of the mind, are you not one hundred times more quiet than in the world? Ask the men of the world, even those who seem the most pleased with their position, and you shall be convinced that they at every moment are exposed to great many contradictions and anxieties of which the monks are rid."

III.—*Hundred Fold relatively to Honors.*

"As to dignities, you are one hundred times more honored under your religious habit than you could have been in the world; for the princes, great lords, bishops, and magistrates, who would have not considered you remaining in the world, now surround you in religion with regard and respect; and why? Because you wear the religious habit.

"Again, God gives you the hundred fold as to rest and tranquillity of life. Finally, to speak more properly, he bestows upon you the hundred fold in everything, and restores to you with usury all that you have left for his sake."

(Idem—vol. 3d, p. 154.)

What hypocrisy! Do not the Jesuits exhaust all means of seduction to deceive their novices? Do not they trample on reason, honesty, feeling, and truth, to fire their young, ardent and impulsive imaginations? Do they not trample profanely on the gospel, the word of Christ, in using them to sanction, to seal their quackery and falsehoods? What! we have seen them teaching contempt and hatred to the world, society, and family. They term the world and society "Egypt, Babylon;" their advantages, "abomination, muddy waters, obscenities." They term the parents "enemies of the spiritual interests of their children;" and now they say that their Order is the philosopher's stone, which changes these "Egypt, Babylon, abominations, muddy waters, obscenities, condemnable family love," into lawful, holy, and spiritual, advantages.

What! because they deny their families, according to Nature and God pretending that family love is a sinful pleasure, will they be allowed, and that in the name of Christ, of God, to enjoy one hundred times in the love of their unnatural family? Because they vow poverty, will they be allowed to swim one hundred times more in silver, gold, and property? Because they wear a religious habit, shall the unlawful honors of the world be lawful for them? And it is, I repeat it, in the name of Christ, of God, a profanation of the gospel that they try to rest this doctrine!

What a crime!—chiefly when they aim to tie the hands and feet of these confident and inexperienced novices, by flattering their senses, after having fired their minds with fanatical and pretended celestial considerations; above all, by painting heaven open over their head, if they enter into religion; and hell reserved for them if they remain in society, in their families.

SECTION XXIII.—*Vow of Chastity.—Remedies against Impurity.*

After having expatiated on the vows of chastity . . . which dissertation we are not allowed to produce, the Reverend Father Rodriguez opens his apothecary and delivers gratis omnipotent remedies against the disease of impurity, as follows:

First Remedy.—"We must stand a certain while on one foot, fast, sleep very little, extend the arms in the form of a cross, kneel, strike our breasts, pinch ourselves, administer to our body some lashes; above all, recite often the following prayer addressed to Mary:

"'O Virgin! always virgin, always helpful, give us favor with your Son. Grant us, tender and pure Virgin, softness of spirit and purity of heart.'"

Second Remedy.—"Likewise to carry in our pocket a good book is a powerful remedy. As proof: an old man, named Nicolas, entered on a certain day into a brothel . . . but, having in his pocket a New Testament, he was repelled by the prostitute, who told him that she saw in him marvellous things. Moved by this miracle, Nicolas went to Corinth, where Saint Andrews cured his bad habits in obliging him to fast."—(Idem—vol. 3d, p. 237.)

"Another very efficacious remedy is an ardent devotion to the Saints and their relics." It is demonstrated by the following instance:

Divine Demonstration of the Efficacy of this Remedy.

"Saint Cesarius relates that a monk named Bernard, who

still lived in the world, went through the country, and was tempted against chastity. Being but little scrupulous about it, he was careless in avoiding temptation. However, it happened that a shrine which he wore customarily hanging upon his neck, and which contained some relics of Saint John and of Saint Paul, began to strike his breast. As he did not understand what it was, he did not pay a serious attention to this admonition, and kept his impure thoughts, until the sight of some object having averted his mind, the strokes of the shrine ceased suddenly. Shortly after, the temptation coming again, the holy relics renewed their strokes, advising him to repulse his impure thoughts. Then he understood why this shrine repeated these strokes. Thus he overcame the temptation."

(Idem—vol. 3d, p. 231.)

Third Remedy.—"Sometimes, to rebuke the devil is efficacious. For instance, we must say to him: 'Go back, demon, miserable. What are you? Are you not ashamed? You must be very dirty to present to me so many obscene fancies.' The reason of it is, that the devil is proud, and gives up rather than to bear such contempt."

Divine Demonstration of the Efficacy of this Remedy.

"Saint Gregory relates that a holy bishop of Milan, named Dacius, was passing at Corinth to reach Constantinople. Having found, in which to lodge, only a house uninhabited for a long while on account of the ghosts, he went there with all his attendants.

"Whilst he at midnight was sleeping, the devils, under various forms of beasts, began to make a dreadful noise; several imitated the roaring of lions, several counterfeited the hisses of serpents, and others the lowing of bulls. The holy bishop, who had been awaked by such noise, looked at them with indignation and contempt: 'How admirably you have succeeded?' said he. 'You have tried to equal God, and you have been changed into beasts: you represent exactly what you are.' 'This jest,' says Saint Gregory, 'confused them so much, that, disappearing suddenly, they left the house without coming back again.'

"Saint Athanasius relates, that Saint Anthony was incessantly tempted against chastity; and that on a certain day, a small negro, dirty, ugly, and disgusting, fell down to his feet, saying: 'I have defeated a great many people, and you alone are invincible.' Then the Saint asked him what he was. The devil having answered that he was the spirit of fornication, 'Well,' replied the Saint, 'henceforth, I will despise you much more, since you are so despicable.' The vision disappeared immediately."

(Idem—vol. 3d, p. 240.)

Thus, some absurd and fanatical gymnastical exercises of the body, some prayers to Mary, a great devotion to the Saints, and a strong faith in the effect of their relics, and some insults to the devil, are the supreme remedies which the jesuitical apothecary contains against the disease of impurity; I do not say, against love, because their hearts being killed, they do not feel and do not know what it is, but I mean against their brutal passions. Also their lasciviousness is stopped and radically cured! they too are chaste, as their remedies are efficacious! Ah! if their tender devotees were less faithful to them, and less afraid to lower their own reputation in disclosing * * * if decency did not prevent us to write the mysteries of their convents, how whitely pure they would shine! What dazzling angels they would be! But we must seal our lips.

As to the ridiculous miracles related, to demonstrate the efficacy of their remedies, we have nothing to say, except that they are absurd and blasphemous lies. We ought not to be surprised at the impious falsehood of the Jesuits; for not to care for truth, provided they reach their aim, is their principle. And at what aim they in raising their novices? They aim to blind their minds and to kill their hearts, to put them into the coffin of their doctrines, and to bury them in the tomb of a passive submission and obedience.

SECTION XXIV.—*Laymen Under the Dominion of the Devil, but the Jesuits Holy.*

"An anchorite of Thebaida, who was a son of a priest of idols, related, on a certain day, to many fathers of the wilderness, that in his youth he customarily accompanied his father to a temple and witnessed the sacrifices. 'But once,' said he, 'it happened that entering in secretly, I saw Satan sitting on a very elevated throne, and all the infernal court near him. One of the chiefs of the devil approached and adored him.'

"'Whence do you come?' Satan asked him.

"'I come,' answered he, 'from such a province, where I have stirred up a sedition, kindled war, and set all on fire and in blood. I come to report that to you.'

"Then Satan asked him for how long a time he had done that. The devil having answered 'one month,' Satan gave orders to whip him instantly, for he had lost his time."

"Another approached and adored.

"'Whence do you come?' Satan asked him, 'and what have you done?'

"'I come from the sea,' answered the devil. 'There I have excited furious tempests, sunk a great many ships, and drowned a crowd of people. I come to report that to you.'

"Then Satan asked this devil what time he had spent to do that. He answered 'twenty days.' Thereupon Satan condemned him to the same punishment as the first, and for the same cause.

"Another devil came, whom Satan questioned in the same manner as the others. This devil having answered that he was coming from a city, in which nuptials were celebrated; that he had stirred up quarrels and caused the death of many people, even of the spouse—and all these in ten days—this devil was whipped too, because he had lost his time.

"A fourth devil approached and adored. Satan questioned him in the same manner as the others. On the answer that he came from the wilderness, where having struggled forty years in tempting an anchorite, he had succeeded the last night to make him sin against chastity, this prince of darkness, rising from his throne, kissed him, crowned him, gave him a seat near his, and praised him extremely on account of his victory.

"'In seeing that,' added the hermit, 'I thought that the condition of the anchorites must be much more excellent than that of the other men. Thereupon, I resolved to fly from the paternal home, and to come to the wilderness.'

"An anchorite having been in a vision carried away into a monastery, where the friars were very numerous, saw a crowd of devils running to and fro through all the monastery. The angel who guided him, led him to a city which was in the neighborhood. Being astonished at seeing there only a devil, who even rested quietly at one of the doors, he asked the angel what was the cause of this difference. He answered him, that in the city every body obeying the devil, one of them was sufficient to keep it in sin; that on the contrary, all monks of the convent trying to resist the temptations, a great many devils were necessary to tempt and pull down the friars.

"A monk being proud of his own holiness, the devil appeared to him under the form of a handsome woman, who feigned to have lost her way in the desert. He received her in his cell, conversed with her, and his heart giving up to criminal desires, he was ready to yield to them. But the woman suddenly disappeared from his arms, crying out. Then he heard in the air great bursts of laughter, and many voices of demons, who, to insult him by bitter mockeries, said to him:

"'O, anchorite, you raised yourself up to heaven, and now you are lowered into the abyss! Learn, henceforth, that he who is proud will be humbled!'"

(Idem—vol. 3d, pp. 252–254.)

SECTION XXV.—*Vow of Obedience.*

"Saint Ignatius, writing about obedience in the third part of our Constitution, teaches us that we must obey, not only externally—which is this first degree of obedience—but internally, viz., in conforming our will to that of the Superior—which is the second degree of obedience—that even we must conform our judgment to his, so much so, that we think exactly as he thinks, believe all that he orders is right—which is the third degree of obedience."

(Idem—vol. 3d, p. 266.)

Americans, pay the most serious attention to the explanation of those principles about obedience. Then you will see that they have been the first spring of all the crimes of the Jesuits, of all their impious and immoral doctrines, of all their dreadful history.

The author continues as follows:

First Degree of Obedience.—"As to the first degree of obedience, I say, that we must be very diligent and exact in doing what we are ordered to do by the Superior; even as promptly as a man extremely famished rushes upon food; or like a man who, loving passionately his own life, grasps all which will preserve it, and even more ardently.

"Our holy founder, writing about the punctuality of obedience, says, that when either the bell rings or the Superior orders, we ought to be as ready to obey as if God himself called us; consequently, that we must not complete a letter half-formed. God has showed by many miracles how much he loves punctual obedience."

"A holy friar writing, the bell rang while he formed a letter. He immediately left the letter half formed and obeyed. At his return he found it completed with a gold dash."

"Another time, Jesus Christ appeared to another friar under the body of a very handsome child. The bell of Vespers having rang nearly at the same moment, this friar left him to go to Vespers. It happened that in coming back, he found in his cell this divine child, who told him: 'I have remained because you went out; but I would have gone out, if you should have remained.'

"Another friar, having been favored with a similar apparition, and having left the infant Jesus with the same motive, found him at his return, under the form of a young man, who told him: 'As much as I have grown since you left me, so much I have grown in your soul, and that on account of the punctuality of your obedience.'"

(Idem—vol. 3d, p. 267.)

"Saint Ignatius wills that we obey with punctuality, not only either the ringing of the bell, or the voice of our Superiors, but the smallest sign of their will."

(Idem—vol. 3d, p. 267.)

Second Degree of Obedience.—"The second degree of obedience consists first, in an entire conformity of our will to that of our Superiors, so well that ours may be identified with theirs.

"Second, in an entire conformity of understanding to theirs, and in the identification of our feelings with theirs. We must believe that all which they order is right, submit our judgment to theirs, and that so strictly, that ours may be ruled by theirs. The proof of it is that we are a burnt sacrifice: then the whole victim ought to be consumed. Though the eyes of Saint Paul were open, he saw nothing in entering Damascus; likewise, we must see nothing though our eyes may be open. We must judge nothing by ourselves, be led by our Superiors, and lay motionless in their hands."

(Idem—vol. 3d, p. 267.)

Americans, you see what lovers of freedom are the Jesuits, what kind of republicans they may be. However, they apparently praise your liberal institutions, and for that you give them your children to educate. Later, when you shall regret it, and shall bewail your confidence, you will try to paralyze the consequences, but it will be too late; the evil will be irremediable, perhaps, as it is now in many liberal countries of Europe. You believe they love your Republic—how much you are mistaken! Really is it possible, that men holding such principles about obedience, can like your political institutions, and are fitted to raise your Republican youths, or fit to inculcate into them the love of their country, of the wise freedom, for the conquest of which their ancestors have shed their blood, and which they have bequeathed to their posterity? O! certainly not. We could believe, rather that the absurd and impious tales which they impose upon their novices are true and holy miracles, than to believe that they will and can bring up as good citizens, the youths whom they educate. The calamitous consequences of the teaching of the Jesuits, still, are but little palpable in this Union; but, Americans, beware—they are artful, and have borrowed a false skin.

Third Degree of Obedience.—"Saint Ignatius our founder in teaching us, says: 'There are in religion two kinds of obedience, viz: the imperfect and the perfect. The first has two eyes, but, to its own misfortune, the second is blind; but it is precisely in its blindness that its wisdom and perfection consist. The first reasons on the orders, the second obeys without reasoning. The first is always more inclined towards one thing than towards another—never stands indifferent; the second is like the tongue of a balance, standing without inclining to one side or another, and is always ready to execute what is ordered. The first obeys externally in executing what is ordered, but disobeys internally by the resistance of its mind; thus it deserves not to be termed obedience: the second performs not only what is ordered, but submit its judgment and will to the judgment and will of its superiors, supposing always that they are right in ordering what they order; it neither searches reasons why to obey, nor gives attention to the reflections coming to its mind, but obeys merely for the consideration that it is commanded, and because to obey in this manner is to obey blindly. This is the blind obedience which the Saints and the teachers of the spiritual life recommended to us so earnestly, and of which they have given us so many striking examples."

(Idem—vol. 3d, p. 280.)

Moreover, when we term this obedience a blind one, we do not pretend that it must be submitted to all things which could be ordered, though they should be criminal, for that would be a dangerous error. Saint Ignatius says so expressly—we call this obedience blind, because, in all cases in which we do not find a sin, we must obey simply, and without reasoning; supposing always that what is ordered is agreeable with the will of God, and not look for another motive, except the obedience itself and the commandment.

(Idem—vol. 3d, p. 280.)

This explanation is hypocritical, for the Superiors of the Jesuits will never order a crime without exhibiting reasons which will justify it, and will change it into a virtuous deed:

witness their doctrines and history, which further shall be exposed.

"Cassinus terms the blind obedience 'an obedience without discussion and examination,' because we must execute what is ordered without intruding ourselves into the seeking again and examining the motives. Saint John Climacus says the same, viz., that obedience is a motion of the will without discussion and examination, a voluntary death, a life rid of all kinds of curiosities, and a deprivation of one's own discerning.

"Saint Basilius, on these words of Jesus Christ, addressed to Saint Peter, and to all Ecclesiastical Superiors in his person, 'Feed my sheep'—St. John, xxi. 17—says, that as the sheep yield to the leading of their shepherds and follow them wherever they intend to lead them, in a like manner, a monk must yield to the leading of his Superiors and apply himself to obey plainly, without reasoning about what they prescribe."

"Saint Bernard, writing on the same obedience, says that the perfect obedience, chiefly for the beginners, ought to be without discernment, namely, adds he, that you must examine neither what you are ordered, nor why you are commanded; but apply plainly yourselves to accomplish faithfully and submissively what you are ordered to execute."

"The true obedience," says Saint Gregory, "examines neither the commandments of the Superiors, nor their intentions; because he who has abandoned the direction of himself to his Superiors, is never more pleased than in executing what they have ordered. One does not know what it is to interpose one's own judgment when one knows how to obey with perfection."

(Idem—vol. 3d, p. 281.)

"Saint Ignatius, intending to instruct us about the duty of obedience with palpable things, uses two comparisons very proper and very useful to that purpose. 'Let all those,'

8

says he, 'who live in obedience, be convinced they ought to yield to the leading of Divine Providence by the way of the Superiors, as a dead body which yields to an arbitrary handling and carrying out indifferently.'"

"This comparison is also made by Saint Francis, who taught it often to his monks, using these words in Christ: 'You are dead and your life is hidden with Christ in God.' Col. iii. 3."

"Effectively, a true monk ought to be so dead to the world that his entrance into religion may be called a civil death. Then, let us be as though we were dead. A dead body sees not, answers not, complains not, and feels not. Let us have not eyes to see the deeds of our Superiors. Let us be without a word to reply when we are ordered. Let us not complain, and when we feel displeased at an order let us stifle the feeling. Ordinarily the dead bodies are buried with the oldest and most worn-out winding-sheets; a monk must be the same for everything . . . .

"Again, Saint Ignatius says (and it is the second comparison which he uses): 'We must yield to our leading by Divine Providence, declaring his will by the mouth of our Superiors, as a stick which one uses to walk. The stick follows everywhere the one who carries it. It rests where he puts it, and it moves only as the hand which holds it. A monk ought to be the same: he must yield to the leading of his Superior, never move by himself, and follow always the motion of his Superior; wherever he may be placed, charged with a high or low employment, he must keep this place or employment without reluctancy. If the stick which supports you when you walk, would resist even slightly your will, and would intend to go to the left hand when you go the right, it would be more cumbersome to you than useful. Soon you would throw it away.

"Likewise, when you resist the hands of your Superior;

when you show reluctancy for the places, employments, and charges assigned to you; when in your actions, will, and judgment, he finds opposition to the motion which he intends to impose upon you, certainly you are more cumbersome to him than useful. Consequently, if you stand in such a spirit of indocility, you will shortly be tiresome to all the Superiors who govern you, and nobody being either pleased with you or able to make use of you, everybody will try to get rid of you. Thus, you will be tossed from one house to another.

"One carries a stick, because, bending itself, it is slight in the hands. A monk must be the same in the hands of the Superiors.

"Saint Basilius treating the same subject uses another and very right comparison. 'A house-builder,' says he, 'uses according to his own will the tools of his art, and it has never been seen that a tool has resisted the hands of a mechanic, and has not bent itself to all his motions. Likewise a monk ought to be a useful tool, and malleable to his Superior who is rising a spiritual building. Moreover, as the tool does not choose its office, in like manner a monk ought not to choose his employment, but leave entirely this care to his Superior. 'Finally,' continues this father, 'as the tool does not move in the absence of the mechanic, because it wants movement by itself, and has only that which it receives from the mechanic; in the same manner, a monk ought neither to do anything without being ordered by his Superior, nor dispose of himself even momentarily for the smallest thing, but to comply always and in all circumstances with the movements and direction of his Superior.'

"Behold precisely the obedience of the monks. And *apropos* of it, I remember that one of our fathers, who having been a long while Superior among us, said, that for fifteen years he had never given to the monks the reason of his orders.

"We read in the life of Saint Ignatius, that being General of the Company, he assured several times, that if the Pope ordered him to embark in any boat whatever, anchored in the harbor of Ostia near Rome, and to sail on the sea without mast, without sails, without oars, without rudder, in one word, without the instruments of navigation, even without food, he would obey immediately, and not only without anxiety and repugnancy, but with a great internal satisfaction."

(Idem—vol. 3d, pp. 285–287.)

"The following will confirm what we have said:

"When the Abbot Nisteron entered into religion, he told himself: 'I profess, now, that I and the ass of the monastery are identical. All which is put upon his back he carries, whether it may be heavy or light he does not murmur or resist. He bears without resentment the blows of the stick which are inflicted upon him, and the contempt of every body. He works incessantly, and is satisfied with a pinch of straw granted to him as food. I ought to be in the same disposition of spirit. Again, as an animal of burden does not go where he wishes to go, does not rest when he wants it, does nothing that is pleasing to him, and obeys always; in like manner a monk ought to submit in all things, to the orders of his Superior, and as an ass works, rests, and eats, for the service of his master and not for his own interest; in the same manner, the work, the rest, the sleep, in short, all the life and actions of a monk ought to reach a sole aim, the benefit of religion, of God, and not his own.'

"Surius, in the life of Saint Mélany, relates an instance which he daily related to his nuns:

"'A young man went on a certain day, to one of the fathers of the wilderness, asking permission to enter into religion. The holy old man, to show him in what disposition of spirit he should be, ordered him to strike a statue which was near his cell. He obeyed. Then the old man asked him if the statue had either complained or resisted. He answered, "No." The old man ordered him to renew his blows, and to add insults to strokes. He obeyed. After this exercise was repeated three times, he asked him if the statue had showed either any impatience or resentment. The young man answered, "No," adding that a statue is incapable of feeling.'

"'Then the old man told him: "If you can bear without murmuring, without complaining, without reluctancy, that I should treat you as you have treated this statue, remain, I consent to it, you will be my disciple; if you cannot bear it, go back to your home, you are not fitted for the religious life."'

"Saint Gertrude entreated God to soften her Superior, whose behavior was very exemplary, but who, ordinarily, was cross and rough. Our Lord answered her: 'I will not rid her of a defect which humiliates her, and withal, is useful to you.'"

(Idem—vol. 3d, pp. 295, 296.)

"An old hermit had a vision of heaven. There he saw four classes of the just. The highest was that of the obedient. They wore gold chains, necklaces, and were more glorious than the three other classes."

(Idem—vol. 3d, p. 299.)

The author fills four chapters of seventy pages each, to prove by the Scriptures and the reason, that the Superior of the Jesuits ought to be considered as God himself; that they must obey him as God himself; that they are as criminal in disobeying him as in disobeying God. And having written on the obligation of blind obedience, even when it injures our health, he tries to confirm this last doctrine by the following instance:

"A tyrant having cut off the breasts of Saint Agathe, Saint Peter appeared to her in prison under the form of a venerable old man, and wished to cure her. She would not, answering him that she had never used corporal remedies."

(Idem—vol. 3d, p. 346.)

Americans, I have laid before you the organization and administration of the Jesuits—their artfulness in getting novices—the tools with which they begin to work upon their souls—the degrading bodily exercises to which they submit them—the wrong, unnatural, and anti-Christian doctrines by which they mislead and delude them. I have represented the Jesuits imposing upon the minds of these unfortunate novices the belief, that the mystical science and perfection are acquired in thirty lessons; that prayer is an organic exercise; that they ought to be bound to mystical conversations, to be without eyes, to speak with affectation; that the Jesuitical Order holds from God the sublime mission to cast down Protestantism; that the rules of their Order are perfect, the Order itself a divine one; and that, to deny its divine perfection is a heresy, consequently that its smallest rules ought to be observed scrupulously; that we are manure and pigs; that humility consists in kissing the feet, in eating below the table, in lying down at the door of a refectory, and so on; that they ought to reveal all their thoughts and feelings; that friendship is condemnable and denunciation a sacred duty; that to die to their families, even to hate them, are sacred obligations; that they must not write to their fathers, mothers, etc., or visit them, or think of them, because these are the best remedies against the disease of their love; that the religious vows are sublime, for the reason that they rid them of the care of wealth, of raising a family, of directing themselves; that these vows are valuable enough to remit sin without previous confession and absolution; that laymen swim in mud and filth; that wealth, pleasures, honors, love of one's family, which they declare unlawful in society, are lawful in the Jesuitical family. I have exposed to you the absurd remedies which they apply to cure the brutal passions of their bodies, and the proofs which they give of their efficacy. I have related to you the instances which they allege to demonstrate divinely, that laymen are under the dominion of the devil, but themselves holy. I have showed their teaching on obedience, which doctrine kills in the human soul all the noble faculties with which God gifted us.

Now, Americans, draw the conclusions. Judge for yourselves whether I was right or wrong in telling that the houses of noviciate of the Jesuits are novel and monstrous butcheries, where they immolate, not animals, not human bodies, but souls created in the likeness of God; that their noviciate is a kind of pneumatic machine, extracting one after another all the faculties of the soul; that their novices having been wrought upon, are in the world with living bodies but without souls, having left them at the disposal of their Superiors, and being merely tools in their hands and blind executors of their arbitrary, capricious, and criminal orders. Judge whether the moulders and moulded, the masters and disciples, are not monsters in society—whether the doctrines which they hold and scatter all over the world, in preaching, confessing, teaching, invading families, are any thing else than monstrous and subversive of society. They are so dreadful that strength would fail us, and our pen would fall from our hand, if the obligation to unveil them were not imposed upon us by the highest and most imperious considerations, namely, the interests of religion, of society, of the American Republic.

CHAPTER VI.

SUMMARY OF THE DOCTRINES WHICH THE JESUITS HAVE HELD AND STILL HOLD, HAVE TAUGHT AND STILL TEACH.

SECTION I.—*Impieties.*

"We can with difficulty determine when we are, strictly speaking, obliged to love God."

(The R. F. Jesuit John Cardenas—Crisis Theologica, p. 241.)

To us it is very easy. Good sense informs us that we are bound to love God as soon as our intellect can appreciate his gifts, and our hearts feel gratefulness. Then we must infer that the Jesuits want good sense and feeling.

"We are bidden rather, not to hate God, than to love him."

(The R. F. Jesuit Anthony Sirmond—Defence of Virtue, Tract 2, sec. 1.)

Christ, however, answered the doctor of the law asking him what was the first and great commandment: "Thou shalt love the Lord thy God with thy whole heart and with thy whole soul, and with thy whole mind. This is the greatest and first commandment." St. Matthew xxii. 37, 38. We must conclude that the Jesuits, in holding an opposite doctrine, not only are not Christians, but profess the deepest contempt for Jesus Christ, his gospel, and style themselves ironically "The Society of Jesus."

"We may act by fear and hope" (consequently without love).

(The R. F. Jesuit Anthony Sirmond, in the aforesaid book.)

'Tis not surprising that the Jesuits, despising Jesus Christ, despise Saint Paul writing in his first epistle to the Corinthian x. 31: "Whether you eat or drink, or whatsoever else you do; do all things for the glory of God." But when we act without love, only by fear or hope, we do not glorify God;

we are slaves working at the sight of the whip, or mercenaries moving but by money. Again, are we not sons of God? May we throw off this noblest of our titles, without offending our father? And, to act without love is it not to throw off this title?

O Jesuits, you are very logical in not loving God, since you condemn the love of your families . . . . fathers and mothers!

"We are not bound by feeling to love God."

(The R. F. Jesuit Anthony Sirmond, in the aforesaid book.)

If we are not bound by feeling to love God, how will we be bound by feeling to love our fellow-creatures, fellow-citizens, friends, kindred, fathers, and mothers? Does not such doctrine grind the human heart? Are not the ties binding the members of the same family, of the same nation, of all mankind, to one another, thus rudely broken? And, can thus a family, a government, society, stand even for a short time? But let us not be astonished that the Jesuits hold this doctrine, for let us recollect that their hearts have been killed during their noviciate, when their masters taught them forgetfulness, contempt, hatred, for society and their own family.

"If you believe by an invincible error, that God orders you to blaspheme, blaspheme."

(The R. F. Jesuit Casnedy—Theological Judgment. Explanation of the first commandmont of God.)

We have delight in our belief, that not one among our fellow-creatures, civilized or uncivilized, is ignorant and savage enough to think that he is ordered by God to blaspheme. We feel sorry in being obliged to say, that the proposition of Jesuits is an insult to the human family and a blasphemy against God.

"A penitent cursing, provoking his Maker, and, in his anger being carried on to scandalous words, will only sin venially, for passion prevents him from appreciating what he says."

(The R. F. Jesuit Etienne Bauny. — Somme des péchés, ch. v. p. 66. Work published in 1655.)

Anger prevents him from appreciating what he says? But does not he admit the consequences who holds the principle? Does not he will the effects who wills the cause? And it is the case when a penitent becomes angry.

"Jesus Christ may say to you: 'Come, blessed of my father. You have lied and blasphemed, believing that I had ordered you to lie and to blaspheme.'"

(The R. F. Jesuit Casnedy—Theological Judgment.)

O Jesuits, how far you are from the love of God! Can you dare to blaspheme your Creator so dreadfully!

"Absolution must be bestowed, though an ignorant penitent does not know or believe expressly the mysteries of the holy Trinity and Incarnation."

(The R. F. Jesuit Lessius—Sacramentum pœnitentiœ.)

But if this penitent does not know expressly the mysteries of the Holy Trinity and Incarnation, he will not know the mystery of Redemption; not knowing the mystery of Redemption, he will not know what is the absolution, by whom it was instituted, and by whom he will receive the forgiveness of sins. Then, in confessing and being absolved he will act as an unreasonable being.

We suppose, reply you, that he knows and believes understandingly these mysteries. If we understand your meaning, you will know and believe these mysteries in his stead, namely, he will give you a kind of power of attorney to do his spiritual business, but in matter of faith it is not so. Jesus Christ said to the blind man: "Thy faith hath made thee whole." St. Mark x. 52. As you see, it is not a question of the faith of the priest, but of one's own. St. Paul says: "Even the justice of God by the faith of Jesus Christ, unto all and upon all them that believe in him: for there is no distinction, for all have sinned, and do need the glory of God. Being justified gratis by his grace through the redemption that is in Christ Jesus, whom God had set forth to be a propitiation through faith in his blood to the showing of his justice for the remission of past sins. We account a man to be justified by faith." Epistle to the Romans iii. 22–28. These texts mean most clearly our own faith, and not the faith of the others, not an implicit, but an explicit one.

Reverend Fathers, we should be very much astonished at your absurd distinction, if we did not know that you, according to your rules and vows, must know and believe only what know and believe your Superiors. It is very logical that you carry out among Christians those principles, which generate the deepest ignorance, blindness, and tyranny of intellect, and kill, with the reason, the individual freedom.

"The Christian religion evidently is credible, but not evidently true, because it teaches obscurely or teaches obscure doctrines. Again, he who professes that the Christian religion is true, must confess that it evidently is false. Infer, then, that at least, it is not evident a true religion exists in the world: for in what manner do you hold that among the various religions the Christian is the most probable? Were the oracles of the prophets inspired by God? And if I deny the prophecies . . . ? If I maintain that the miracles attributed to Christ are not true?"

(Thése Philosophique des Jesuites de Caën, Soutenue au College Bourbon.)

Reverend Fathers, you attack the learning and teaching of the universities; you found colleges everywhere; you privately and cunningly insinuate and make public, by your creatures and Jesuits of the short gown, among all ranks of society, that you are the most learned and best teachers; you daily deliver lectures on philosophy—then we are very much astonished at your reasoning. We must infer, either that you do not know, or have forgotten the first rules of logic, for you say: "The Christian religion evidently is credible, but not evidently true." Reverend Fathers, listen to us. The third among the old rules of the syllogism (I quote them because they are your beloved, as all are which are superannuated), this third rule, I say, is this: "Nunquam contineat medium conclusio fas est." Viz.: "That the conclusion may not contain the middle term." However, you say: "The Christian religion is not evidently true (still) it is evidently credible." Then you suppose that what is not evidently true, is evidently credible, which proposition is contrary to good sense. Moreover, you are bound to infer this conclusion: then the Christian religion is evidently credible—which conclusion contains the middle term if the argument is logically performed.

But it is not all. You say that "the Christian religion is not evidently true, because it teaches obscurely or teaches obscure things." Certainly, the essence of the dogma being impenetrable, these doctrines are not evident, but their truthfulness is evident since what God teaches is evidently true. And as—if I am not mistaken—you admit that Christ is God, then the religion which he taught is evidently true.

You add that he who professes that "the Christian religion is true, must confess that it evidently is false," etc. We deny such anti-Christian conclusion, because it is contrary to the rules of logic and to good sense, and are compelled to proclaim that you are most illogical. When, on the other hand, you dare affirm that "we may not hold, that among the various religions the Christian is the most probable," etc. . . . we are obliged to denounce you to Christians as anti-Christian, and to say, that Voltaire never spoke and wrote better than you in attacking the Christian religion.

"Besides purgatory known to every body," says Lacroix after Bellarmine and Guimenius, "there is another place which is a beautiful meadow, covered with all sorts of flowers, lighted brilliantly, exhaling a delicious odor, which is a delightful spot where the souls do not suffer the pain of the senses. This spot is the dwelling of the slight sinners, a very mitigated purgatory, and a kind of sanatorial prison where we may live without dishonor. Then, there we will not be displeased.

"As to the other purgatory, not a sinner has spent there more than ten years."

(Life of the Reverend Father Jesuit Claudius Lacroix.)

Advertisement to slight sinners! Children may disobey their parents, be disrespectful and ungrateful toward them. Girls may dress themselves immodestly, frequent with worldly intentions soirees and balls, plot sinful intrigues of love without the cognizance of their fathers and mothers. Every body may lie million of times, deceive, steal thousand and thousands of dollars—provided it may be in small thefts, namely, up to fifty-nine cents each time and from various persons, detract, slander, etc., etc. . . . . for all these sins are declared slight by the Jesuits and by the most of the Romish Theologians. It is an article of faith in the Roman Catholic Church that a sole purgatory exists, but it makes no difference. Since the Jesuits pretend to be, even by Divine confirmation, the chief soldiers of this church, its strongest defenders, and sent by God himself to support it and cast down Protestantism, evidently they are allowed to change the creed of this Holy Papal Church.

Then, all you slight sinners be informed that, with your money for venial sins, you will be admitted "into a beautiful meadow, covered with all sorts of flowers, lighted brilliantly, exhaling a delicious odor," into "a delightful spot, where your souls will not suffer the pain of the senses." This abode

9

will be to you "a very mitigated purgatory, a kind of sanatorial prison where you will live without dishonor. There you will not be displeased." Do not fear to be excluded from this residence of delight, for if your venial sins are not light enough they will open to you the other purgatory, where not a sinner has spent more than ten years.

I said [advertisement to you slight sinners !] because, as to myself, I will never be admitted into "this beautiful meadow, this delightful spot, this sanatorial prison," even into the other purgatory, considering that I am the greatest sinner among all in unveiling the Jesuits, and consequently deserving a copious dose of their poison called "Aqua Toffana;" and to be buried in hell as soon as possible.

O Jesuits, what kind of mountebanks you are ! Your fellow-quacks are injurious to the people merely in stealing from them money, in altering their health ; but you steal from them incalculable treasures, and kill their souls : all this in the name of God. How criminal you are !

"Mary would prefer to be eternally damned, deprived of seeing her Son, and necessitated to live with the devils, rather than to be bred in original sin."

(Rev. Father Jesuit Oquett—Sermon preached at Ascala, 1600.)

In truth, we do not know at what the Jesuits aim in holding a so unnatural belief. If they intend to extol Mary, they on the contrary degrade her the lowest possible, in denying to her the most natural and noblest feelings.

What is the strictest duty of a mother ? The maternal love. What is the glory and crown of a mother ? The maternal love. What is the happiness of a mother ? To see her son continually ; to live near him, beneath the same roof ; to partake of his troubles, anxieties, sufferings, successes, joys, pleasures ; to mingle and identify her mind and heart with his mind and heart; in one word, to lavish on him her cares, solicitude, tenderness, and boundless love. Her irremediable sorrow is to live far from him, without hoping to meet him again—to see him dying. However, the Jesuits dare assure that "Mary would prefer not to see her Son . . . . rather than to be bred in original sin." What insult, what injury, to the maternal heart of the mother of Christ!

Again: all men coming into life are guilty of original sin. Then, Mary being one of the daughters of Adam, ought to partake of the condition of her fellow-creatures, and like them to be guilty of original sin. It follows, that to suppose she would claim such a privilege and stand above the human family, is a slander against her humility, and is to charge her with selfishness, blind pride, despising and denial of her family. Also, how far from truth, from the feelings of Mary, the Pope and the Bishops have been and are, in celebrating annually, and that with a solemn rite, the feast of the "immaculate conception," and in exhibiting Societies under this calling.

The Jesuits add, that "Mary would prefer to be eternally damned and necessitated to live with the devils, rather than to be bred in original sin." Decidedly they forget logic, for the Scripture informs us that the sinners only shall be eternally damned and necessitated to live with the devils. Then, the Jesuits suppose that Mary would prefer to be guilty of actual sins rather than of original sin.

We must infer from the above reasonings, that if the Jesuits intend to extol Mary with such doctrine, they on the contrary degrade her as low as possible; that if they intend to injure her, they succeed wonderfully. If Mary lived among us, she would reproach them with the same.

"Saint Ignatius saw the souls of his fellows arising to heaven and stopping to converse with him. They foretold to

him that every Christian wearing the Jesuitical habit should have the privilege to go straight to heaven."

(Compendium, p. 43—Several mystical books.)

We could laugh at such a modest tale, if it were not a deceitful and profane lie.

Question.—"What will we see in the Paradise?"

Answer.—"We will see the very sacred humanity of Jesus Christ, the adorable body of the Virgin Mary, and those of the other Saints, without reckoning thousands and thousands other beauties."

Question.—"Will our senses enjoy the pleasures which pertain to them here?"

Answer.—"Yes. And, O admiration! they will eternally enjoy them without disturbance."

Question.—"What! the hearing, the smelling, the taste, the touching; will they have all the pleasures of which they are capable?"

Answer.—"Yes, undoubtedly, the hearing will be charmed with the softness of sounds and harmony. The smelling will enjoy the pleasures of odors and perfumes. The taste will be flattered with savors. Finally, the touching will be entirely satisfied."

Question.—"If we speak in the Paradise, I should be desirous to know in what language it will be?"

Answer.—"Likely in the Hebrew language, which God taught the first man, and which Jesus Christ has spoken. We will be allowed, too, to speak the language of our choice, since all are familiar to the blessed."

Question.—"How will the blessed be dressed?"

Answer.—"They will be dressed with glory and light. All parts of their bodies will shine according to what they will have suffered for God."

(The Reverend Father Jesuit Pomet—Catechism of Theology, published in Lyons, France, 1675.)

What! Reverend Fathers, we will see in the Paradise the adorable body of the Virgin Mary? Then you are idolaters. We will see the bodies of the other Saints, without reckoning thousands and thousands other beauties. But you are lascivious, even blasphemously lascivious. Our senses will enjoy the pleasures which pertain to them here! Beware; you are voluptuous, and profanely voluptuous. The hearing will be charmed with the softness of sounds and harmony! Then we will find, in the Paradise, instrument-makers and music-teachers, artists. . . . . What do you say? You materialize the Paradise. The smelling will enjoy the pleasure of odors and perfumes! Then we will have gardens, parterre, flowers, trees . . . . . What material and epicureal Paradise! The taste will be flattered with savors; namely, our tables will be delicate, our meals the most refined, our drinking the most exquisite and exciting. What delight for the gluttons! The touching will be entirely satisfied! O, Reverend Fathers, we refuse to go to your Paradise; the society will be there too impure . . . .

We close our reflections about it, in recalling to you these words of Christ: "In the resurrection they shall neither marry nor be given in marriage, but shall be as the angels of God in heaven." St. Matthew xxii. 30.

Reverend Fathers, you add, that likely we will speak in Paradise the Hebrew language . . . . . that we will be allowed, too, to speak the language of our choice, since all are familiar to the blessed. Dear Fathers, we are very grateful to you for this precious discovery; but we could feel more grateful had you informed us whether we will be obliged to get teachers of these languages, or will learn them by intuition. You add, that all parts of the blessed bodies will shine according to what they may have suffered for God! What encouragement for the young men and girls, for the chaste men and women . . . . . We stop; it is odious and disgusting above all expressions.

Chapter 73.—"Men and women will enjoy in the Paradise masquerades and ballets."

Chapter 74.—"The angels will dress themselves as the women—will appear to the Saints with rich female ornaments, curled hair, with petticoats, and fardingales, and muslin shirts."

Chapter 58.—"Each blessed will have in heaven a particular residence. Jesus Christ will dwell in a splendid palace. There will be wide streets and large public squares, castles and citadels."

Chapter 22.—"The supreme pleasure will be to kiss and embrace the bodies of the female blessed. They will bathe in springs destined for the purpose, and will sing like the nightingales."

Chapter 65.—"Women will have beautiful and long hair. They will adorn themselves with ribbons; their dress and head-dresses will be the same fashion as here below."

(The Reverend Father Jesuit Hendriquez—Occupation des Saints dans le ciel.)

Reverend Fathers, you assure us that men and women will enjoy in Paradise masquerades and ballets! But the masquerades and ballets are the pomps of the world, the works of Satan. Then the Paradise in which dwell the blessed, Jesus Christ and God, is the world which Christ has cursed; the kingdom of Satan, of which the blessed, Jesus Christ and God, are the subjects. Jesuits, you are dreadfully impious.

You add, that the angels will dress themselves as women, will appear to the Saints with rich female ornaments, curled hair, with petticoats, and fardingales, and muslin shirts! Then Paradise is an angel's retiring-room, a parlor of coquetry. The gospel, even the Roman Catholic church, teach that the angels are pure spirits; and still you give them curled hair, petticoats, muslin shirts. The lascivious ought to be very glad of your discovery, and vote thanks to you; the merchants of novelties, too, for they will make money in keeping splendid stores, and, with greater reason, the manufacturers of these angelical dresses.

According to you, Reverend Fathers, the blessed will have in heaven their particular abodes. Jesus Christ will dwell in a splendid palace. There will be wide streets and large public squares, castles and citadels. Please tell us what will be the material of these particular houses, of this splendid palace of Jesus Christ, and where they will be situated—whether in cities, surrounded by fragrant trees, or in the country, among amorous woods. Still you give us a kind of information, in assuring us that in Paradise we will find wide streets, large public squares, castles and citadels. But you lead us into another labyrinth; for, who traced these streets and squares? Who built these houses, palaces, castles, and citadels, and on what ground? On a planet or a star? Moreover, you suppose that Paradise will be organized into a feudal political system; that the blessed will be divided into bondmen and lords; that the lords will war against each other, will have armies, and will keep garrisons in these citadels. O Jesuits, be kind enough to inform us in what page of the gospel you have read your teaching.

Moreover, you say that the supreme pleasure of the blessed will be to kiss and embrace the bodies of the female blessed; that these female blessed will bathe in springs suited for the purpose; that they will sing like the nightingales. Reverend Fathers, let us say to you that your Paradise is merely that of Mahomet, and worse—that it is a brothel, and nothing else; that you must keep it for yourselves and your devotees.

When you add, that in Paradise women will have beautiful

and long hair, that they will adorn themselves with ribbons, that their dress and head-dresses will be in the same fashion as here below, we feel sorry on account of your blasphemy, but not at all surprised. Christ has said, "Out of the abundance of the heart the mouth speaketh." St. Matthew xii. 34. You are so fond of ladies finely dressed, chiefly to confess them! Also, they know your blind side, and surround your confessionals, particularly when they are tired of their husbands, and, with your hand on your conscience, you know who averted them from the love of their husbands; you know why you confess them weekly, and make them come to you, under the pretext of direction of conscience, many times a week. Of course you answer that your motives are laudable; but were you sincere, you should recite a great "meâ culpâ —meâ culpâ—meâ maximâ culpâ."

Americans, however the Jesuits declare with a loud voice that they are the Saints of the Roman Catholic Church, her strongest pillars, particularly against Protestantism, and the main soldiers of Popery . . . . if you must judge the other monks, the nunneries, and secular priests, by them, the consequences will be mostly honorable to the Romish Church; you will have for its leaders the most favorable opinion, the highest consideration and esteem.

"The Reverend Father Jesuit Cotton, confessor of Louis XIV., King of France, asked the devil, in exorcising a pretended possessed, whether or not he had nails before the seduction of Eve." (Compendium—p. 53.)

This demand at the first sight seems a foolish one, but it is a will of ability and artfulness. As this Reverend Father Jesuit was very influential on the mind of the King (witness the history of France), he tried to blind and deceive the public opinion, in giving the people occasion to say, that a man of so feeble spirit was not dangerous.

"In Malabar and China, the Jesuits allowed the converts to worship the images of idols, provided they would secretly carry a crucifix."

(Magnum Bellarium Romanum—p. 388.)

Is not this compliance an idolatrous one? Of course. But religion in the hands of the Jesuits is merely a political lever to grow up wealthy, powerful, and to reach their criminal aim, viz., to obtain for the Pope the universal monarchy. Also let us listen to Pascal, the celebrated mathematician:

"By their easy and obliging behavior, as the Father Pétau terms it, the Jesuits yield to every body. If any one comes to them resolved to restore what he stole, fear not they prevent him from it. They will, on the contrary, praise and encourage a so holy determination. If another come to them and by absolution without the previous restitution of which he stole, it shall be the most entangled case if they do not absolve him. Thus they keep their friends, and justify themselves against all their enemies. They answer, when accused of an extreme compliance, by exhibiting the names of their austere confessors, and by showing noisily some of their books which treat about the severity of the Christian law. Then it happens that the ignorant, and those who do not investigate carefully their artfulness, are satisfied with such justification.

"The Jesuits have answers for all tastes, and are so complying, that, when they are in a country where a God crucified is considered as a folly, they suppress the scandal of the cross, preach a Christ glorious, and no Jesus Christ suffering. They did so in China and in India, where they permitted to the Christians even idolatry, by the cunning invention of an image of Christ hid under their clothes, to which they should mentally offer the public adorations, addressed either to the idol Cachinchoam or to their Keum-fucum."

(Pascal—Cinquième Lettre Provinciale, sec. 5, 6, et 7.)

The same writer adds, on the impious compliances of the Jesuits:

"I went to an obliging casuist of their Society. After some indifferent themes of conversation, I told him that to fast is tiresome for me.

"This Father urged me to make an effort. He still felt moved, and tried to find some grounds of dispensation . . . . Finally, he asked me if I did not rest well in going to bed, having not supped.

"'No,' I answered, 'and by this reason I must sometimes take my light meal at noon, and sup in the evening.'

"'I am very glad,' replied he, 'to have found this lawful way to relieve you. Be quiet,' assured he; 'you are not bound to fast. I will not that you believe merely on my decision: come to the library.'

"I went there. He took Escobar, and looked for the case. Then he told me:

"'Behold the Tract, ex. 13, No. 67.' *(Question.)* 'Is he who cannot sleep, having not supped, obliged to fast?' *(Answer.)* 'Not at all. Are you not pleased?'

"'Not quite,' I answered, 'for I can fast in taking my light meal in the morning, and my supper in the evening.'

"'Look at the sequel,' added he, 'they have foreseen all cases.'

"'And what shall happen,' I asked, 'if I sup in the evening? Is it not necessary to take the light meal in the morning?'

"'I am ready,' replied he; 'even in this case we are not bound to fast, for nobody is obliged to change the hour of his meals.'

"'O, what good reason!' I exclaimed.

"'Tell me,' pursued he, 'if you drink a good deal of wine?'

"'No, my Father,' I answered, 'I cannot bear it.'

"'I asked you this,' replied he, 'to inform you that you may drink wine in the morning, and according to your want, without breaking fast. Moreover, wine fortifies a little. Look at this decision, No. 57.'—'May we, without breaking fast, drink wine even a good deal, and according to our will?'—'Yes, even hypocras.'

"'I had forgotten this hypocras,' said he; 'I must write it in my records.'

"'This Escobar is an honest man,' I said.

"'Every body likes him,' replied the Father Jesuit."

Pascal adds:

"Will you say, Jesuits, that the profane and coquettish picture of piety which traces Father Lemoine in his book, 'Devotion Aisée,' does not inspire rather contempt than respect for Christian virtue? Is not all his book of moral pictures written the same way? Is this Ode of the seventh book, headed 'Eloge de la Pudeur,' worthy of a priest?—ode in which this Father Jesuit says, in each stanza, that the most prized things are roses, grenads, mouth, and tongue? And it is among these gallantries, shameful to a monk, that he dares haughtily mingle these blessed spirits who stand before God, and of which Christians ought to speak only with veneration:

"'Les Chérubins, ces glorieux
Composés de tête et de plume,
Que Dieu de son esprit allume,
Et qu'il eclaire de ses yeux;
Ces illustres faces volantes
Sont toujours rouges et brûlantes,
Soit du feu de Dieu soit du leur,
Et dans leurs flammes mutuelles
Font du mouvement de leurs ailes
Un eventail à leur chaleur,
Mais la rougeur éclate en toi,

Delphine avec plus d'avantage,
Quand l'honneur est sur ton visage
Vêtu de pourpre comme un roi.'
* * * * *

[TRANSLATION.]

"The cherubs, these glorious beings, composed of head and feather, whom God with his spirit fires, and with his eyes lights; these illustrious winging faces are always crimson and burning, either with the fire of God or with their own; and, in their mutual flame, with the motion of their wings, fan their ardor. But redness shines in thee, Delphine, more attractively when honor is on your face colored with purple as a king."

* * * * * * *

"Do you think, Jesuits, that the preference of the redness of Delphine to the ardor of these spirits, who have but that of charity, and the comparison of a fan with these mysterious wings, are very Christian in a mouth which consecrates the adorable body of Jesus Christ? Is it not true that, if justice was rendered to him, he could not escape censure? Of course, he, to preserve himself, would allege what he reports in the first book, and which is not less censurable, namely, that Sorbonne has not jurisdiction over Parnassus; but is it not forbidden to blaspheme, either in poetry or in prose? Suppose that this allegation may justify him, at least this other passage of the preamble of the same book could not be spared, viz., that the water of the river, on the bank of which he composed these verses, is so fit to inspire poets, that, though it could be changed into holy water, it could not expel the demon of poetry.

"Moreover, is it possible to justify the passage of the Father Garasse in his book—'Somme des Vérités Capitales de la Religion'—in which (p. 649) he unites blasphemy to heresy, in writing on the sacred mystery of incarnation as follows:

'The human individuality has been grafted, or put on horseback, on the individuality of the word.'

"Likewise, is it possible to justify what the same author says about the name of Jesus, ordinarily represented with the letters I H S, viz., that many have blotted out the cross to keep only these letters, meaning a Jesus-stripped!'

"O Jesuits! this shows how unworthily you treat the religious doctrines."

(Pascal—Lettres Provinciales—Onzième Lettre, p. 25, 26.)

"We may discard our title of Christian, and act as the worldlians act, though what we will do may not be, properly speaking, permitted by the gospel."

(Compendium—p. 61.)

O Jesuits, with what fidelity you paint yourselves! What a precious key you give us to unlock and penetrate the sanctuary of your crimes! What leading thread you put in our hands to explore the windings of the labyrinth of your history! How faithfully and carefully you have practised this hypocritical maxim! In feigning humility, you grew up powerful. In feigning chastity, you were allowed to be refinedly licentious. In feigning piety, you reached consideration. In feigning devotedness to youth and solid learning, you obtained by gratuitous donations many thousand colleges, filled with numberless scholars, who paid very dear for the superficial instruction sold to them by yourselves. In feigning poverty, you acquired immense wealth. In feigning prodigality, you became lucratively covetous. In feigning idolatry, you obtained from the Emperor of China money, dignities, even a living in his palace. In feigning sensibility, you gained the devotedness of the rich and noble ladies. In feigning commiseration towards the poor, you harvested a countless amount of alms which you either pocketed, or politically distributed to obtain the brutal favor of the mob. In feigning servility before the secular clergy, you oppressed them. In feigning zeal in the dioceses, you usurped the jurisdiction of the bishops. In feigning a sublime and mystical doctrine, you gained the consciences and all the faculties of the soul, and between us I could add, the bodies of the devotees. In feigning to have discovered a rosy road leading to heaven, namely, in dancing, immodestly dressing, tissuing sinful intrigues of love, spending time frivolously and voluptuously, etc., you became the confessors and directors of the rich, influential, and noble ladies, who paid largely for your sacrilegious compliances with money and protection, and in getting for you charges, dignities, wealth, in serving all your ambitious and criminal desires. In feigning to find an easy way to lead to Paradise the mistresses of kings, you obtained their favor, gratitude, gifts, and rewards, of every kind. In feigning that the gospel may be understood for the great of the world differently than for the people, you won their benevolence and support. In feigning love of royalty, and in widening the narrow way of the gospel, you obtained the confidence of Kings and Emperors; were admitted to their councils; imposed your views upon them in God's name; confessed, absolved, and gave them the sacrament, in spite of their tyrannical and criminal behavior. And for what? All this, to kill them after a while if they did not obey passively your wishes, which were in the style of the court imperious orders. In feigning friendship for the ministers of Kings and Emperors, you disgraced and banished them from the courts. In feigning republicanism, you invaded the Republics, fomented disunion, hatred, and kindled civil war, to dissolve them—to reach by these means your pretentious and criminal aim, viz., to conquer for the Pope the "universal monarchy," which through him you would possess. Finally, in feigning devotedness to all forms of governments, you disturbed all. In feigning the most sincere attachment for the Princes, Kings, and Emperors, you betrayed them all, except the Popes, or at least Papacy.

O Jesuits, how faithfully and carefully you have disregarded your title of Christian — I mean your Christian obligations — and acted as the worldlians act, and worse than them; though what you did was not, properly speaking, permitted by the gospel!

"The obligation of hearing mass is fulfilled though we do not intend to hear it."

(The R. F. Jesuit Vasquez, in his Theology, Article, Mass.)

According to the belief of the Roman Catholic Church, mass is the renewing of the sufferings and death of Christ to redeem us. Christ leaves heaven at the order of the priest pronouncing the words of consecration, and replaces the bread and the wine, which are no longer called bread and wine, but the body, the blood, the soul, the Divinity of Jesus Christ, and keep only the form and appearance of bread and wine.

Thus, to assist at the mass is one of the most serious and sacred actions which we can imagine: to fulfil respectfully and devotedly this service, is the most sacred duty. And we can fulfil the obligation of hearing mass without intending to hear it! O! certainly not: it would be to laugh at Jesus Christ. Such a doctrine is an insult to him.

"The obligation of hearing mass is fulfilled, even while beholding women with concupiscence."

(The R. F. Jesuit Escobar — Moral Theology — Tract 1.)

Jesuits, can we be astonished at seeing, that in the Catholic countries you are surnamed the Fathers with wide sleeves? at seeing your confessionals crowded with dissolute men and women, chiefly with the rich and noble families whom you absolve, and to whom you administer the sacrament although they give public scandal? But you make your trade; you get honors and money; it is all. Why care for the remainder? Deny that, if you are impudent enough.

"I have been taught by the blessed Mary . . . . that in looking upon a woman with unchaste desires, we fulfill the obligation of hearing mass, even if we had not intended to fulfil it."

(The R. F. Jesuit Masarrennas— Tract 5.)

Advertisement to the licentiousness. If they want money to go to the theatres, or rather to the * *, they may go to church. There they will enjoy very cheap, for they will pay nothing. Even they will hear the mass; they will fulfil a religious and sacred obligation. It is so true that the blessed Mary has revealed it to the Jesuits. And, Reverend Fathers, you do not feel ashamed!

"Is not a man having unworthily taken the sacrament at Easter, obliged to commune anew? I answer, 'No: because he has fulfilled the duty imposed upon him by the Church. The law which obliges to take communion binds only to the substance of the action, and a sacrilegious communion is sufficient."

(The R. F. Jesuit George Gobat—Ouvres Morales. Tome 1, Traité 4, p. 253—Publiées à Douai en 1700.)

The Jesuits must suppose that the laws of the Roman Catholic Church are very despicable, to lower them in such a manner. But do they care for the laws of the Roman Church, when, as we will see in the summary of their history, they handle religion as a political lever; when they consider the laws of their church as a way for making money? So it has been by their counsel that the pretended and celebrated dress of Jesus Christ has been honored at Trêves, France, which quackery afforded to the priests an immense annual revenue. It has been by their counsel, too, that My Lord Affre, Archbishop of Paris, had exposed to the veneration of the people a nail which, even now, affords a great amount of money.

SECTION II.—*Simony.*

"If we bestow a sacrament or another holy thing, aiming at a lascivious pleasure which we consider as a reward of our compliance, and not merely as a pure gift, we shall be guilty of Simony and profanation. It is the case of a man who would grant a benefice to a brother for the favor of lasciviousness committed with his sister. However, if this man, having * * * with the sister, grants the benefice to the brother under color of gratefulness, he commits only a kind of irreverence."

(The R. F. Jesuit Vincent Filliucius—Moral Questions—Tome 2, ch. 7, p. 616.)

What can we infer from this doctrine? We may and are logically compelled to infer, that religious things are a spiritual merchandise of which the Jesuits are the storekeepers; that, according to a greater or less ability and artfulness in dealing, they will be allowed to get less or more money; that the sole difference between the goods-merchants and them will be, that the first shall be termed profane dealers, and the Jesuits sacred dealers. What must we infer again from this doctrine? That the Jesuits would imitate Judas: would sell Jesus Christ for a few pieces of money if he should come again into this world. This conclusion is evident, for, since they deal with the gospel of Christ, they undoubtedly would deal with his own person.

O religion of the Saviour, into what hands art thou fallen!

"Simony and Astrology are lawful."

(The R. F. Jesuit Ars. de Kin—Theol. Tripartita, Tome 2, Tract 5, ch. 12: published in 1744.)

Astrologers, fortune-tellers, mountebanks of every denomination, flock together! The Jesuits will grant you licenses and letters-patent for exercising your honorable and useful

10*

trade. These licenses and letters-patent will be valuable, for the Jesuits (at least they say so) hold such power from God by letters of attorney, which He bestowed upon them as His lieutenants in this world.

Simony has been declared lawful by fifteen theologians of the Jesuits.

SECTION III.—*Perjury.*

"We may swear in a slight or grave matter without the intention of holding our oath, if we have good reasons to swear."

(The R. F. Jesuit Cardenas—Crisis Theologica—Question Oath.)

"If a woman hides her dowry after the confiscation of the property of her husband, she may answer, at request, that she hid nothing, by understanding, 'nothing belonging to her husband.'

"When a crime is secret we may deny our guilt, by understanding, 'public crime.'" (The R. F. Jesuits Stoz—Tribunal de la pénitence.)

"We may swear in a slight matter intending not to hold our oath, if our reasons for swearing are valuable.

Question.—"To what is a man bound swearing fictitiously, and aiming to deceive?

Answer.—"To nothing by the virtue of religion, since his oath is false. He is still bound by justice to fulfill what he has sworne" (Compendium à l'usage des Séminaires, par l'abbé Moullet—publié á Strasbourg en 1843.)

"A man who has been compromised, and who is now necessitated to swear that he will espouse the girl with whom he has been surprised, may swear that he will marry her, by understanding, 'If I am compelled to it, or if after a while she pleases me.'

"If any one wishes to swear without keeping his oath, he may mutilate the words. For instance, he may say 'uro,' instead of 'juro;' in suppressing the 'j,' then he says, 'I uro,' which means 'I burn,' instead of 'juro,' which means 'I swear.' Then it is merely a venial sin." (The R. F. Jesuit Sanchez—Theological works.—Question Oath.)

"Questioned about a theft, which you have committed intending a compensation, or about a loan which you owe, not having paid it, or which you at least owe not actually, either because the term is out, or because your poverty excuses you from paying, you may, in such case, swear that you did not receive a loan, by understanding, 'in order that you may be bound to pay instantly,' for the judge aims only at the end." (The R. F. Jesuit Castropaolo—Virtue and Vice, p. 18.)

"We may swear that we did not a thing, though we have done it, by understanding within ourselves either 'any particular day,' or 'before we are born.' Likewise, such expedient is frequently convenient and justifiable, when it is necessary or useful to our health, honor, or social station." (The R. F. Jesuit Sanchez—Opera Moralis.—Part 2, Book 3, ch. 6.)

"If you have killed Peter in defending yourself legally, you may swear before the judge that you did not kill him, by understanding, 'unjustly.'

"If you are a merchant, you may, when the purchasers tax your goods too low, use a false weight, and in conscience deny your action with oath before the judge, by understanding, 'the purchaser did not suffer on account of it.'" (The R. F. Jesuit Gobat—Moral Works, Tome 2d, p. 319.)

Then, Americans, down with oath! Down with your magistrates! Down with your judges! Down with justice! Down with your tribunals! Down with your courts! Down with the officers of your States! Down with your Governors! Down with your Legislative Assemblies! Down with your Senates! Down with your Representatives to Congress! Down with your Senators! Down with your President!

Down with your Republic! Down with your nation! Down with society! Live disorder, injustice, hatred, civil war! Live anarchy!

What consequences! And still, perjury generates them directly. O Jesuits, what deadly foes of society you are! What profanation, what impiety, to dare to teach perjury, chiefly in the name of God!

Perjury has been taught by thirty theologians of the Jesuits.

Section IV.—*Probabilism.*

"A confessor may follow the probable opinion of his penitent without caring for his own, and that, even when the probable opinion of the penitent is injurious to a neighbor, as for instance, if it is a question of not restoring what has been stolen." (The R. F. Jesuit N. Baldel—Disputes sur la Théologie Morale, Livre 4, p. 402.)

Then we may act against our own conscience, provided that we follow the opinions of the others. We consider such teaching from the Jesuits as a natural consequence of their principle of blind obedience.

Moreover, we must infer from such doctrine, that we may steal—for, to cause the spoliation of another is an injustice, a pure theft.

"An opinion is probable when it is taught by a single doctor, and we may follow it." (The R. F. Jesuit Peter Nicole.)

This doctrine is the most injurious to society that we can conceive. It is the spring of all misdeeds; for the Romish and chiefly Jesuitical Theologians having authorized and taught all kinds of crimes, without one exception, the wicked are allowed to give way to their criminal propensities, and to believe that their crimes are virtuous deeds.

"The followers of Probabilism ought to be called 'virgins,' because they do not commit a venial sin." (The R. F. Jesuit Caramuel—Fundamental Theology, p. 134.)

Then drunkards, liars, slanderers, perjurers, thieves, murderers, etc. . . . all the members of this virtuous family shall be called not only "holy," but "virgins" for in following Probabilism their crimes are changed into acts of virtue.

God alone knows what numberless and deadly fruits this doctrine has yielded since it has prevailed.

SECTION V.—*Gluttony.*

Question.—"Is not gluttony a mortal sin?"

Answer.—"Yes and no. To eat and drink without necessity to vomit, provided still that health may not be injured, is a venial sin. Even if vomit is previously foreseen, it is but a venial sin." (The R. F. Jesuit Busembaum.—Theologia Moralis—Article, Gluttony.)

Cheer up, Reverend Fathers, bring customers to your confessionals! It is preferable to get the friendship of the rabbles, rather than that of honest men. Enjoy drunkards! Do not fear hell! Christ either mistook or deceived you in saying by the mouth of Saint Paul: "Nor drunkards, nor . . . shall possess the kingdom of God." 1st Epistle Cor. vi. 10. Since you are guilty only of a slight venial sin, you will be admitted into "a beautiful meadow covered with all sorts of flowers, lighted brilliantly, exhaling a delicious odor," into "a delightful spot where the souls do not suffer the pain of the senses," into "a sanatorial prison where you will live without dishonor. There you will not be displeased!"

"A man is not drunk whilst he can discriminate somebody from a cart loaded with hay." (The R. F. Jesuit Busembaum.—Theologia Moralis—Article, Gluttony.)

Bravo! Reverend Fathers, exclaim in clasping hands the friends of brandy and whisky. What soft fathers and tender friends of human frailty you are! You, however, understand and appreciate all the inebriating, all the voluptuousness lying in the bottom of the bottle. Since you are worthy of our society, let us touch glasses and drink to our friendship and fraternity! Let us not fear to empty many glasses: can we not always discriminate our fellow creatures from a cart loaded with hay?

Section VI.—*Falsehood.*

"Amphibologies are permitted for a just cause. Thus, as the Latin word, 'Gallus,' means either a 'cock' or a 'Frenchman,' though I have killed a Frenchman, I may answer 'no,' by understanding a 'cock.' Likewise, as the Latin verb, 'Esse,' means either, 'to be,' or 'to eat,' when I am asked if Titius is at home, I may answer, 'no,' though he is at home, by understanding, 'He does not eat there.' (The R. F. Jesuit Sanchez—Moral Theology.)

"You may have two confessors; the one for the mortal sins and the other for the venial, in order to keep the esteem of your customary confessor. You must, however, not remain in the mortal sin by abusing this latitude." (Common teaching of the Theologians of the Jesuits and of other Romish Doctors.)

"This man does not lie who says: 'I did not such a thing,' though he did, provided he fashion his negotiation as an able man ought to do." (The R. F. Jesuit Sanchez—Opera Moralis.)

"If you believe invincibly that you are ordered to lie, lie." (The R. F. Jesuit Casnedy—Theological Judgment, p. 278.)

"Intention regulates the righteousness of our actions. Consequently, a man does not lie in swearing that he did not such an act when he did it, by understanding, 'this day,' or if he pronounces aloud, 'I swear,' and mentally inserts 'I say that I did such a thing." (The R. F. Jesuit Filicitius.—Moral Theology—Tract 25, p. 11.)

Americans, as to the authorization of having two confessors : the one for the mortal sins, and the other for the venial, I assure you that devout men and women practise largely this license. Also they become so hypocritical this way, that in society, devout is synonymous with devotee, bigot.

As to the principles of the Jesuits on lying and deceitfulness, we say that they are most pernicious. Can confidence, devotedness, and love, reign in families, when their members know that they lie and deceive one another? Can commercial transactions, the citizens' exchange of social and business relations be sustained, when they know that sincerity does not exist among them; that in lying they deceive each other? Can a government, can society stand when they rest upon falsehood? What a spectacle Europe has presented and still presents, where this Jesuitical doctrine has prevailed and still prevails.

Section VII.—*Detraction and Calumny.*

"According to the Jesuits, men may without scruple attack one another by detraction and slander, even they may attempt the civil and natural life of each other." (Chauvelin, Counsellor in the Parliament of Paris.—See his Memorial to the Parliament on the Principles of the Jesuits.)

"To calumniate for the preservation of one's honor is not a mortal sin." (The R. F. Jesuit Caramuel—Fundamental Theology.)

When the Jesuits teach that calumny is not a mortal sin, namely, that it is not gravely opposed to justice and charity; that we may calumniate to preserve our honor, we shrink with horror, so dreadful are the consequences of this doctrine; we thus see the citizens slandering and hating each other; when the Jesuits add, that we may attempt the natural life of our fellow creatures, we see society as a compound of bands of murderers, sharpening their poignards to slay each other in the dark; we see her falling exhausted and dying in waves of hatred and blood.

SECTION VIII.—*Injustice.*

"A judge may receive money to pass according to his arbitrary will, a sentence favorable to one of both parties, when their rights are equal."

"A judge, having been bribed to pass an unjust sentence, is not obliged to make restitution." (The R. F. Jesuit Escobar—Moral Theology, vol. 1, Book 2.)

Question.—"Is not a judge obliged to restore what he has received to administer justice?"

Answer.—"He is bound to restore when he has taken any thing to pass a just sentence. If he has received money to pass an unjust sentence, he may keep this money because he has gained it." (The R. F. Jesuit J. B. Taberna—Abridgment of the Practical Theology.)

Question.—"If we take money for a bad action, are we obliged to restore it?"

Answer.—"We must distinguish. If we should not have done it, we could not keep this money. If we should have done it, we might." (The R. F. Jesuit Molina, Works—vol. 3d, p. 138.)

"A Judge may receive gifts from the parties, under the color of friendship, or of gratitude for precious justice done to them; or because they intend to oblige him to do it later, or to be more careful, or to despatch the suit." (The R. F. Jesuit Molina—Works, vol. 1, Tract 2.)

Americans, what are your tribunals, your courts, your Judges, good for, since justice will be done according to a less or greater deal of money? Can your institutions, your government, your Republic stand, if such a doctrine prevails among you—and that, too, sanctioned by religion? Still, it soon or late shall happen if you do not beware, as I shall demonstrate in the course of this exposition.

SECTION IX.—*Duelling.*

Question.—"Can we accept a duel?"

Answer.—"Yes and no. To accept it openly with scandal is a sin. To accept it with prudence, in defending one's property, even by the death of one's enemy, is lawful." (The R. F. Jesuits Escobar and Mendoza—Moral Theology.)

Which is to say, that we may administer justice to ourselves, but secretly; that we may kill our enemy, but in darkness, according to the axiom of robbers and murderers, "Pas vû pas pris," viz., "Not seen not seized."

SECTION X.—*Theft.*

"If one cannot sell his wine according to its value, either on account of the injustice of the judge, or on account of the malice of the purchasers, he may lessen his measure, mingle some water with the wine, and sell it as wine pure and without alteration." (The R. F. Jesuit Tollet—"Des Sept Péchés Mortels," p. 1027.)

Merchants, take and keep carefully this lesson of artfulness. In remaining honest, you will remain poor; but in stealing, you will get rich. Since you are allowed by the Jesuits, in the name of God, to steal, avail this opportunity!

"If we see a robber resolved to steal from a poor man, we may dissuade him in pointing out a rich one whom he shall rob in his stead." (The R. F. Jesuits Vasquez and Castropaolo—Tract 6; and Escobar, Tract 5.)

"To steal without previous deliberation, is merely a venial sin." (The R. F. Jesuit Dicastillo—Cardinal Virtues, Book 2, Tract 2.)

"God forbids theft when it is considered sinful, but not when it is considered lawful." (The R. F. Jesuit Casnedy—Theological Judgment, vol. 1, p. 278.)

Encouragement to the robbers accustomed to steal; for,

habit being a second nature, they do not deliberate and extemporize their crimes. They have not to fear hell, though Christ threatens them of this endless punishment; the Jesuits assure them that, in stealing, they are guilty merely of a venial sin, and will be admitted, either into "the beautiful meadow which is covered with all sorts of flowers, lighted brilliantly, exhaling a delicious odor," into "the delightful spot, where the souls do not suffer the pain of the senses," into the "sanatorial prison, where they will live without dishonor," or at least will be admitted into "the other purgatory, where no sinner has spent more than ten years." But what say we ? The Jesuits send robbers straight to Paradise; for in proportion as they become wicked, the light of their mind grows dark; the remorse of their conscience decreases, at length is silent, and then they believe they are right in stealing. As on the other hand, at least according to the Jesuits, God forbids theft when it is considered sinful, not when it is considered lawful — consequently the most wicked among thieves are not guilty even of a venial sin, and will go straight to heaven.

"It is lawful to steal in necessity." (The R. F. Jesuit Lessius — Tract of Justice, Book 2.)

Reverend Fathers, explain at least what kind of necessity you mean, for nobody will term "theft" the taking of some food or cloth in extreme necessity, namely, to preserve one's own life.

Question. — "Is it not permitted, in certain cases, to kill an innocent man, to steal, or to commit fornication ?"

Answer. — "Yes, in consequence of a commandment of God; becanse, he being master of death and life, to fulfil his order in this manner is a duty."

Question. — "Are we permitted to steal on account of our necessity ?"

Answer.—"Yes, we may steal either secretly or otherwise, when we cannot supply our wants." (The R. F. Jesuit Peter Aragon—Abridgment of the Theological Summary of Saint Thomas, pp. 214, 365.)

"The small thefts which are committed at intervals of several days, and in different degrees, either on the same person or many, shall never constitute a mortal sin, how considerable soever the amount may be." (The R. F. Jesuit Bauny—Somme des Pèchés, ch. 10, p. 143.)

Then thieves in retail will go either into the "beautiful meadow," "the delightful spot," "the sanatorial prison," or into the other purgatory in awaiting Paradise.

Now, Jesuits, you are very logical. We apprehend perfectly your reasoning. Having sent straight to heaven the biggest rogues, you ought to allow to the rest at least the gratification of being admitted into your "beautiful meadow," your "delightful spot," your "sanatorial prison," or into "the other purgatory, where no sinner has spent more than ten years."

"A man is not bound to return what he stole in small sums, whatever may be the total amount." (The R. F. Jesuit Tamburin—Explication du Décalogue, Livre 8, Traité 2.)

Cheer up, Jesuits, do not stop in your way; trample on the natural law, the Bible, and the gospel! Enjoy yourselves, petty thieves, you may here below use the fruit of your crimes; and afterwards wing your way into heaven, with your conscience light as a feather!

"A servant may, intending compensation, steal from his master; still on the condition that he will not be caught in stealing." (Manuel du Confesseur, p. 137.)

Masters, send your servants to the confessionals of the Jesuits; this is one of the lessons which they will teach them:

"The domestics may either appeal against their masters

who are unjust, or administer justice to themselves, or to use secret compensation." (The R. F. Jesuit Cardenas—Crisis Theologica, p. 214.)

Masters who have difficulties with your servants, beware! lock your doors, for it is easier and more sure to administer justice to one's self than by a judicial sentence.

"When we fear to be not paid by our debtors, we may use the secret compensation." (Traité de C'Incarnation, p. 408.)

"The domestics who believe that their wages are not worth their labor, may steal secretly from their masters." (The R. F. Jesuit Cardenas—Crisis Theologica, Diss, 23.)

"A wife may take the property of her husband when he is a gambler, in order to supply her spiritual wants, and in order that she may do as other wives do." (The R. F. Jesuit Gordonus—Universal Moral Theology, Book 5.)

What consequences for the benefit of the confessor! Also, poor husbands, you cannot suspect what a vast deal of your money goes in the dark, to the chests of the Jesuits, who privately laugh at you.

"If fathers and mothers refuse money to their children, they may steal some from them."

What a lesson for youth! what results for families!

"When one man is so indigent and another so rich, that the last ought to aid him, he may purloin from him without sin and without being obliged to restitute. Yet, he must steal secretly, without scandal." (The R. F. Jesuit Longuet—Question 4, p. 2.)

Rich men, be cautious, for to steal from you is a holy bread.

"A child who serves his father, may rob secretly from him as much as his father should have paid a stranger." (The R. F. Jesuit Escobar—Moral Theology, vol. 4, Book 4.)

Then a father of a family will lavish his cares, anxieties, sufferings, and health; will spend day and night in hard and constant labor, to feed, clothe, educate, and give instruction, to his children; it makes no difference, all these sacrifices are worth nothing: his children, when being raised, and able to aid him, will be allowed to steal from him as much money as he should have paid a stranger who would have served him.

"You ask if you are obliged to make restitution when you have aided another to steal with greater security and facility.

"I answer, with probability, no; though you have held the ladder of the thief, or though, obeying your master, you have carried off a box stolen by him, and which he would have taken off without your help." (The R. F. Jesuit Trachala — De la Régle du Confesseur, publié à Ramberg, en 1759.)

Thirty-five theologians of the Jesuits have taught theft.

Americans, in reading these immoral lessons, does it not seem to us that thus we assist at a meeting of thieves in their lurking-holes? Does not theft become a right and a sacred right, since the Jesuits teach its Divine lawfulness? How can a society in which theft will have an apotheosis stand? Also, what is the condition in Europe of the Roman Catholic countries, where the Jesuits and the Popes have caused it to prevail? Honesty has pretty much disappeared from them in the transaction of business.

Section XI.— *Usury.*

"We may purchase an article lower than its value if it is sold by necessity, because this kind of sale diminishes the price of the object which is offered, but may not be suitable. Not only in this case the object loses the third of its value, but even the half. The tavern-keepers may mix wine and water together, and the farmers mingle straw and wheat, to sell these goods at the current price; provided, still, that this wine and wheat may not be worse than those which are daily sold." (The R. F. Jesuit Amédée Guimènius.)

We understand easily that the Jesuits advocate usury, for in the suit of Afnair, which took place a few years ago, it was demonstrated that they discount, buy and sell goods, by secret agents; that they lend money at an usurary rate, and that they make such a trade on a capital of more than six million francs. The whole of France was filled with the scandal of this suit.

Section XII.—*Rebellion.*

"The revolt of a clergyman against a king is not a crime of high-treason, because he is not his subject." (The R. F. Jesuit Sâ—Aphorisms—word *clericus.)*

Advice to all governments! Advice to you Americans! Since the Jesuits and the priests are not bound in conscience to obey your laws, since they are only subjects of the Pope, they will be allowed to rebel and to preach rebellion according to his will—what they will undoubtedly do, as they have done two years ago in Switzerland.

"Who could be simple enough not to admit that, when a tyrant has endangered a nation, all means are lawful to cast off his yoke." (The R. F. Jesuit Marianna—De Rege.)

At least, Reverend Fathers, let us at the first use the legal means.

Section XIII.—*Murder.*

"'Tis permitted to kill an aggressor in defending one's self, whoever he may be. A father may kill his son, a wife her husband, a servant his master, a layman his parish priest, a soldier his general, an inferior his superior, an accused his judge, a scholar his teacher, a subject his prince." (The R. F. Jesuit Azor—Abrégé des cas de conscience, Livre 3.)

Any one who would not know the monacal history, would not suspect such crudity of language from men professing, or at least being obliged to profess, mercifulness.

Question.—"Is it not permitted to defend ourselves against an aggressor?"

Answer.—"If this murder is practicable without scandal, it is not unlawful." (The R. F. Jesuit Francis Amicus—Theological Cursus, published in 1642.)

Reverend Fathers, how much you like darkness! How fond you are of the axiom of rascality: Pas vû pas pris—"not seen not seized."

"A man is allowed to kill a false accuser, the witnesses produced by him, and the judge himself." (The R. F. Jesuit Francis Amicus—Theological Cursus, Tract 29, ch. 2.)

What respect for the laws, the rules of justice, and for the magistrates!

"If a priest officiating at the altar is attacked, he may lawfully kill the aggressor, and straightway continue the mass." (The R. F. Jesuit Francis Amicus—Theological Cursus, Tract 29.)

The Jesuits hold and preach, that the mass is the renewing of the sacrifice of mercifulness and redemption of Christ on the cross; but it makes no difference, a priest may complete the mass, his hands red with the human blood which he has shed. What insult to Christ!

"A priest who commits adultery is not criminal in killing the husband who assails him." (The R. F. Jesuit Henriquez—Summary of Moral Theology, vol. 1, book 4.)

O Jesuits, how dreadfully tolerant you are when it is a question of sacerdotal lasciviousness! We see full well that you plead your own cause.

Question.—"Is a husband allowed to kill his wife surprised in adultery, and a father to kill his daughter for the same cause?"

Answer.—"First, a husband killing his wife before the sentence of the judge, sins mortally. . . . .

"Secondly, a husband may, after the sentence of the judge, kill his wife without sin. The reason of it is, that he becomes a volunteer executor of the judgment, and is authorized to murder his wife if he pleases." (The R. F. Jesuit Vincent Filliucius—Moral Questions, vol. 1, p. 372, published in 1833.)

Reverend Fathers, can we not admire your so penetrating mind and so tender feelings? All governments owe to you a brief of discovery, for the economical way which you teach them of executing the judicial sentences. Really, what is the use of paying the hangman, since the husbands will hang their wives gratis, and the fathers their daughters? Your invention is a wonderful one in matter of economy, especially of feeling.

"Regularly, we may kill a man who steals from us a crown-piece." (The R. F. Jesuit Escobar.)

"You are allowed to kill a man for stealing from you six or seven ducats, though he flies after his robbery. I would not declare sinful the act of a man killing another who has stolen from him the value of a crown-piece." (The R. F. Jesuit Molina—vol. 4, Disp. 16.)

Jesuits, if you esteem yourselves a crown-piece, we have nothing to say about it; you ought to know your own value better than anybody else. But, ask the husbands, the fathers and mothers; they will answer you that they esteem more than the value of a dog, even above all money, their wives, sons, and daughters. Ask everybody that is neither a Reverend Father Jesuit nor a Jesuit of the short gown; ask even the savage Indians the value of human life: all will give you a like answer. Now, let us ask you in what manner you reconcile this principle with your teaching?

You hold that Jesus Christ descended from heaven to redeem us. Still, in murdering a man, you send him straight to hell; since you declare that the theft of a crown-piece is a mortal sin. But we are mistaken; we forget that with your left hand you will bestow upon him absolution, and with the right you will poniard him. O barbarous mountebanks, what deadly foes of mankind you are!

Question.—"If somebody attempts to ruin my reputation by calumny, am I allowed to kill him directly?"

Answer.—"Certainly; you may fitly kill him, still not publicly to avoid scandal." (The R. F. Jesuit Airault—p. 319.)

Since everybody may take vengeance privately and in darkness, what are the tribunals good for? What security possible for the citizens? And what compassion can be between the calumny and the murder of the slanderer? But the Jesuits do not care for justice and society. If they give so good and so fruitful lessons to murderers, let us not be astonished, for they are familiar with the fact, old and able practitioners of their teaching, as it will be demonstrated further in the summary of their history.

"You may falsely accuse your enemy to take away his credit, even to kill him." (The R. F. Jesuit Guimenius—7th proposition.)

"We may kill by treachery a man banished." (The R. F. Jesuit Escobar—vol. 4, p. 148.)

Can the Jesuits teach more clearly slander, treason, destruction of the public justice, assassination, etc. . . . .

"It is lawful to kill any man to save a crown." (The R. F. Jesuit Molina—vol. 3.)

Very well, Reverend Father, you are right and logical. Is not the sheep the property of the wolf? Still, you killed kings. "But only," reply you, "when they were noxious to our Order or to Papacy. When they supported us or Papacy, we declared them crowned by God, and advocated their power against the people with all our influence."

Reverend Fathers, we thank you for this explanation; we

remain convinced that, in this case, you are logical and consistent with yourselves.

"A monk who, instead of flying, kills his aggressor, does not sin against justice, for he is not obliged to fly." (The R. R. Jesuit Lessius—Art. Obligationes Clericorum, in his Moral Theology.)

Stop, Jesuits! what fierce, fighting fellows, or rather cold butchers, you are. In flying, you would save the life of your aggressor, and you prefer to kill him, even without bestowing upon him absolution. What humanity; what sensibility of heart!

"To fly would be shameful," reply you. But where is the humility which you boast to profess? Where is your solemn contempt of the prejudices of the world? Where is your death to all things, even to your reputation? Do you despise this maxim of Christ: "To him that striketh thee on the one cheek, offer also the other?" (St. Luke vi. 28.) Have you forgotten the treatise on the Christian and Religious perfection, which is your manual? Are you bad Christians, or rather, avowed worldlians? Still you noise abroad that you profess publicly the councils of Christ; that laymen swim in mud and filth; that they are on the road of the eternal damnation, but that you are holy; that you, in being Jesuits, go straightway to Paradise, and that you practise not only the Christian but the Religious perfection.

Then Reverend Fathers, why do you not practise this divine perfection? . . . . You smile, and remain without an answer . . . We understand your silence . . . All your piety is on your lips; all your fair words of true and perfect followers of Christ are for the pretence. They are the veil of your deceitful, barbarous, and sanguinary quackery.

"In all cases, when any man has the right to kill another, he may, if he feels moved, authorize a neighbor to do it in his stead." (The R. F. Jesuit Busembaum; Moral Theology, vol. 1, p. 295.)

Is a lover lying at the feet of his beloved, more attentive and careful in guessing in her eyes and in her smile the smallest wishes, than the Jesuits are with murderers? Fearing that these tender hearts may be a little moved in killing their fellow-creatures, either because they are not quite accustomed to this honorable trade, or for other considerations, the Jesuits allow them—and let us not forget it—"in the name of God," to authorize others, having stronger hearts, to kill them whom they are entitled to slay.

"If a man does not believe to commit a great sin in killing another, his sin is only venial, because he does not know the grievousness of his action. (The R. F. Jesuit Georges de Rhodes; Scholastical Theology, tome 1, p. 322.)

It follows that almost all murderers sin only venially; for we hardly encounter, in perusing the judicial histories of their holy portion of society, that some of them believed to commit a great sin in assassinating.

O Jesuits, with what brilliant society you people "your beautiful meadow," "your delightful spot," "your sanatorial prison, where one may live without dishonor." Can all Christians not be flattered and passionately desirous to swell their number, and enjoy among them?

"It is certainly permitted to kill a thief in order to keep goods that are necessary to life, because the aggressor assails not only the goods, but life itself. Still it is dubious whether or not we may kill a thief who assails only property unnecessary to our life. When in killing the thief we can defend efficaciously our goods, it is probable that we may murder him; by the reason that charity binds no one to lose a considerable fortune to keep the life of his neighbor." (The R. F. Jesuit Moullet; Explication du Décalogue.)

Bravo! Jesuits, the murderers ought by gratitude to stamp medals and erect statues to your honor, you are so zealous in advocating them!

"A father may wish the death of the husband who is rough with his daughter, because he must love his daughter more than his son-in-law.

"A son is allowed to desire the death of his father, still not on account of the death but of the inheritance." (The R. F. Jesuit John Cardenas; Crisis Theologica, p. 242—published in Cologne in 1702.)

The R. F. Jesuit Thomas Tamburini, casuist, says: "May a son desire the death of his father to enjoy his inheritance? May a mother desire the death of her daughter in order not to be obliged to feed and endow her; May a priest desire the death of his Bishop hoping to replace him?

"In answer to these questions: If you wish to enjoy merely these events, you are allowed to desire them and to enjoy when they happen. You do not sin, because you are not glad of the ill of your neighbor, but of your benefit." (Méthode de la confession aisée, p. 20.)

"A son who being intoxicated kills his father, may, without sin, enjoy this event by which he inherits great wealth." (The R. F. Jesuit Gobat—Moral Works, vol. 2, Tract 5.)

"A son may lawfully kill his father when he is noxious to society." (The R. F. Jesuit Escobar—Moral Theology, vol 4, Book 31.)

What wonderful filial love! O Jesuits, your doctrines and teaching on death to the love of your families . . . . even father and mother, and hatred of them, have been very fruitful in your hearts, and unfortunately too fruitful in society! How numberless are in Europe the families which your odious and barbarous principles have thrown into the deepest mourning.

Thirty-seven theologians of the Jesuits have taught murder.

Americans, I ask you if the Jesuits are not fond of human blood, happy only among bloody flesh and bones. The tigers do not devour each other; but according to the doctrines of the Jesuits on murder, society ought to be a compound of human tigers devouring each other, even friends their friends, brothers their brothers, husbands their wives, fathers their sons, sons their fathers. Are they not the most deadly foes of mankind?

SECTION XIV.—*Regicide.*

"We are allowed to kill an unjust aggressor, though he might be General, Prince, or King—innocence is always more useful than injustice—and a prince who persecutes his subjects is a wild, cruel, and noxious beast, which ought to be killed." (The R. F. Jesuit Paul Comitolo—Moral Decisions, Book 4, p. 458.)

Jesuits, explain at least in what circumstances a king will be a tyrant. If you term "tyrant" a King who does not favor you and the Pope, he certainly is not a tyrant; witness Henry VI., King of France, whom you have poignarded, and so many others whom you have immolàted with iron or poison.

"Every subject may kill his Prince in the case of usurpation. It is so right that the murderers of such tyrants have been in all nations highly honored. However, it is to be supposed that he is a usurper, for if he has a probable right it is sinful to kill him." (The R. F. Jesuit Martin Bécan—Opuscules Théologiques, p. 130.)

According to you, Jesuits, a usurper is that one who is not King or Emperor by Divine right. But he is King or Emperor by Divine right who has been crowned and anointed with the holy chrism, or he who favors your Order and the Pope: your history strongly induces us to believe so. Then all the other Princes are reputed usurpers and ought to be killed. Kings, Emperors, chiefly Presidents of Republics, who govern by the free will and election of the people, and not by pretended Divine right, study this lesson and keep carefully in your mind that every one of your subjects or fellow-citizens may kill you, not only without sin, but even in the name of God, whom the Jesuits represent (at least they say so) in this world and in his church.

"A tyrant may be killed by open force and arms. However, the best way is to use fraud and stratagem, in order to preserve the country from private and public dangers." (The R. F. Jesuit Marianna.—Reg. Institut. Liber. 6. 1.)

Jesuits, what kind of owls you are! You show never your sharp nails except in darkness. You never sharpen and handle your poignards except in the night.

"A tyrant is not a lawful king. Then any one of the people may kill him—Unusquisque de populo potest illum ouidere." (The R. F. Jesuit Emmanuel Sâ.)

And the constitution? And the laws? Have not the people legal means to get rid of a tyrant? May a single individual manage the interests of the citizens without their consent? And do you believe that a nation will be low and infamous so far as to murder its chief? O! no, you alone Jesuits and your disciples, are capable of such criminal meanness and cruelty.

"Any one may kill a tyrant who is such really—tyrannus quoad substantiam—It is glorious to exterminate him—illum exterminare gloriosum est." (The R. F. Jesuit Adam Tanner.)

"The Catholics honored Garnet as a martyr. Every body has heard of the ear of wheat, upon which a drop of blood had fallen: the face of father Garnet was painted on it with the most striking likeness." (The R. F. Jesuit Feller.—Dictionnaire Historique.)

However, who was this strange martyr? The principal leader of the conspiracy termed "Gunpowder Plot;" a cruel fanatic who prayed publicly in the following manner: "God destroy a perfidious nation (England); exterminate her from the land of the living, that we may joyfully pay to Jesus Christ the praises which we owe to him." Who was this Reverend Father Jesuit? A monster who, asked if it was lawful to cause the death of several innocent in killing many culpable, answered cruelly and without hesitation: "If it is useful to the Roman Catholic faith, and if the culpable are more numerous than the innocent, it is right to cause their death."

The conspirators Catesby, Greenwell, Tesmond, Garnet, and Oldercorn, had spent one year in digging a mine below the Parliament (England). They intended to blow up the Halls of the Commons and Lords, and thus kill all their members, the King and his Ministers. Moreover, the Reverend Father Jesuit Garnet made many clear and important confessions, which lie in the archives of England, signed by the hands of this regicide.

In 1594, the Reverend Father Jesuit Commolet chose for the text of a sermon the passage of the book of Judges, in which it is related that Ehud killed the King of the Moabites. He exclaimed, in pointing out Henry IV., King of France: "We want an Ehud whoever he may be, whether monk, or soldier, or shepherd!"

This Reverend Father Jesuit termed Henry IV. a "Nero," a "Moab," a "Holofernes," a "Herod." On a certain day, he summoned his auditory, because, said he, they endured on the throne a false convert. (History of Paris by Dulaure.)

The Reverend Father Jesuit Nicolas Serrarius praised the murder of the King Eglon by Ehud. In writing about this fact he said: "Many learned think that Ehud was right, because he was inspired by God, and for many other considerations, chiefly because such a deed is an ordinary right against Tyrants." (Commentaries of the Bible by this Reverend Father Jesuit.)

"To kill an heretical King is an action meritorious before God. Neither Henry III., nor Henry IV., nor the Elector of Saxony, nor Queen Elizabeth, are true sovereigns. The action of James Clement killing Henry III. was an heroical one. If it is possible to war against the Béarnais (Henry IV.), let us war; but, if we cannot war, let us kill him." (The R. F. Jesuit Guignard — who was hung — Fragment of the Suit.)

"Rome sees this driver (Henry IV.) ruling France — this Anthropophagi — this monster bathing in blood. Will not one rise to take arms against this wild beast? Will we not have a Pope using his axe for the salvation of France?" (The R. F. Jesuit Charles Scribanius.)

The Reverend Father Jesuit Gabriel Malagrida plotted, during the ministry of Pombal, against the life of Joseph I., King of Portugal. He had assured the conspirators that the murder of the King should not be guilty even of a venial sin, because Joseph did not like the Jesuits. This Reverend Father was hung and burnt with his colleagues Mathos and Alexander. (History — Fragments of the Suit.)

"The world witnessed lately a magnificent and great deed for the instruction of the impious princes. Clement acquired, by killing the King, an illustrious name — ingens sibi nomen fecit. He died, Clement, the eternal honor of France — æternum Galliœ decus — according to the opinion of a great many. He was a youth with a candid spirit and delicate body, but a superior strength fortified his arm and his mind." (The R. F. Jesuit Marianna — De Rege, Liber 1, p. 14.)

This book "De Rege" was dedicated to Philip III., King of Spain, Such a deed characterizes the Jesuits, who live but supported by poignards, and by applying the most odious principles. "To corrupt in order to get power and to govern," has been always one of their devices.

"When a Prince governs tyrannically, he may lawfully be killed by his vassals or subjects, even with aguettes and poison, in spite of the oath of faithfulness taken in his hands; this is lawful even without previous sentence or order of any judge."

"Any one may kill a usurper if there is no other way to get rid of him." (The R. F. Jesuit Emmanuel Sâ.)

"Certainly," exclaims the Reverend Father Jesuit Andrew Delrio—"any one is allowed to kill a usurper if he can not be dethroned by other means!"

"Is it not strange that men professing to be monks, to whom I have never been and will never be noxious, daily attempt my life?" (Words of Henry IV., King of France. Mémoires de Sully Ministre de Henry IV.—Tome 1, Lettre de Henry IV.)

The same Henry IV. told Sully and others of his friends:

"You do not approve of my calling again the Jesuits; but can you guaranty my life? I know by my own experience that they have designs against me; for I already carry the cicatrices of their wounds. We must neither irritate them longer nor push them to extremities. I consent, then, to their repeal, but quite involuntarily and merely by necessity." (Mémoires de Sully.)

"Monks and other clergymen are not allowed to kill the kings with ambushes—and the Popes are not accustomed to this proceeding. When the Sovereign Pontiffs have corrected them paternally, they retrench them by censures from sacraments. They afterwards, if it is necessary, release their subjects from their oath of allegiance; deprive them of their royal dignity and authority; and then, it is the right of others besides the clergymen to act—Executio ad alios pertinet." (The R. F. Jesuit Bellarmine.—De Sumni Pontificis auctoritate, Tome 4, p. 180.)

This Reverend Father Jesuit was such a fanatical worshipper of the Pope, that we read in the "Historical Dictionary," by the Reverend Father Jesuit Feller (word Bellarmine), that whilst dying, when the Pope entered his room, he exclaimed: "Lord, trouble not thyself, for I am not worthy that thou shouldst enter under my roof; wherefore neither thought I myself worthy to come to thee: but say in a word, and thy servant shall be healed." Luke vii. 6, 7.

Seventy-two of the Theologians of the Jesuits have taught regicide.

Americans, does not your hair stand up whilst reading such details? whilst hearing such language? What fanaticism! What cruelty! Could we find words to term, to stigmatize so odious teaching, teaching so horrible!

Section XV.—*Infanticide.*

"We are asked if a woman may cause to herself a miscarriage?

"We answer first: When the child is not animated and the great belly dangerous, she is allowed to cause to herself a miscarriage, either directly or indirectly: directly, in taking potions which * * *; indirectly, by bleedings, or by taking remedies relieving her and being injurious to the child.

"Secondly: When the child is already animated, and she is expected to die with him, she may, before the childbed, take remedies indirectly offensive. This decision is justified by this following, which is admitted by the Theologians: when a woman about finishlng her time is pursued by a wild beast, she may fly to preserve her life, though it is certain that she will miscarry.

"Thirdly: When a young girl has been corrupted violently, she may, though the child be animated, . . . arbitrarily, lest she may lose her reputation, which is more precious than life itself; (The R. F. Jesuit Airault.—Propositions sur le cinquième précepte du Décalogue, p. 322.)

Navarrus, Henriquez, Sà, Sanchez, Castropaolo, Diana, and great many other Theologians, who are the most celebrated among the doctors of the Jesuits, have taught infanticide, and have, in certain cases, enjoined the most unnatural and cruel modes of destroying the children, resting their thesis on the value of female reputation.

As to those who know the Jesuits and other monks, the moving motive of so dreadful a doctrine and teaching is not the preservation of the female reputation, but—we regret to be obliged to say—of their own.

Section XVI.—*Suicide.*

Question.—"When a Chartreux is ordered by a physician to take a remedy which will save him from impending death, is he obliged to take it?"

Answer.—"This question is controverted. Yet, I believe the negative decision is more probable, and it is the common opinion of Theologians." (The R. F. Jesuit Moullet—Compendium for the use of the Ecclesiastical Seminaries.)

This doctrine is merely fanaticism and folly.

Section XVII.—*Lasciviousness.*

Forgive, Americans, if I foul my pen in writing what follows; I still must do so in spite of my reluctancy. I will choose the less obscene among the muddy doctrines of the Jesuits.

"A man and woman who undress themselves (and are even without a shirt) to kiss each other, do not sin. This action is an indifferent one." (The R. F. Jesuit Vincent Filliucius—Moral Questions, Tome 1, p. 316—published in 1633.)

"A monk casting off his dress, does not fall under excommunication, though it might be for a shameful action; for instance, to commit fornication, to steal, or to go more secretly to brothels." (The R. F. Jesuit Escobar—De Luxuriâ.)

"Clericus vitium bertialitatis perpetrans non incurit bullæ pœnas . . . [We do not dare translate it], except if he is frequently guilty of this sin." (The R. F. Jesuit Escobar and Mendoza—De Luxuriâ, vol. 1, p. 213.)

"Clericus Sodomiticé patien nonincidit in pœnas bullæ, [likewise, we do not dare translate it], if he commits this sin only once or twice." (The R. F. Jesuit Escobar and Mendoza—vol. 1, p. 144.)

"When a domestic is obliged to serve a lustful master, necessity authorizes him to perpetrate the worst deeds. Thus he is allowed to look for and bring home concubines, to lead him to brothels; and if his master wishes to scale a window to * * * a woman; he may support his feet, or bring a ladder—quia sunt actiones de se indifferentes—for these actions are indifferent in themselves." (The R. F. Jesuit Castropaolo—Virtue and Vice, p. 18. published in 1631.)

"Suzanna says in Daniel: 'If I yield to the criminal desires of those old men, I am lost.' As in this extremity, she feared infamy on the one hand and death on the other, Suzanna was allowed to say, 'I will not consent to their shameful action, still I will bear it, and I will not speak of it to preserve my life and reputation.' But inexperienced females, believe that in order to remain chaste, they must exclaim: 'Corrupter!' . . . We sin only when we consent and coöperate to a voluptuous action.

"Suzanna ought to have abandoned herself to the old men, still without consenting inwardly or coöperating. She was not obliged in order to preserve her chastity, to make known her dishonor by cries, and to expose herself to death, because reputation and life are preferable to the purity of body." (The R. F. Jesuit James Tirin—Commentaries of the Bible, p., 787—published in 1648.)

"We may haunt the brothels to convert the prostitutes, though we will likely be exposed to sin with them. We are allowed it, even when we have already sinned with them, having been seduced by their eyes and courting. If a virgin consents to the * * * we may not endow her, and with greater reason not marry her, because in corrupting her we have not injured her." (The R. F. Jesuit Etienne Bauny.—Somme des péchés, p. 77.)

The Reverend Father Caramuel taught that fornication is lawful. My Lord Bouvier, actual Bishop of Mans (France), has written extensively about it in his obscene and infamous book, "Supplementum ad Sacramentum de Matrimonio," which book is taught in the Ecclesiastical Seminaries of France to all clergymen.

"Women do not sin mortally in adorning themselves with superfluous ornaments, in uncovering their breasts, and * * * if it is a habit in their country, and if they have not bad intentions." (The R. F. Jesuit Simon de Lassau.—Explanation of the Decalogue.)

The tract on marriage by the Reverend Father Jesuit Sanchez, is so lascivious, so obscene, that decency forbids us to translate and produce it.

"Suppose that a clergyman—knowing full well, that he will be in danger in going to the room of a woman, with whom he entertains amorous relations—should be surprised in adultery by the husband, whom he kills to preserve his life or limbs, he is not irregular, and may continue his ecclesiastical functions." (The R. F. Jesuit Henriquez.—Summary of Moral Theology, work published in 1600.)

Cheer up, Jesuits, plead yours and the sacerdotal cause.

"A confessor may and must bestow absolution on a woman who cohabits with a man, when she cannot honestly send him out of her house, or has some other reasons."

Question.—" For how much may a woman sell the pleasure which she causes ?

Answer.—" We must, for an exact appreciation, consider the nobility, beauty, and honesty, of this woman . . . . . an honest is worth more than one who opens her door to the first comer. Let us distinguish. If this woman is a prostitute, she may not with justice charge one more than another; she must have a fixed price. 'T is a kind of contract between her and the 'Pointer' who pays . . . . . The 'Pointer' gives money, she her body.

" If this woman is honest, she may charge as she pleases; because, as such things have not a common and established rate, she has the same right as a merchant, who may dispose of his merchandise according to his own will. A maid and an honest woman may sell their honor as dear as they prize it." (The R. F. Jesuit Tamburini — De la Confession aisée, Livre 8, chapitre 5.)

" A prostitute may justly require a salary, but she is not allowed to charge too much. A girl and a prostitute who secretly deal alike with their bodies, have the same right. A married woman is not allowed to ask money, because the benefits of her prostitution are not stipulated in the contract of marriage." (The R. F. Jesuit Gordon — Morale Universelle, tome 11, livre 5.)

" May a bridegroom and his bride . . . . . before their marriage ?" The R. F. Jesuits Navarrus, Sanchez, and many others, answer, " Yes."

Section XVIII. — *Rape.*

" Rape is not a circumstance grave enough in order that we must aver it when we confess; we suppose that the girl has assented to it." (The R. F. Jesuit Facundez.)

" He who deflowers a girl with her consent, incurs only the

penalty of making penitence. The reason of this decision is, that she, being the owner of her body, may grant her favors as she pleases, even against the consent of her parents." (The R. F. Jesuit Francis Xavier Fegelli—Questions pratiques sur les fonctious des Confesseurs, p. 284—Ouvrage publié a Augsburg en 1750.)

"He who by violence, or threat, or fraud, or importunity of prayers, has . . . . . a virgin without promising to marry her, is bound to indemnify the girl and her parents by endowing her, in order that she may find a husband. If he cannot pay this indemnity, he is obliged to espouse her. However, if his crime has remained absolutely concealed, 'tis more probable that he is not bound to reparation." (The R. F. Jesuit Moullet—Compendium for the use of the Ecclesiastical Seminaries.)

SECTION XIX.—*Adultery.*

"If any one entertains criminal relations with a married woman, not because she is married, but because she is handsome—as he abstracts the circumstance of her marriage, these relations do not constitute the sin of adultery." (The R. F. Jesuit Moullet—Compendium for the use of the Ecclesiastical Seminaries.)

Lasciviousness, with all its degrees, has been taught by eighteen theologians of the Jesuits.

Americans, I will abstain from reflections about such muddy doctrines. Yet it is for me a duty to say to you:

The Jesuits hold and apply in practice and in the confessional all these principles, though more secretly and more artfully than formerly. I warn you because I know—have seen this in confessing their penitents. Then beware! take care of your wives and daughters. When they will say that they are sick and want their confessor, beware! Very often it will be a rendezvous. When they will say that they go to confess, beware! Very often it will be a rendezvous. When they will say that they visit the Jesuits for direction of conscience, beware! Very often it will be a rendezvous. Remember, that if their doctrines about lasciviousness are so widely immoral, they are very deeply interested in it.

SECTION XX.—*Intolerance.*

"The children are obliged to denounce their kindred and parents who are heretics, though knowing they will be burnt. They may either starve them to death, or kill them as enemies of humanity." (The R. F. Jesuit Escobar—Moral Theology, book 31.)

"Parents may desire the death of their children, and of any one who disturbs the Catholic church." (The R. F. Jesuit Fegelli—Practical Questions, Part 4, ch. 19.)

"The Christian and Catholic children may accuse their parents of heresy, though they foresee that they will be burnt and killed; and not only they will be allowed to refuse them food if they avert them from the Catholic faith, but they will be permitted to kill them, without sin, if they have tried to dissuade them violently from the Catholic faith." (The R. F. Jesuit Etienne Facundez—Traité sur les Commandments de l'Elise, Tome 1, Livre 1, ch. 33—Ouvrage publié en 1626.)

Question.—"May a son kill his father expatriated?"

Answer.—"A great many theologians decide that he is allowed it, if his father is noxious to society. I partake of their opinion." (The R. F. Jesuit Dicastillo—De Justitiâ et de Jure, Liber 11, pagina 511.)

"It is of faith that the Pope has the right to dethrone the Kings who are heretics and rebels. But a monarch dethroned by the Pope is no longer either a King or a lawful Prince: if he refuses to obey the Pope after his degradation, then he must be styled a 'tyrant,' and may be killed by the first comer — cuilibet de populo licet illum interficere." (The R. F. Jesuit Suarez — Defensio fidei, Liber 6, caput 4.)

This Suarez is the same who, next after Saint Thomas, is considered the first theologian of Catholicism; the same Doctor of whom it is said, in the history of his life, that in his youth he was without talent, but that on a certain night the blessed Mary opened prodigiously his intellect.

"The pope may kill with a word (potest verbo corporalem vitam assumere). For the right of feeding the sheep having been granted to him, was not the right of killing the wolves granted to him (potestatem lupos interficiendi)?" (The R. F. Jesuit Emmanuel Sâ. — In his Theology — Questions on the Authority of the Church.)

"The pope may reprimand Kings, and punish them with death." (The R. F. Jesuit Sanctarel. — Of the Pope, ch. 30, p. 296, work published in 1625.)

"A man condemned by the Pope may be killed anywhere." (The R. F. Jesuit Lacroix — vol. 1, p. 294.)

"We may kill anywhere a man proscribed by the Pope, because the Pope has at least an indirect jurisdiction over all the world, even in temporal things." (The R. F. Jesuit Busembaum — Theologia Moralis.)

Many sovereign courts issued decrees which condemned the work of Busembaum, and ordered that it should be burnt by the hand of a hangman.

Americans, in reading these sentences of denunciation, persecution, proscription, blood, and death, we ask ourselves if the authors and apostles of these principles are not fiends with the human face. At least we feel relieved in thinking that they are denied by everybody, and looked upon as monsters in the human family. But we fall overthrown when the Roman Catholic Church answers us that they, the Jesuits, are her main soldiers, her most learned, strongest, and the most devoted supporters. We feel horrified in thinking of our ancesters, who have been victims of these principles; in thinking that citizens, friends, and kindred, denounced and drove one another to the sacerdotal prisons, and thence to the scaffolds; in thinking that husbands were butchers of their wives, and wives of their husbands: that sons starved their fathers and mothers to death, or drove them to the dungeons, under the poniards and wood-piles of Bishops, Monks, and Popes; that fathers and mothers, with hearts oppressed, drove to monacal and papal butcheries the children to whom they had given life. And all these things, Jesuits, you taught and imposed upon our ancestors, in the name of Christ the Merciful, the Redeemer; in the name of God! Ah! their ghosts will never be silent; we will hear them always remembering us that in Europe you caused their blood to run abundant as rivers; that you fattened the fields with their flesh; that you scattered their bones through nearly all Europe. We will never forget that our forefathers, the first inhabitants of the American land, were compelled to leave their native country, to come to bury themselves in unknown and far-distant wildernesses to escape your tyranny and cruelty. Who have been for centuries peopling the deserts of the United States? The victims of your principles! You will accuse, to justify yourselves, Kings and Emperors. But though you killed some of them, did you not unite with them to support one another? And, what say I? were they not the instruments, the tools of your and papal will? Did they not hold the sword which you handled? "We were suppressed," reply you. Yes, but not everywhere. You lived in Prussia. You breathed freely in that atmosphere of tyranny, deadly to freedom and to generous hearts. You were dead, say you. Can you die? Are you not a hydra which never dies? The papal sword alone could cut off your numberless heads, but he is your first head—he will be careful not to kill you, lest he may die himself; lest he may be bound to restore his temporal and spiritual thefts; lest he may let fall his blinding, anti-social, and anti-Christian tyranny, which maintains a whole and noble people in a political, intellectual, and moral barbarity, and the whole Roman Catholic church in ignorance, fanaticism, and superstition.

O Jesuits! How can you clear yourselves in the tribunal of society? Will you quote the Reverend Father Jesuit Cérutty who published a book for your justification? But the Reverend Father Jesuit Feller is obliged, in his "Universal Biography," to confess that Cérutty left your Order a short time after his publication. And why? Because, devoured by remorse, he listened to his conscience, and would give to all humanity a public acknowledgment of his crime against truth, against the gospel, against man's welfare. Then he became your martyr, and since that time you attack his name, his memory, in your biographies. What can you produce for your justification? Your feigned death, your apparent inoffensiveness? but you know, full well as I, that you have borrowed a false skin, the skin of darkness; that slowly and without noise, as a worm eating silently the wood in the heart of a timber, you loose the ties of families, the ties of the American Republic. And what are you doing now in Russia, in Austria, in Prussia, in Rome, etc. . . . where you appear with a less false skin, because you are stronger and favored by their Kings and Emperors, or rather tyrants? In Russia, in Austria, in Prussia, you surround and support the thrones of the enemies of freedom and democracy. In Rome you surround the bloody steps of the throne of the Pope; fill the prisons with the victims of the papal tyranny; confiscate their property; banish them, and disgrace, persecute, deprive their families of the necessities of life: every day you wash the pavement of the city with innocent blood. In France you support the half throne of the half President of the half French Republic. There you send to the National Assembly, by the priests, the devotees, the wives, and the peasants, aristocratic representatives, enemies of democratic principles and of the Republic. The proof of your misdeeds and intolerance in these and other European countries, the ports of the United States are daily obstructed with the victims of political and religious tyranny, coming to this hospitable land, and looking for a shelter and a living, thirsty to breathe the vivifying air of liberty.

O Jesuits! Whatever you may try to justify your past conduct, you will never accomplish it. You are now a Cain marked on the forehead with the iron pen of history, as the most deadly foes of the human family. You still are powerful, even exceedingly powerful; you demonstrate it in Europe. There all true friends of improvement, of freedom, of democracy, of the gospel, and of social welfare, tremble in contemplating the future; and if you are not stopped and carefully watched in America, you will prove to the United States that they warm in their bosom a snake that will kill them.

Americans, pray give a special attention to the following reflections.

In reading the summary of the doctrines which the Jesuits have held and taught—which they still hold and teach; in reflecting on their principles, so impious, so inhuman, so immoral, so obscene, so intolerant, and so anti-Christian, you likely were astonished, and thought that the writers who taught and professed such doctrines were the villians of the Society of Jesus: but you were mistaken. These writers have been always, and still are, considered the main Theologians and the light of the Society. Their Theology is taught now to all the secular clergy in the Ecclesiastical

Seminaries, and applied by all the priests in their ministry; not only in a few countries but all over the Roman Catholic world. The Pope himself has beatified several of the aforesaid Theologians of the Jesuits.

These Theologians have been always and still are oracles among the Jesuits. All these Reverend Fathers, in preaching, in writing, in confessing, in short, in exercising the sacerdotal ministry, have followed and still follow their teaching, all their doctrines, except a few points of morals which the Pope, in order to delude the people, politically has condemned. I notwithstanding can solemnly assure you, that from my relations with the Jesuits, my sacerdotal ministry, chiefly that of confession, they certainly hold, practise, and apply all these doctrines.

Perhaps you will ask me if these principles have been approved by all the Society of Jesus. I answer to your question in quoting this article of their rule:

"No volume shall be published by one of the members without a previous approbation of the Superiors."

Paschal reproached them for this article of their rule, in unveiling some immoral points of their doctrine. (See the fifth and ninth of the Provincial letters.)

Therefore, Americans, we must necessarily infer that the whole society of Jesus is responsible for the principles contained in the books published by its Theologians, and for all their consequences.

"Do the Jesuits," continue you, "proclaim actually from the pulpit these principles?"

Certainly not. They are too artful to show what they are, especially in the United States. Feeling that the ground is still moving under their feet; that they are not the majority; knowing that an imprudent and impolitic behavior would risk their prospects among you, they are very cautious and fearful. They confine themselves in a subterraneous and almost invisible work, to become after a while the majority. Be not astonished if they bend themselves to these mean proceedings, for, witness their past policy, they know and apply admirably this principle, "that they must crouch and creep unseen, in order to reach power and to tyrannise."

Again. "Do the Jesuits," ask you, "apply their immoral principles in confessing?"

I feel sorry to be obliged to answer: yes. They apply their immoral principles which have been exposed, and even many others which are more immoral; but they are so incredibly immoral that I am not allowed to write them. Moreover you could not believe me, because, knowing them only by the confessional, I cannot exhibit proofs. You still can judge the mysterious and unwritten doctrines of the Jesuits by those which they have avowed and written.

Americans, we have related summarily, how the Jesuits are educated or rather moulded during their noviciate—what doctrines they have held, taught, and still hold and teach. Let us, at present, group, summarily, some facts of their history. We say some facts, for several volumes might scarcely contain the details of their crimes. You will see, Americans, what faithful and careful practitioners they have been, and in our days are, of their doctrines and teaching.

CHAPTER VII.

SUMMARY OF THE HISTORY OF THE JESUITS.

YEAR 1534.—Paris was the first cradle of the Order of the Jesuits. Saint Ignatius Loyola, a man unfortunately too famous for mankind's welfare, was its founder. Having exalted the ambitious and fanatical views of Francis Xavier, Peter Le Fevre, James Laynez, Rodriguez, they united with each other by vows in the Church Montmartre, near Paris. Soon after they came to Rome; exposed their aim, designs, and plans to the Pope, and promised to add a fourth vow to those of poverty, chastity, and obedience, namely, that of obeying him and his successors on the throne of Saint Peter. (Various Histories—Universal Biography by the R. F. Jesuit Feller, at the word Ignatius.)

Year 1540.—The Pope Paul III. accepted their proposal, and introduced them into the political life, by approving and confirming them as a religious body under the calling of "Society of Jesus," with the Bull "Regiminis militantis Ecclesiæ." (Idem works.)

Year 1541.—Saint Ignatius Loyola was appointed General of the Order. Hardly born, the Jesuits began the stout tissue of their criminal history. Finding obstacles in the way of their ambitious aims, they diffused themselves everywhere, under the color of zeal and devotedness to the Roman Catholic Church. They inflamed talented but fanatical and inexperienced youth; and thus won a great many proselytes. To overcome difficulties, they applied the principle, which henceforth was to be their favorite one, "Divide et regna," "Divide and you shall reign." They sowed discord and hatred among families, provinces, nations, Kings and Emperors whom by intrigues they succeeded in surrounding. They disturbed chiefly all Germany in wearing all sorts of masks, playing all parts, stirring up all the popular passions against the Protestants, and still feigning to calm the parties.

The Jesuits displayed under the aforesaid circumstances, a hypocrisy so mean and so artful, that in Bavaria they declared expressly, in order to deceive the Protestants, that they intended to restore the former Christian faith; and that Saint Ignatius had solicited and obtained an introduction to Luther, by the intercourse of Paquier, the celebrated lawyer of the University of Paris. (History of Christian Empire, from the Reformation to . . . . by Schrockh—3, 515—Reflections on the history and Constitutions of the Society of Jesus, by Spitler—work published in 1819—History of the Jesuits in Bavaria, by the Chevalier De Lang—work published in 1819.)

At the same time, the Jesuits excited the Pope and the temporal powers against the Reformation. The Reverend Fathers Jesuits Bobadilla and Lejay, who, nearly at the same moment were troubling by the lowest duplicity the Diet of Ratisbonne, and the religious conferences moved there from Worms, were the leaders and responsible Papal agents of this important and machiavelistic mission. (See above cited works.)

Year 1545.—The Pope Paul III., appointed as Theologians of his holiness, for the council of Trent, the Revered Fathers Jesuits Laynez and Salmeron. Thus he rewarded the Jesuits for the solemn vow of obedience to the Papacy, taken by their Society. However, the principal end of the Pope in choosing these Fathers, was to find in them devoted and able creatures; deadly enemies of Protestantism, and zealous defenders of the Papal usurpations, against a great many Bishops opposed to them.

The Jesuits appreciating all the advantages of such a proposal, and chiefly knowing that it was a sure title to the highest favors and privileges of the Popes, through whom they might become rid of the jurisdiction of the Bishops, accepted it gratefully, and sent to the council the Fathers Laynez and Salmeron, who fulfilled heartily and successfully their mission.

The Jesuits had not been mistaken in their hopes, the Popes after a short while, granted them the famous Bulls; which emancipated them from all Episcopal jurisdiction, and excommunicated even the laymen who would dare contradict their rules. (Various Catholic and Protestant Histories of the council of Trent.)

Year 1549.—The Reverend Father Jesuit Bobadilla, by cringing and flattery, became confidential confessor and director of Ferdinand I. By him he governed Germany from 1541, to 1549. Fortunately for that country which he disturbed, and by the political and religious dissensions which he fomented, impoverished, he trusted too much in his influence over the mind of the Emperor. Having plotted and thwarted the interim of Charles, he fell from his power, and was finally disgraced. (History of Germany, by J. C. Pfister—vol. 7, edition 8.)

Year 1551.—The Jesuits surrounded the fanatic Duke of Bavaria, who was displeased on account of the interim; excited him against Ferdinand I., and were authorized by him to teach at Ingolstadt. The Reverend Father Jesuit Cassius, who had been appointed Provincial in Germany, and who was to be, during about thirty years, so noxious to that country, was their leader and head of these intrigues. (Stumpt—p. 291.)

Year 1553.—Ferdinand was obliged to yield. He called them in Vienna to stop—at least said he—the ruin of the Romish Church. He appointed the Reverend Father Jesuit Canisius Visitor of the University of Vienna. If Maximilian II., was threatened to be poisoned, as it is ascertained from the writers of the two parties, this crime took place at this epoch, and was ascribed to the vengeance and policy of the Jesuits.

(Schneller æsterr—einfluss, 1, 168—De Hormayr, æsterr—Plutarch, 7, 29.)

From the year 1554 to the year 1556.—In 1554 the Jesuits had invaded all classes of society, and alarmed all powers; so thick, so powerfully they had grown up. And, in what manner? By artful policy, in changing with circumstances; in by turns, flattering, lying, slandering, stooping, threatening, promising; in one word, in handling masterly the deepest hypocrisy.

In France the Jesuits succeeded in gaining the protection of the Cardinal De Loraine, and by his interference, obtained from the king, Henry II., the right of collecting money, building chapels and opening colleges all over the territory of France.

The third of August, the Parliament alarmed, decreed that the letters patent of Henry II. and the Brief of the Pope Julius III., should be communicated to the Bishop of Paris, and to the Faculty of Theology.

The formula follows:—

"Considering; 1. That the new 'Society' attributes to itself the strange name of 'Society of Jesus.'

"2. That it admits indifferently in its bosom, every kind of people, bastards, rascals . . . .

"3. That it has neither rules nor constitutions, nor the manners and behavior which discriminate the monks from the laymen.

"4. That it obtained many privileges, liberties and indemnities; principally relative to the administration of sacraments, thus damaging the Bishops, Clergy, Lords, Princes, citizens and Universities. . . . ."

The Faculty of Theology passed on the first of December of the same year, the following Decree:

"The Faculty of Theology considering:

1. "That the Society of Jesus dishonors the Monastical and

Religious Orders, of which it enfeebles the discipline by its want of the pious practices, which generate fervor and keep up virtue.

2. "That it causes the transgression of the vows, escapes from submission to the Prelates; dispossesses unjustly the ecclesiastical Lords and others of their rights; generates in the civil and religious governments, disturbance, complaints, dissensions, lawsuits, contentions, jealousies, rebellions, and divisions of every kind.

"Declares for all these motives, that the aforesaid Society is dangerous to religion; to the church which it disturbs; to the monastical discipline which it enfeebles; and that it is organized rather for the ruin than for the edification of the faithful . ."

Year 1556.—Many years before the Jesuits had invaded Portugal and Spain. In Portugal they had been, at first, extraordinarily influential. In Spain, Charles V. who had pondered the consequences of the power of the Jesuits, had not favored them. Melchior Cano, a Dominican, who was undoubtedly the most celebrated Doctor of the University of Salamanca, had denounced them publicly as forerunners of Anti-christ. Don Martinex Cilicio, Archbishop of Toledo, had expelled them from Ascala, and the people of Sarragossa, from their city. In 1556, the Jesuits availed themselves of a circumstance with the greatest ability. Donna Maria of Portugal having died, they engaged the young King of Naples, Sicilia, and Low Countries, to marry the daughter of Henry VIII. of England. They withal invited Charles V., under the pretext of the salvation of his soul being at stake, to abdicate his crown. They sent to London, to solicit the hand of the daughter of Henry, Edmond Campion, who, afterwards convicted of high treason, was condemned to be tortured and beheaded in London, on the 28th of November, 1581. By this compliance and political intrigue, the Jesuits gained the gratitude and confidence of Philip II., and began to rule Spain. At the same time, they founded colleges in Ingolstadt and Vienna. (Jel Pfister—History of Germany, vol. 7.)

Saint Ignatius Loyola, Father, Founder, and General of the Jesuits, died, having been in turn a page, a licentious soldier, penitent fanatic, poet, apostle, philosopher, politician, legislator, manufacturer of men walking with living bodies but dead souls, King of such extraordinary people, and, by handling them artfully, ruler of many countries in India, and of the most powerful Kings and Emperors in Europe ; in short, ruler of the temporal, intellectual, moral and religious interests of the greatest nations. His power had been so astonishing, that the epitaph following was engraved upon his tomb :

"Whoever you may be who imagine to yourself the great Pompey, Cæsar, or Alexander, open your eyes : you shall see on this marble, that Ignatius has been greater than these conquerors." (Les Convents, p. 71.)

From the year 1557 to the year 1560.—The Jesuits tried to obtain more credit by profane and sacred means. To adorn their Order with a pretended divine seal, they published everywhere that God empowered them to perform miracles—but being careful to say that these miracles happened in far distant countries, but their existence might be controlled. They proclaimed from the pulpit, in their writings, in the parlors, in their colleges, in every manner and everywhere, that India, where they had missionaries, was a country which God blessed ; that there all civilized or uncivilized kingdoms, provinces and colonies, resounded with the supernatural deeds, with which God had favored their apostle Francis Xavier, during and after his life. They extolled, to the skies chiefly the following miracles :

"This extraordinary man," they preached and wrote, "appeared eight feet tall when he taught the people. His worn out surplice shone suddenly with fine embroideries. He brought to life again dead bodies in the presence of the largest assemblies.

On a certain evening, whilst he preached in a religious meeting, a volcano broke out and the earth shook : all fell, but he stood up. Alaradin, a Mahometan Prince, besieged Malacca with an army and a fleet, but the Saint, though having only seven small boats to defend the people, advanced against him ; his voice resounded as thunder, and Alaradin alarmed, turned and fled." Read the relation of these miracles and many others in the lives of Saint Francis Xavier by the R. F. Jesuits Turselin and Bouhours. The first is written in Latin, the second in French.

Years 1560 and 1561.—The Parliament of Paris ordered that the Jesuits should sue for their Institute in the great Council of Trent. The tenth of October, John Prévost, Rector of the University (France), was compelled to forbid them to teach, because they excited and misled youth. Then they asked to be incorporated in the University, but they entangled so much the conditions of their admission, that their petition was disregarded.

In 1561, they intrigued powerfully, seduced the Bishop of Paris, and corrupted the Rector of the University.

[See for the above and following quotations, "Annales de la Société des Soi-dissant Jésuits, ou, Recueil historique et chronologique de toutes les pièces écrites, contre les Jésuites." Edition in 4 volumes. In this work are related the most authentic and official pieces written, decreed, and published about the Jesuits. This work being a living condemnation and sentence against them, they have spent a good deal of money to cause all the copies to disappear, but many remain in the public libraries of France.]

Year 1564.—In France, the Jesuits seduced Les Guizes in flattering and promising them support in their political and ambitious views. So powerfully protected, they corrupted the celebrated lawyer Versoris and attacked the University. In spite of the talent of the famous Pasquier, and of his well-grounded pleading : in spite of the Parliament ; even in spite of the will of the people, they were authorized in all their plans to monopolize the public instruction. The Reverend Father Jesuit Odon Pigenat, styled by Arnaud "Le Corybante fanatique," "The fanatic Corybante," and by the historian De Thou, "Le Tigre," "The Tiger," was the hero of all those mean intrigues. (Annales . . . Arnaud—De Thou.)

Year 1569.—In France, De Póntas, Bishop of Razas, refused but in vain, his consent to their establishment in Bordeaux, where they excited the Catholics against the Protestants. (Annales . . .)

Year 1570.—Elizabeth, Queen of England, expelled the Jesuits from her kingdom. (Annales . . .)

Year 1571.—In Belgium, the misdeeds of the Jesuits were so hideous and so subversive, that Arias Montanus wrote to Philip II., King of Spain, assuring him that the deluge of their works of destruction covered all society. He entreated him to take some measures to stop, or at least paralyze the jesuitical power, and proposing a series of instructions, which should be executed by the Governor of these disturbed provinces.

At the same time, Catharine of Austria complained urgently and bitterly in a letter to Borgia, against the enormities of the Jesuits, who, she said had revealed her confession, and profaned criminally the most respectable and sacred things. (Annales.)

Year 1572.—In France, the Jesuits directed by Gregory XIII., that worthy Pope who celebrated so solemnly in Rome the news of the massacre of the Protestants all over the kingdom, the Jesuits, say I, advised the counsellors of Charles IX., and of Catherine De Médicis. It was in their lurking house at Paris that these counsellors deliberated during the mournful night of the massacre, known under the name "Massacre de la Saint Barthélemy."

At the same time, as the Jesuits had previously fired Germany, stirred up the Catholics who were in the majority against the Protestants who were in the minority, two armies were organised, frightful battles fought, and blood ran everywhere. (Annales . . . . and various extracts.)

We read in the 2d volume, page 613, edition octavo of the History of France by Anquetil, a Roman Catholic priest who died in the Roman communion, who, thereby, is undoubtedly not chargeable with partiality when he avers some too visible misdeeds of Bishops, Jesuits, and Popes:

"La nouvelle de la mort du General Coligny fut reçue à Rome avec les transports de la joie la plus vive. On tira le canon. Ou alluma des feux comme pour l'évènement le plus avantageux. Il y cut une messe solennelle d'actions de grâces, à laquelle le Pape Grégoire XIII. assista avec l'éclat que cette cour donne aux cérémonies qu'elle veut rendre célébres. Le Cardinal De Lorraine récompensa largement le courrier et l'interrogea en homme instruit d'avance. Brautôme raconte que le Souverain Pontife versa des larmes sur le sort de taut d'infortunees. Je pleure, dit il, taut d'innocents qui n'auront pas manqué d'être confonpus avec les coupables, et, possible qu'à plusieurs de ces morts Dieu ait fait la grâce de se repentir."

[TRANSLATION.]

"In Rome, the news of the death of General Coligny was received most joyfully. The cannon was fired. Bon-fires were kindled as for the most fortunate events. A solemn mass of thanksgiving was celebrated, at which mass the Pope Gregory XIII. assisted, with the splendor given by this Court to the ceremonies considered by it as worth solemnization. The Cardinal de Lorraine rewarded largely the courier, and showed, in questioning him, that he was informed in advance. Brantôme relates that the Sovereign Pontiff shed tears on the fate of so many unfortunate victims. 'I mourn,' he said, 'so many innocent victims, who undoubtedly have been confounded with the culpable, and God will have perhaps granted to many of them the grace of repentance.' "

Ah! Jesuits, Popes, Cardinals, and other religious butchers, if you did know how strong, how revengeful, arise in our minds and hearts the remembrance of our forefathers whom you assassinated! If you did know how their cries in falling agonized and dying under your poignards, resound thundering through our ears, and stir up all the power of our filial love! If you did know how heroical it is to forgive you! But Christ the merciful orders us: we stop and are silent. We will only borrow and apply to you the language which he addressed, under almost similar circumstances, to your ancestors the Pharisees:

" Wo to you, Pharisees, because you love the uppermost seats in the Synagogues, and salutations in the market-place. Wo to you, because you are as sepulchres that appear not, and men that walk over them are not aware. Wo to you lawyers, because you load men with burdens which they cannot bear, and you yourselves touch not the packs with one of your fingers. Wo to you who build the monuments of the prophets: and your fathers killed them. Truly you bear witness that you consent to the doings of your fathers: for they indeed killed them, and you build their sepulchres. Therefore also the wisdom of God saith: I will send to them prophets and apostles, and some of them they will kill and persecute: that the blood of all the prophets which was shed from the foundation of the world, may be required of this generation, from the blood of Abel unto the blood of Zacharias, who was slain between the altar and the temple. Yea, I say to you, it shall be required of this generation. Wo to you lawyers, for you have taken away the key of knowledge: you yourselves have not entered in, and those that were entering in, you have hindered." St. Luke, xi: 43 and following.

Year 1579.—Saint Charles Borromeo, Archbishop of Milan,

wrote to Cæsar Spetiano, his apostolical pronotary and agent in Rome, complaining about the undertakings, enormities, and rascalities of the Jesuits in that city. He ordered him to claim from the Pope a sentence against them, styling them "Fathers Du Jesus," because they dishonored the Sacred name of Jesus. He did not succeed, for they were too powerful in Rome, the too beloved idols of Papacy. Pius IV. had told an ambassador of Portugal, that the Jesuits were his troops. (See Ribadeneira, one of the authors of the Jesuits.—Annales . . . .)

Year 1581.—The Jesuits were expelled from Bourges, Rouen, and Tournon (France,) where they had opened colleges; were discredited in Monomotapa, suspected and threatened in London after the execution of Campion, Skerwin, Briant; and expelled from Anvers for having disturbed Gand, a city of the Low Countries.

The Reverend Father Sammier was deputed to the Princes of Germany, Italy, and Spain, to induce them to unite against France. (Pfister—History of Germany, 7 vol.—Mézeray, French Historian.)

Year 1584.—The murderer of the Prince of Orange, Balthazar Gérard, declared that four Jesuits of Trêves, to whom he had revealed his project, had encouraged him in assuring him, that if he fell and died in his pious design, he should be a martyr. (De Thou—French History of France, Book 79.)

By the intrigues of the Jesuits, the Princes of Guise and Philip II., King of Spain, united on the first of December, against the Protestants of France and those of the Low Countries, for the double purpose of crowning King of France the Cardinal Bourbon, after the death of Henry III., and of banishing all the heretical Princes. At the same time, the Jesuits being immensely rich, forestalled the victuals, famished France and preached rebellion against the King Henry III. (Annales Mezeray—History of France.

From the year 1586 to the year 1590.—In England the Jesuits organised and directed a new conspiracy, not to try again to kill Queen Elizabeth, but to dethrone her, and to crown in her stead Mary Stuart.

They shook France, and were, says the historian Mezeray, "Les trompettes de la Ligue," "The leaders of the League." Their Provincial of Paris, the Reverend Father Mathew, was surnamed "Le courier de la Ligue," "The courier of the League." They struggled to win Henry III. Also, Paquier, in his Catechism, Book 3, ch. 2, says about it: "Anger, confeseur de ce Prince, avait bien tâté son poux et jaugé profondément sa conscience,"—which means, that the Jesuits had carefully and deeply sounded the intentions and conscience of this Prince. But they did not succeed. Then they stirred up the mob in Bordeaux, from which city the Marshal de Martignan expelled them. (De Thou—History of France, Book 10, ch. 4.)

Afterwards, the Jesuits preluded the murder of Henry IV., by deifying James Clement, who killed Henry III. at Saint Cloud, the first of August, 1589. The Reverend Father Jesuit Molina, Theologian of the Jesuits, wrote on these circumstances: "Murder was atoned by murder; and the manes of the Duke of Guises unjustly killed, were avenged by the effusion of the royal blood." Further, he adds: "James Clement made a truly noble, admirable, memorable . . . . . action, by which he taught the Princes of the world, that their impious designs do not remain unpunished." (Molina—His Theology, Article de Regibus.)

Year 1590.—Aquaviva, General of the Jesuits, obtained from the Pope Gregory XIII., a Bull putting them beyond all civil and spiritual authorities, and compelling these authorities under pain of excommunication, to admit and practise all the contents of this Bull.

We give an abridgment of the cases in which this excommunication is incurred:

Are excommunicated,

1. " Kings, Princes, and Administrators who will tax the Society of Jesus, its individuals or property.

2. " All those who will prejudice the Society.

3. " All those who will oblige the Society to lend, either its churches or houses in which to say mass.

4. " All those who will be bold enough to violate the concessions granted to the Jesuits.

5. " All those who will refuse the office of protectors of the Society.

6. " All Regulars and Seculars of whatever estate, rank, and prëeminence they may be, Bishops, Archbishops, Patriarchs, and Cardinals, who will attack the Order of the Jesuits and their Constitutions, either some articles of their Constitutions, or concerning them; though it may be for disputing and seeking truth.

7. " The Rectors of Universities and others, who would molest the Rectors and teachers of the colleges of the Society of Jesus.

8. " All those who would oppose the privileges of the colleges of the Jesuits, etc. . . . .

9. " The fathers of families who would hinder their children from belonging to the Society of Jesus. . . . .

(La Chalottias—Comptes rendus, p. 116, 117, 118.)

At that time, there was seen in many houses of the Jesuits a hall called, " Hall of Meditation," in which these Reverend Fathers instructed murderers of the Kings. Placing in their hands a hallowed poignard, they told the elected:

" Va, mignon de Dieu, élu comme Jephté; voila le glaive de Samson, le glaive de David, duquel il trancha la tête de Goliath, le glaive de Judith duquel elle trancha la tête à Holopherne; le glaive des Machabés; le glaive de Saint Pierre, duquel il coupa l'oreille a Malchus; le glaive du Pape Jules II., avec lequel il arracha dec mains des Princes Immola, Fænza, Ferli, Bologne et autres villes avec grande effusion de sang. Va, sois hormne robuste. Que le Seigneur assure tes pas!

—" Ils le conduisaient eansuite vers un portrait de Jacques Clément et lui disaient:

" A la mienne volonté que Dieu m'eûtélu et choisi en votre place; je serais assuré de n'aller point en Purgatoire, mais tout droit en Paradis."

[TRANSLATION.]

" Go, favorite of God, elected like Jephtha; this is the sword of Samson; the sword of David, by which he beheaded Goliath; the sword of Judith, by which she beheaded Holophernes; the sword of the Machabees; the sword of Saint Peter, by which he cut off the ear of Malchus; the sword of the Pope Julius II. by which he snatched from the hands of the Princes Immola, Fænza, Forli, Bolonia and other cities with great effusion of blood. Go, be a strong man. That God may insure your steps!

" Then they led him before a picture of James Clement, and told him:

" I would desire to have been chosen and elected in your stead; I should be certain to escape Purgatory, and to go straight to Paradise." (Les Convents.)

Year 1592.—Patrick Cullen, by the instigation of the Jesuit Holte, went to England, intending to murder Queen Elizabeth, but he did not succeed. (Les Convents.)

Year 1593.—The Reverend Father Varade, Rector of the Jesuits at Paris, excited Barrière to kill Henry IV., King of France. As proof, this murderer has asserted this declaration in his testament. Moreover, we read in an authentical piece headed "Les remontrances du Parlement à Henry IV."—" Advice of the Parliament to Henry IV." presented to him in 1603: " Jean Barriére avait éte instruit par Varade, et confessa avoir reçu l'absolution sous le serment fait entre ses mains de vous assassiner " —" John Barrière had been instructed by Varade, and has avered to have been absolved from his sins, because he had sworn to murder you."

De Thou says : " This crime stirred up the people against the Jesuits, who had by their seditious sermons exposed the life of the King." (Remontrances du Parlement à Henry IV.—De Thou—History of France, Book 107.)

Year 1594.—The Jesuit Holte excited Williams and Yorck, young Jesuits, to murder the Queen of England, and in order to fortify them for the execution of this crime, bestowed upon them the holy communion. They fortunately did not succeed, and this wicked man was hung with Henry Garnet. (Fragments of the law-suit in the Archives of London.)

Year 1595.—Achille de Harlay proposed to the Jesuits the following oath, which they refused to take because Aquaviva, their General, favored the Roman Catholic Spain, against the half Protestant France.

This was the formula:

" I swear to live and die in the Catholic, Apostolic, and Roman faith, and to submit to Henry IV. I renounce all confederacies against his service, and I will do nothing against his authority." (De Thou—History of France, Book 109.)

John Chatel tried to kill Henry IV. He had for accomplice the Reverend Father Jesuit Guignard, who was hung for this regicide on the seventh of July of the same year. John Chatel stabbed the King with a knife, but by God's providence he was wounded but slightly.

This wretched murderer endured torture and death firmly and without repentance. " Such a circumstance," writes Anquetil, a Roman Catholic priest, in his History of France, vol. 3, p. 199, was attributed to the lessons of the Jesuits. They were seized and critally questioned. Many seditious books having been found in their convent, and many facts and circumstances having been charged upon them, John Guignard was condemned to be hung. All the other Jesuits were expelled forever from France. They left Paris on the eighth of January. "Behold," says the journalist of Henry IV., "how a simple usher accomplished on that day with his switch what four battalions could not have done!"

"The King was deeply afflicted at this attempt." 'Is it necessary,' said he in sorrow, 'that the Jesuits be convinced by my mouth!' The murderer had struck and cut his lips, and broken two of his teeth.

"A pyramid was erected in Paris to perpetuate the horror of this monstrous crime." (Anquetil—History of France.)

Americans, hoping to be agreeable to you in placing under your eyes more extensive documents about this Regicide, a fact which embraces in itself all that the Jesuits are able to do, I will extract from the 9th vol. p. 283, of the memoirs of Sully, Minister of Henry IV., these long but interesting and authenticated quotations: I say interesting, because, thanks to the artfulness of the Jesuits, this 9th volume, which is a complement of the work, has been taken off in great many editions.*

* These are the sentences passed against John Châtel, and the Jesuits—against John Guignard—against John Gueret and Peter Châtel—I produce them with their old French style:

"Arret Contre Jean Chastel et les Jesuits.—Vu par la Cour, les Grand'Chambre et Tournelle assemblees, le procès criminel commencé à faire par le Prévôt de l'Hôtel du Roi, et depuis parachevé d'instruire à la Requête du Procureur-Gènéral du Roi, demandeur et accusateur à l'encontre de Jean Châtel, natif de Paris, Ecolier, ayant fait le cours de ses études au College de Clermont, prisonnier ès prisons de la Conciergerie du Palais, pour raison du très-exécrable et abominable parricide attenté sur la Personne du Roi: interrogatoires et confessions dudit Jean Châtel: Oui et interrogé en ladite Cour ledit Châtel fur le fait dudit parricide: Oui aussi en icelle Jean Gueret, Prêtre, soi-disant de la Congrégation et Société du Nom

Inscriptions of the Pyramid.

"The Pyramid erected to eternalize the remembrance of the crime of the Jesuits, was drawn and engraved by John Le Clerc,

de Jesus, demeurant audit College, et ci-devant Précepteur dudit Jean Châtel, Pierre Châtel et Denise Hazard, pere et mere dudit Jean : Conclusions du Procureur-Général du Roi, et tout considéré IL EST DIT que ladite Cour a déclaré et déclare ledit Jean Châtel atteint et convaincu du crime de le-ze-majesté divine et humaine aupremier chef, par le très-méchant et très-détestable parricide attenté sur la personne du Roi. Pour réparation duquel crime a condamné et condamne ledit Jean Châtel à faire amende honorable devant la principale porte de l'Eglise de Paris, nud en chemise, tenant une torche de cire ardente du poids de deux livres, et illect à genoux dire et déclarer, que malheureusement et proditoirement il a attenté ledit très inhumain et très abominable parricide, et blessé le Roi d'un couteau en la face ; et par fausses et damnables instructions il a dit au procés être permis de tuer les Rois et que le Roi Henri IV à présent regnant n'est en l'Eglise, jusqu'à ce qu'il ait l'approbation du Pape, dont il se repent et demande pardon à Dieu, au Roi et à la Justice. Ce fait, être mené et conduit dans un tombereau en la place de Gréve : illec tenaillé aux bras et cuisses, et sa main dextre, tenant en icelle le couteau duquel il s'est efforcé de commettre ledit parricide, coupée : et après, son corps tiré et démembre avec quatre chevaux, et ses membres et corps jettés au feu, et consumés en cendres, et les cendres jettées au vent ; a déclaré tous et chacun ses biens acquis et confisqués au Roi. Avant laquelle exécution sera ledit Jean Châtel appliqué à la question, tant ordinaire, qu'extraordinaire pour savoir la vérité de ses complices, et d'aucuns cas résultants du procès. A fait et fait inhibitions et défenses à toutes personnes, de quelque qualité et condition qu'elles soient, sur peine de crime de lezemajesté, de dire ni proférer en aucun lieu public lesdits propos, lesquels ladite Cour a déclaré et déclare scandaleux, séditieux et contraires à la parole de Dieu, et condamnés comme heretiques par les saints Decrets. Ordonne que les Prêtres et Ecoliers du College de Clermont, et tous autres soi-disant de ladite Societe, comme corrupteurs de la Jeunesse, perturbateurs du repos public, ennemis du Roi et de l'Etat, vuideront dedans trois jours après la signification du present Arrêt, hors de Paris, et autres villes et lieux où sont leurs Colleges, et quinzaine après hors du Royaume, sur peine où ils y seront trouves, ledit tempts passe, d'être punis comme criminels et coupables dudit crime de leze-majeste. Seront les biens father of Sebastian, engraver of the King. The inscriptions or stamps have been erased by the Jesuits: we find them only in the cabinets of the amateur.

tant meubles qu'immeubles à eux appartenants, employes en œuvres pitoyables, et distribution d'iceux faite ainsi que par la Cour sera ordonne. Outre fait defenses, à tous Sujects du Roi d'envoyer des Ecoliers aux Colleges de ladite Societe qui sont hors du Royaume pour y être instruits, sur la même peine de crime de leze-majeste. Ordonne la Cour que les extraits du present Arrêt seront envoyes aux Bailliages et Senechaussees de ce ressort, pour être execute selon sa forme et teneur. Enjoint aux Baillis et Senechaux leurs Lieutenants generaux et particuliers, de proceder à l'execution dedans le delai contenu en icelui, et aux Substituts du Procureur-General de tenir, la main à ladite éxecution, faire informer des contraventions, et certifier la Cour de leurs diligences au mois, sur peine de privation de leurs etats. *Signê* Du Tillet. Prononce audit Jean Châtel, execute le 29 Decembre 1594.

Arret Contre Jean Guignard, Du Janvier 1595.—Vu par la Cour, les Grand'Chambre et Tournelle assemblees, le procès criminel fait par l'un des Conseillers d'icelle, à la Requête du Procureur-General du Roi, à l'encontre de Jean Guignard, Prêtre, Regent au College de Clermont de cette ville de Paris, prisonnier ès prisons de la Conciergerie du Palais, pour avoir ete saisi de plusieurs Livres contenant contr'autres choses, approbation du très-cruel et très-inhumain parricide du feu Roi, que Dieu absolve, et inductions pour faire tuer le Roi à present regnant; Interrogatoires et confessions dudit Guignard, lesdits Livres representes, reconnus composes par lui, et ecrits de sa main: Conclusions du Procureur-General du Roi; oui et interroge ledit Guignard sur les cas à lui imposes et contenus es dits Livres, et tout confidere.

Il sera dit que ladite Cour a declare et declare ledit Guignard atteint et convaicu du crime de leze-majeste, et d'avoir compose et ecrit lesdits Livres contenant plusieurs faux et seditieux moyens, pour prouver qu'il avoit ete loisible de commettre ledit parricide, et etoit permis de tuer le Roi Henri IV. à present regnant. Pour reparation de ce, a condamne et condamne ledit Guignard à faire amende honorable, nud en chemise, la corde au cou, devant la principale porte de l'Eglise de Paris: et illec etant à genoux, tenant en ses mains une torche de cire ardente du poids de deux livres, dire et declarer: "Que mechamment, malheureusement et contre verite il a ecrit le

"This Pyramid was twenty feet high. It had four faces at the four corners, where were painted the four cardinal virtues. On the top was a cross, below which was the following verse :

"feu Roi avoir ete justement tue par Jacques Clement, et que si le Roi à "present regnant ne mouroit à la guerre, il falloit le faire mourir, dont il se "repent, et demande pardon à Dieu, au Roi et à la Justice.' Ce fait, mene et conduit en la place de Greve, pendu et etrangle a une potence qui y sera pour cet effet plantee : Et apres, le corps mort reduit et consume en cendres en un feu qui sera fait au pied de ladite potence. A declare et declare tous en chacun ses biens acquis et confisques au Roi. Prononce andit Jean Guignard, et execute le septieme jour de Janvier 1595.

Arret du Meme Jour, Contre Jean Gueret, et Pierre Chastel.—Vu par la Cour, les Grand'Chambre et Tournelle assemblees, le procès criminel commence à faire par le Prevôt de l'Hôtel du Roi, et depuis paracheve d'instruire en icelle à la Requête du Procureur-General du Roi, demandeur et accusateur à l'encontre de Jean Gueret, Prêtre, soi-disant de la Congregation et Societe du nom de Jesus, demeurant au College de Clermont, et ci-devant Precepteur de Jean Châtel n'aguere execute à mort par arrêt de ladite Cour, Pierre Châtel, Marchand Drapier, Bourgeois de Paris, Denise Hazard sa femme, pere et mere dudit Jean Châtel, Jean le Comte et Catherine Châtel sa femme, Magdelaine Châtel, fille desdits Pierre Châtel et Denise Hazard, Antoine de Villiers, Pierre Roussel, Simonne Turin et Louise Camus, leurs serviteurs et servantes, maître Claude l'Allemant, Prêtre, Cure de Saint-Pierre des Arcis, maître Jacques Bernard, Prêtre, Clerc de ladite Eglise, et Maître Lucas Morin, Prêtre habitue en icelle, prisonniers ès prisons de la Conciergerie du Palais; Interrogatoires, confessions et denegation desdits prisonniers, confrontation faite dudit Jean Châtel audit Pierre Châtel son pere ; information faite contre ledit Pierre Châtel ; confrontation à lui faite des temoins ouis en icelle; le procès criminel fait audit Jean Châtel pour raison du très-execrable et abominable parricide attente sur la personne du Roi ; le proces-verbal de l'execution de l'Arrêt de mort donne contre ledit, Jean Châtel le vingt-neuvieme de Decembre dernier passe : Conclusions du Procureur-General du Roi : ouis et interroges en ladite Cour ledit Gueret, Pierre Châtel et Hazard sur les cas à eux imposes et contenus audit procès. Autres interrogatories et denegations faites par lesdits Gueret et Pierre Châtel, en la question à eux baillee par ordonnance de ladite Cour, et tout confidere :

"The fifth of January, year of salvation 1591, by decree of the Court.

> "Hic domus immani Quondam fuit hospita monstro
> Crux ubi nunc cœlsum tollit in astra caput:
> Sanciit in miseros pœnam hane sacer ordo Penates
> Regibus ut scires sanctius esse nihil."

[TRANSLATION.]

"This house (of Chatel) on the top of which a cross raises now its head to the stars, once sheltered a wild monster: the Sacred Order of Penates inflicted upon them this punishment, in order that they might know that nothing is holier than Kings."

Il fera dit que ladite Cour, pour les cas contenus audit procès, a banni et bannit lesdits Gueret et Pierre Châtel du Royaume de France, à favoir ledit Gueret à perpetuite, et ledit Châtel pour le temps et espace de neuf ans et à perpetuite de la Ville et Fauxbourgs de Paris: A eux enjoint de garder leur ban, à peine d'être pendus et estrangles, sans autre forme ni figure de procès. A declare et declare tous et chacuns les biens dudit Gueret acquis et confisques au Roi: et a condamne et condamne ledit Pierre Châtel a deux mille ecus d'amende envers le Roi, applicables à l'acquit et pour la fourniture du pain des prisonniers de la Conciergerie, et à tenir prison jusqu'à plein paiement de ladite somme: Et ne courra le jour du bannissement, sinon, du jour qu'il aura icelle payee. Ordonne ladite Cour que la maison en laquelle etoit demeurant ledit Châtel, sera abattue, demolie at rasee, et la place appliquee au Public, sans qu'à l'avenir on y puisse bâtir. En laquelle place pour memoire perpetuelle du très-mechant et très detestable parricide attente sur la pensonne du Roi, sera mis et erige un pilier eminent de pierres de taille, avec un table auauquel seront inscrites les causes de ladite demolition et erection dudit pilier, lequel sera fait des deniers provenants des demolitions de ladite maison. Et pour le regard desdits Hazard, le Comte, Catherine et Magdelaine Châtel, de Villiers, Roussel, Turin, Camus, l'Allemant, Bernard en Morin, ordonne ladite Cour que les prisons leur seront ouvertes. Pronounce auxudits Hazard, le Comte, Catherine et Magdelaine Châtel, de Villiers, Roussel, Turin, Camus, l'Allemand, Bernard et Morin, le septième de Janvier, et auxdits Gueret et Pierre Châtel, le dixieme du dit mois mil cinq cent quatre vingt quinze.

First Inscription.

"On the face before the bridge *Au Change.*

"D. O. M.

"Pro salute Henrici quarti, clementissimi and fortissimi regis, quem nefandus parricida, perniciossimœ factionis hœresy pestiferâ imbutus; quœ nuper abominandis sceleribus pietatis nomen obtendens, Unctos Domini, vivas que Majestatis ipsius imagines occidere populariter docuit, dùm confodere tentat, cœlesti numine scelestam manum inhibenti, cultro in labrum superius delato, et dentium occursu fellciter retuso, violare ausus est. Ordo amplissimus, ut vel conatus tam nefarii pœnoœ terror, simul et prœsentissimi in optimum principem ac regnum, cujus salus in ejus salute posita est, divini favoris apud posteros memoria extaret, monstro illo admissis equis membratim discerpto, et flammis ultricibus consumpto, œdes etiam, undè prodierat, hic sitas funditùs everti et in earum locum salutis omnium ac gloriœ signum erigi decrevit."

[TRANSLATION.]

To God, Good and Omnipotent.

"In remembrance of the deliverance of the Most Clement and Most Valiant King Henry, whom a monstrous parricide, infatuated with the most pernicious and destructive heresy, (which lately, hiding the most abominable crimes under the appearance of piety, has taught publicly men to murder Kings, the anointed of the Lord and living images of his majesty,) undertook to kill; whose wicked hand, at the same moment, the arm of God stopped, the knife which stabbed the upper lip having been repulsed, in happily meeting the teeth. Thereupon, the Court of Parliament passed the sentence—that the monster should be quartered by four horses, and his members reduced to ashes— that the house where he was born should be utterly destroyed—and that in its place, should be erected the image of salvation and glory, in order that thereafter, the fear of his punishment should repress these horrible attempts, and that the memory of the very extraordinary favor of God towards this good Prince and this nation, whose safety depends on his, be preserved by posterity."

Second Inscription.

"On the face before the Palace, was engraved the sentence passed against John Chatel and the Jesuits, as it is related in the foregoing notes."

Third Inscription.

"Before the bridge *Saint Michael.*

D. O. M.

"Duplex potestas ista fatorum fuit
Gallis saluti quod foret, Gallis dare
Servare Gallis, quod dedissent optimum."

[TRANSLATION.]

"Providence could both grant to the French what their safety required, and preserve to the French the best which she had granted them.

"Cùm Henricus Christianissimus, Francorum et Navarræ Rex bono Reipublicæ natus, inter cœtera victoriarum exempla, quibus, tam de tyrannide Hispanicâ, quam de ejus factione, priscam regni hujus majestatem, justis ultus est armis, etiam hanc urbem et reliquos regni hujus penè omnes recepisset, ac denique felicitate intestinorum Franciæ nominis hostium furorem provocante, Joannes Petri filius, Castellus, ab illis submissus, sacrum Regis caput cultro petere ausus esset, præsentiore temeritate, quam feliciore sceleris successu: ob eam rem ex amplissimi Ordinis, consulto vindicatâ per duellione, dirutâ Petri Castelli domo, in quâ Joannes ejus filius inexpiabile nefas designatum patri communicaverat, in areâ adœquatâ hoc perenne monumentum erectum est, in memoriam ejus dici in quâ seculi felicitas, inter vota et metus urbis liberatorem regni fundatorem que Reipublicæ quietis, a temoratoris nefando incæpto, Regni autem hujus opes attritas ab extremo interitu vindicavit, pulso præterea totâ Galliâ hominum genere novæ ac maleficœ superstitionis, qui Rempublicam turbabant quorum instinctu piacularis adolescens dirum facinus instituerat."

[TRANSLATION.]

"When Henry the Most Christian King of France and Navarre, born for the welfare of the Republic, had, among other instances of his victories, chastised the Spanish tyranny, and the league which Spain had formed. When he had justly avenged by his arms the former splendor of this Kingdom, and even received the submission of this city (Paris), and of nearly all the others of this Kingdom. Finally, when his successes had excited the furor of the intestine foes of France, a certain John Chatel, son of Peter, seduced by these people, attempted with a knife the sacred life of our King with more temerity than success. Therefore, the Court of Parliament having by a sentence punished the crime of high treason, cast down the house of Peter Chatel, (in which John Chatel had imparted to his father this inexpiable attempt,) this eternal monument has been erected on the place of his house demolished in remembrance of this day in which the happiness of the world, among the hopes and fears, the city, has preserved from this bloody design our King, savior of the country, founder of public tranquility, and repairer of the debilitated strength of this falling Kingdom. Moreover, the Court of Parliament has banished from all France the kindred of a new and noxious superstition which disturbed the nation and by whose instigation this wretched young man had undertaken this odious parricide."

"S. P. Q. P.

"Extinctori pestiferæ factionis Hispanicœ, incolumitate ejus et vindictâ parricidii læti, majestati que ejus devotissimi."

[TRANSLATION.]

The Senate and the People of Paris.

"To him who has destrroyed the pestilential Spanish sect, happy on account of his preservation, and of the parricide, the very obedient subjects of his Majesty.

"*Fourth Inscription.*

"On the face before the *Barnabites.*

"Quod sacrum votum que fit memoriæ, perennitati, longœvetati saluti que maximi, fortissimi, et clementissimi Principis Henrici IV., Galliæ et Navarrœ Regis Christianissimi.

"Audi Viator, sive sis extraneus,
Sive incola urbis cui Paris nomen dedit.
Hic alta quœ sto Pyramis, domus fui
Castelli sed quam diruendam funditus
Frequens Senatus crimen ultus censuit.
Huc me redegit tandem herilis filius,
Malis magistris usus et schola impia.
Sotericum, eheu ! nomen usurpantibus.
Incestus et mox parricida in principem
Qui nuper urbem perditam servaverat
Et qui favente sœpe victor numine
Defflexit ictum audaculi sicarii
Punctus que tantum est dentium septo tenus
Abi, Viator, plura me vetat loqui
Nostræ stupendum civitatis dedecus.

[TRANSLATION.]

"To be consecrated and devoted to the memory, immortality, length, and preservation of the life of the Most High, Most Powerful, and Most Clement Prince Henry IV., the Most Christian King of France and Navarre."

"Hark, passer, whether you may be a stranger or a citizen of the city to which Paris gave his name. I who now am an elevated Pyramid, was formerly the house of Chatel; but by order of Parliament, I was utterly demolished in punishment of a crime. The son of my owner finally reduced me to this condition, from having been taught in an impious school, by wicked professors who boasted, alas! of the title of Saviors of the country. This son, at first incestuous, became soon afterwards, parricide of his Prince who had saved the city, and who helped by the Lord, by whose assistance he had obtained so many victories, avoided the stroke of a too rash murderer, and was only wounded in the teeth between the lips.

"Go your way, passer. The astonishing dishonor of our city prevents me from revealing many things.

"The Pyramid having been demolished in the month of May, 1605, the following verses were written:

J'ote la Pyramide honte de mes sujets,
Pour des malheurs passes arracher la memoire:
Ceux qui n'approuvent pas mes hauts et saints projets,
Feignant d'aimer mon bien, ils envient ma gloire.

[TRANSLATION.]

"I take out the Pyramid a shame for my subjects, to blot out the recollection of passed misfortunes: those who approve not of my sublime and holy projects, in feigning good will towards me are jealous of my glory.

"In 1606, a fountain was built on this place, and below, these two epigrams were engraved:

"Pyramis ante fui: quid not mutabile cum me
Verterit in fontem prefecti cura Myronis,
Hic ubi restabant sacri monumenta furoris
Eluit infandum Myronis unda sce us.
Nunc fous est mauans ubi Pyramis ignea sedit
Pacifico in regno sic temperat omnia princeps."

[TRANSLATION.]

"Formerly I was a Pyramid—what is unchangeable? When I was by the care of the Prefect Myron changed into a fountain. Here, where stood the monuments of fury, the water of Myron washes out a dreadful crime. Now, where a fiery Pyramid stood, a fountain bursts out. Thus the Prince softens all in his pacific reign."

Year 1598.—The Jesuits cause the murder of Maurice de Nassau, and were expelled from Holland.

Having been expelled from France, they cringed, promised, and intrigued; thus gained over Lesdiquiere, and by his intercession were forgiven. Henry IV. let them come again into the kingdom, at least, tacitly. Surprising thing! This great warrior, this destroyer of the League, feared those men of whom he said: "They have correspondences and familiaries everywhere, above all, a great ability and artfulness for bending and directing minds according to their will." (Memoires de Sully, Ministre de Henry IV.)

Year 1604.—The Cardinal Borromeo expelled ignominiously the Jesuits from the college La Breda. (Annales.)

On the second of February, an edict of James I., King of England, Scotland, and Ireland, expelled them from all these States, as being authors of plots, conspiracies, etc., directed against him and the Queen Elizabeth, as corrupting his subjects, and exciting them to rebellion. (Annales—Edict in the Archives of London.)

Years 1605 and 1606.—In England, the Reverend Father

Jesuits Garnet, Oldercon, Gerard and Tesmond, organized and directed the conspiracy known under the name of the "Gunpowder conspiracy." The Fathers Garnet and Oldercon were hung and quartered in London. The Fathers Gerard and Tesmond escaped this fate only by flying from the kingdom secretly and rapidly. (Archives of London.)

In England, James I. issued a new Edict expelling the Jesuits from all the Kingdom.

The Jesuits having betrayed the Venitians to serve the interests and ambition of the Pope Paul V., the Senate banished them by a solemn decree from all the territory of the Republic.

Their misdeeds were so numberless in Prussia, and their teaching so dangerous, that, on the twenty-fifth of August, the Consuls and Senate of Dantzick issued a decree expelling them, and forcing them to leave that city within three days. On the twenty-fourth of October, they issued another decree banishing them from Thorn, a city of the same Kingdom. (Annales.)

Year 1609.—The Jesuits, to defy the friends of the religion of Christ, of the peace and welfare of society, to insult them and deceive the people, solicited and obtained from the Pope Paul V. the Bull of canonization of their worthy father and founder, Ignatius Loyola. (Various Ecclesiastical and other Histories.)

Year 1610.—In Paris, the Faculty of Theology condemned solemnly the doctrine of Marianna, Jesuit, who in his book "De Rege," taught regicide.

On the fourteenth of May, the Jesuits, in spite of the forgiveness and numerous gifts in money, gratifications, and privileges granted to them by Henry IV., (see Memoirs of Sully, vol. 9,) killed him by the hands of Ravaillac, in the Laferronière street. (Anquetil, a Roman Catholic priest, in his History of France, Annales—Premier avertissement de l'Univeristé de Paris, p. 84, publié en 1684.

Thus, within twenty years, the Jesuits had killed two Kings of France and plotted ten times in England.

On the tenth of June, James I. revived his Edicts of expulsion against the Jesuits, who, in intriguing and conspiring again in the dark, were as dangerous as formerly. (Annales—Archives in London.)

Year 1611.—In France, the Parliament passed a sentence against the Jesuits, who had corrupted and enticed away an only son. (Annales—Authentical fragments of the Law-suit.)

Year 1618.—By an Edict of the fourth of June, the Jesuits were expelled from Bohemia and Hungary. (Annales.)

Year 1619.—On the fourth of November, the Jesuits were banished forever from Hungary, by a decree "Des Etâts Generaux." (Annales.)

Year 1620.—On the thirtieth of March, the twenty-third and twenty-ninth of May, Henry Louis De Castaigner De la Roche-posay, Bishop of Poitiers, and La Rochefoucault, Bishop of Angoulême (France), issued various sentences and ordinances against the Jesuits, who usurped the Episcopal jurisdiction.

The Jesuits were expelled from Poland. De Berulle, Founder and General 'De la Congregation de l'Oratoire de France,' wrote several letters to the Cardinal De Richelieu, complaining and petitioning against the ingratitude and enormities of the Jesuits. (Annales.)

Year 1624.—On the twentieth of January, the Reverend Father Louis Sotello, Monk of the Order of Saint Francis, who had been appointed Bishop of Japan by Paul V., protested in a long letter of complaints against the infidelity, the scandals, intrigues, seditious plots and anti-christian principles of the Jesuits in that Empire, where the Reverend Father Jesuit Martinius had solicited and obtained an office of "Mandarin."

Year 1625—On the twenty-first of January, took place the law-suit relative to an hideous crime of Francis Martel, parish priest of Estreu (France). The Reverend Father Jesuits Ambroise, Guyot, and Stephen Chapuy had been his counsellors.

At the same time, the Bishops of Poitiers, Langres and Cornouailles (France), published ordinances against the Jesuits, who had usurped their Episcopal jurisdiction. (Annales.)

Year 1626.—The Jesuits, who, in spite of their banishment from Poland, had succeeded by their artfulness to enter again into that country, were compelled to leave their college in Cracow. (Annales.)

Year 1630.—At Hildesheim, the Jesuits played a comedy against the Comte Tilly and against the King of Sweden. (Annales.)

Year 1631.—They played another comedy against the University of Rheims, which, on the twenty-ninth of August, resolved to inform about it "*Le Procureur du Roi*," and the Rector of the University of Paris. (Registers of the University of Rheims.)

Year 1632.—In 1631 and 1632, the Jesuits attacked secretly and openly the Bishops of France and England, and even published injurious and slanderous pamphlets against them, because they had condemned the infamous writings of one of their Theologians, the Reverend Father Sanctarel. (Annales.)

Savoy, Spain, and France were governed by the Jesuits. We read in the History of France by Anquetil, a Roman Catholic priest:

"What a beautiful, sprightly, and insinuating favorite, had been unable to do, two Jesuits undertook, namely, to cast down Richelieu and to direct the politics and war between Savoy, Spain, and France. 'The Father Caussin, confessor of Louis XIII., was a good man,' said the Cardinal, 'but the Father Monod, director of Christine (of Savoy,) was a spirit full of malice. That is to say according to the meaning of Richelieu : the first followed his will, and the second opposed his views in governing the Court of Savoy and that of France.

"This Jesuit directed for a long while the politics of Savoy. He had been the manager of the marriage between Victor Amédée and Madame, on account of which marriage he went to France, where he studied Richelieu's character. We must confess that he tried to win him. So, he offered him a silver chapel with ornaments of all sorts. However, either antipathy against the Cardinal, or conviction that his designs were opposed to the interests of Savoy, this Father always acted against the Prelate; and, not satisfied in restricting him he endeavored to destroy his power. He imposed upon the conscience of the Father Caussin to enlighten the King about Richelieu, and persuaded him so well, that he used all means, all his power on the mind of his royal penitent to influence him. He, above all, painted before his eyes the dreadful account which God would require from him, for the oppression of the Catholic Church in Germany, caused by his alliances with the Protestants. 'And you shall answer, Sire,' said he, 'on your own salvation for the blood which you shed in all Europe.' Louis, surprised, answered that the Cardinal had showed him the consultations of many Doctors not believing so, and even of the Jesuits, his colleagues. 'Ah! Sire,' the confessor replied ingenuously, 'do not trust in them for they have to build a church;' at that time they were building the church of the House of the Professed in Saint Anthony street," (consequently they ought to be compliant in order to get money.)

"Vainly the King tried to justify his Minister, he was obliged to give up. He asked then his confessor whom he should appoint to replace Richelieu. Caussin proposed the Duke of Angoulême, bastard of Charles IX. and Mary Touchet, but the Duke having declared this proposal to the Cardinal, Caussin was disgraced and sent to Quimpercorantia in Basse-Bretagne.

Year 1642.—The Jesuits stirred up the too lamentable dispute, or rather scandalous battle of the Jansenism. Being jealous of the Monastery of Port Royal, they attacked violently Marie Angélique Arnaud and her brother, the learned and celebrated Doctor. They attacked too Pascal, Nicole, and the most of the French clergy, nor sparing insults, harsh contentions and slander. Their immorality was never more clearly unveiled than in the various periods of this long war; notwithstanding, they were justified and triumphed in Rome, even they were victorious in the court of France, by the intrigues of the Father Annat, confessor of Louis XIV. (Works of Arnaud, Pascal, Renaudot; various histories and extracts.)

Year 1643.—The Jesuits were so malevolent in China, that J. B. Moralés, a Dominican, was compelled to address a request to the congregation of Propaganda in Rome, to petition against the superstitious and heathen rites practised by the Jesuits; against their immorality, and destructive principles. (Annales.)

Year 1645.—The Cardinal Henry de Sourdis, Archbishop of Bordeaux, (France,) issued ordinances against them on account of their usurpations, the wicked behavior of the Reverend Father Marianna and others, and the immorality of all the Jesuits who lived in Bordeaux and other towns of his diocese. They were expelled from Malta. They undertook commercial operations on an immense scale,—witness the contract of association between the Reverend Father Jesuits Biard and Massé, who were their agents, and the merchants Robin and De Liancourt. The matter of this contract was the lading of ships sent to Canada. (Annales . . . .)

Year 1646.—On the 25th of May, they became bankrupts in Seville, (Spain.) They denied that the Reverend Fathers who acted for them were their agents, and avoided the obligation of paying their creditors. (Annales . . . .)

Year 1647.—Don Juan Palafox, Bishop of Angelopolis,

sent the Doctor Silverio Pineda to Innocent X., and Juan Martinez Guyatro to Philip IV., King of Spain, with letters detailing the enormities and misdeeds of the Jesuits in India; exposing their avarice, the low means employed by them to make money, their tithes, and their usurpations on the episcopal jurisdiction.

The Jesuits were wicked enough to organize in Angelopolis, among the students of their college (31st July,) a masquerade, in which these young men drove through the mud of the streets, an ass dressed with episcopal ornaments, cross and mitre, in order to deride the Bishop: whilst they stood at the windows of their house applauding and exclaiming, 'Bravo!'

The king of Spain examined the claims of the Bishop Don Juan Palafox, inquired into the behavior of the Jesuits and condemned them.

Year 1648.—A book entitled "Monarchia Solipsorum" was published in Venice: the author was the Reverend Father Jesuit Melchior Inchofer, who died in Rome, on the 28th of September, 1648. He had been persecuted by the Jesuits so cruelly, that the Roman Catholic Priest Bourgeois and another Romish Clergyman assure us, that he had been condemned to death by the Jesuits, carried out from Rome at night by the General and his Assistants, and saved only by the intervention of the Pope. The Jesuits attribute falsely this book to Scotti, an ex-jesuit, a learned and conscientious man, who though he had taken the four vows, left the order and taught philosophy and canonical jurisprudence in a university of Italy.

This book having at this epoch produced a profound sensation among the public, we give its summary, as a document, an explanation, and a testimony.

In the first chapter, the author reveals the "Monita Secreta," "Secret Instructions;" explains the contents of the fifth Bull (1540,) and of the sixth (1549) of Paul III., which granted to the Jesuits even the power of imprisoning the members who should reveal their rules. The eleventh chapter is a summary of the laws of the Jesuits. "The Jesuits," says he, "being admitted into the order, are bound 1st, to deny all rights, whatever they may be, and to set themselves free from all bonds; 2ndly. to worship God only according to the orders of the General; 3rdly. always to approve the words and deeds of the General; 4thly. to consider as their own enemies those of the General; 5thly. to avoid any correspondence with strangers; 6thly. to keep the deepest silence about the words, deeds, and government of the General; 7thly. to regard the order as being higher than all other things; 8thly. to accept neither dignities nor employments without the consent of the General, and to inform him of everything; 9thly. to report immediately the secret crimes to the General; 10thly. to discard the love of their own reputation, even in the case of reparation of calumny; 11thly. to confess to the General their own faults, and at request, those of their neighbors; 12thly. to accept passively the employments fixed by the General; 13thly. to bind themselves not to examine the secrets of the government of the General; 14thly. to renounce their own will and judgment."

In the twelfth and thirteenth chapters, the author writes briefly, the biography of the Generals of the Order, but too fully to be introduced here.

In the fourteenth chapter, he says: "The General is elected for life. Particular assemblies are held every five years. Each kingdom sends there an assistant, but they do not investigate serious questions, lest they may hurt the General. Pretended conferences are held at the palace of the General,—the important, three times a week; the ordinary, every day. In the first conferences, the Provincials and other dignitaries are appointed; but in these appointments, as in all things, the Assistants answer always 'Amen,' to the wishes of the General."

In the fifth chapter, the author unveils and explains all the ambitious views of the Jesuits, and the criminal means which they use to reach them. He proves irrefutably, by a great many instances, that the writers of the Jesuits steal from authors, in order to adorn themselves with the glory of great men.

In the sixteenth and seventeenth chapters, he relates the scandalous behavior and contentions of the Jesuits against the Capuchins in China.

In the eighteenth chapter, he relates extensively how the Jesuits seduced and hid from his father's search Réné Ayrault, son of Peter Ayrault, a learned and celebrated juris-consult and magistrate of Angers (France.) He points out the covetous and ambitious views of the Jesuits in asking and obtaining from Gregory XIII., against all the canonical laws, the license of practicing medicine.

In the nineteenth chapter, the author shows how meanly the Dominicans and the Jesuits, Aquaviva their General and Clement VIII. vilified one another, in the controversy known under the name "De Congregatione."

In the twentieth chapter, he explains the murder of Henry IV. by Châtel, and declares that the Jesuits had incited him to this crime.

The author says in another part of the book: "the Assistants compose the secret council of the General. Each of them represents a nation. They reside at Rome; still not one of them knows perfectly the laws of the Order. The novices are allowed only to read the apostolical letters of Julius II., the abridgment of the constitutions and the common rules. The Nobles or Professed bow to one another, but the Temporal Coadjutors or the Lay-friars, never. The ignorant monks are favored because they are the best spies. The General has in his palace twelve magistrates, whose business it is to disentangle delicate and difficult affairs, one hundred of them to govern the provinces, and many for each city."

Afterwards, the author details, but too extensively to be introduced here, the policy of the General in appointing the subaltern Superiors, in order to rule through them the monks, and through the monks the Society. "All charges," says he, "are bestowed upon the more artful and wicked: so the Reverend Father Brisacier, the famous slanderer of the Bishops of France, was appointed Rector,—the Reverend Father Malescot, a notorious forger, and condemned for having ante-dated public acts, was appointed Rector at Tournon,—Sivarli Cœsus and Colobodozarus, though publicly convicted of guilt, were appointed Rectors of colleges. . . . . . The Constitutions were printed only in 1607, so interested was the Order to keep them in the deepest darkness."

We read pretty much the same thing in another book, entitled, "The Jesuits on the Scaffold." The author of this book says: "The unworthy alone are promoted to dignities. The Rectors do not consult the learned and talented friars, but may give orders to them, exclusively under the direction of the Provincials, and to all others, arbitrarily. All Rectors are absolute in the Colleges, and act against the will even of all their inferiors. All dignitaries are liable to change after three years of office; but it is not done. The Superiors do not listen to the inferiors, lest they may obtain the ascendancy. The monks, on account of denunciation and jealousy, do not like each other, but it matters not, they are bound by the rules to mutual denunciation.

Another book, published in 1616, headed: "Instruzione a Principi della maniera con la quale si governano li padri Jesuiti, fatta da parsona Religiosa, a totalmente spassionata," "Instructions for the Princes on the behavior of the Jesuits, by an impartial monk," contains very strange and interesting details about the administration and internal government of the Order of the Jesuits, and about their thefts from other monks. So, they stole an abbey from a nunnery, during the reign of Pope Clement VIII. Likewise, they stole the abbey La Flèche, near Angers (France,) from the Augustinians. The author relates their intrigues with Gregory XIII. to obtain the lucrative cures of Rome, and so on . . . . but lest we overstep the bounds of an historical summary, we continue.

In the same year, 1648, the aforesaid Bishop Don Juan Palafox, again petitioned the Pope against the immoral and anti-Christian doctrines and teaching of the Jesuits in the East Indies. Then the Pope, in spite of his own will but for political considerations, was obliged to disapprove of them by a sentence of the sixteenth of April. This Bishop expressed himself as follows: "I have found in the hands of the Jesuits almost all the wealth, all the funds and opulence of South America. They incessantly swell their treasures by dealing artfully; they even hold cattle markets, butcheries, and shops."

At the same time, the faculty of Theology of Toulouse (France.) sent an address to that of Louvaine, to protest against the Jesuits, who had slandered both of them. (Annales.)

Year 1650.—On the fourth of May, the Archbishop of Sens issued ordinances forbidding the Jesuits to exercise the ministry in his diocese, and the faithful, under pain of excommunication, to receive sacrament from them. He ordered public prayers in order that the Church may be rid of the Jesuitical contagion. The general assembly of the clergy in Paris, sent circular letters to the Bishops of France, which condemned the doctrines of the Jesuits, and their irreligious slanders against the Archbishop De Gondrin. (Annales.)

Year 1651.—On the twenty-ninth of December, the same Archbishop De Gondrin censured the book of the Reverend Father Jesuit Brisacier, headed 'Le Jansénisme donfondu'—

which book was a repertory of lies and slanders directed, chiefly against Colaghan, Doctor of Sorbonne. In spite of the partial recantation of this Reverend Father, the Fathers Nouet, Maynier, and others, defended this book. (Annales.)

Year 1656.—On the twenty-sixth of October, the parish priests of Rouen protested against the slanders, bad doctrines, and immorality of the Reverend Father Jesuit Bérard, De La Brière, and of Brisacier Rector of the College. (Annales.)

Year 1658.—The Curates of Beauvais and Paris, alarmed at the licentiousness which the Jesuits inculcated from the sacred desk, by the confession and in their colleges, protested many times against the immorality of the casuists of the Jesuits. The curates of Nevers, too, protested against the impiety of these Fathers, who, by a pretended indulgence freeing souls from Purgatory, attracted to their chapels all the faithful, and harvested by this quackery a large amount of money. (Annales.)

Hitherto, we have seen the Jesuits lying; slandering; preaching among the people immoral, incentive and impious doctrines; disuniting families; stirring up insurrections in the cities and provinces; arming Princes against Princes, Kings against Kings, nations against nations; reddening the soil of Europe with human blood; plotting against Bishops and spoiling them; conspiring against Kings, obliging them to choose Jesuits as their confessors and still killing them. We have seen the Jesuits abusing the ignorance and credulity of the Catholics, in order to steal from them innumerable sums of money; dealing every where; loading ships; becoming bankrupts; denying their agents and robbing their creditors; changing the education and instruction of youth, the sacred desk, the confessional, in short, the religion of Christ into a matter of trade. We have seen them degrading themselves, and rolling from their cradle in the most incessant and odious crimes against the people, society, the gospel, Christ and God—and all these, under the name of the 'Society of Jesus;' 'of apostles of Christ and his gospel;' of the main, the most pious, the most learned, and the most devoted defenders of the Roman Catholic Church; as commissioned miraculously by God to support his true church against Protestantism. Finally, we have seen them feared, hated, condemned by all classes of society, and expelled frequently from several countries.

Undoubtedly we should wish to put down the pen, for their history is so disgusting, so dreadful, that we can discover no virtuous deeds to relate; but we must complete our task, and unroll this chain of crimes up to our days. However, we will hasten to reach the end; we want to breathe.

Year 1670.—The Reverend Father Jesuit Annat was expelled from the Court of France, because he had displeased the King by his haughtiness, immoral behavior, and incessant efforts to reach power and domination. Alexander Gothofred, General of the Jesuits, was, under these circumstances, powerful and artful enough to impose as confessor upon Louis XIII., the Reverend Father Jesuit Ferrier his intimate and faithful accomplice, but who died a short time after. Then he succeeded in effecting the appointment to this office the Reverend Father Jesuit Larier, who some time after, being engaged in a court intrigue, was disgraced.

Year 1675.—In France, the Reverend Father Jesuit Lachaise (the grand nephew of the two famous Cotton, confessor of Henry IV.), then Provincial of Lyons, intrigued so artfully that he obtained the office of confessor of Louis XIV. His name is still alive in Paris, so criminal were his fostering of the loves of the King, his violences against the Port Royalists, his hatred, struggles, and cruelty against the Protestants. (Various Histories of France.)

Year 1685.—The Jesuits, ordered by the Pope and led by

the Reverend Father Jesuit Lachaise, caused the revocation of the Edict of Nantes. To appreciate the criminalty of their views under such circumstances, let us read what Anquetil, a Roman Catholic priest has written about it in his History of France:

"The Court tried all means to attract the Protestants to the Catholic Church. Favors of every kind were granted to the new converts: exemptions from *taille*, from guardianship, from local taxes, from the punctual payment of debts and from other charges. They were freed from the paternal right; and the converted children were allowed to marry without the consent of their Calvinistic parents. Moreover, the new converts were preferred for the charges and offices of the magistracy, finances, commerce, even for military grades.

"Whilst these extensive privileges were conceded to the new converts, sentences of exclusion were pronounced against those who persisted in their religious belief. They at first were excluded only from the lucrative public employments, or merely from the honorable, municipal, judiciary, doctrinal, and mechanical functions, but after a while, those who held them were obliged to renounce them.

"Thus the Protestants were excluded from 'Le corps des métiers,' masterships, apprenticeships, Court, and were not allowed, even to the sergents recors, ushers, register-keepers, procurors, with greater reason, judges and lawyers. The Chambers of the Edict were suppressed; the royal farms and all their accessory employments were interdicted to them, even the subordinate functions. Their names were blotted out of the matriculation books of the Universities, out of the registers of the royal house, out of those of the Princes and of all the Royal family. Not only the Government withheld from the officers, but also from their widows and children faithful to their religion, annual allowances, honors, rights of nobility and other distinctions, ordinarily pertaining to these stations. Finally they were not allowed to practise medicine, surgery, pharmacy, even the art of midwifery.

"It was insufficient to vex the flock if the shepherds were not struck, but the time was not yet ripe to banish them. The Government constrained them only in their individuals and functions. The ministry was forbidden to strangers. The pastors were not allowed to interfere with public affairs; to wear the ecclesiastical dress; to entitle themselves 'Ministers of the word of God;' to term their religion 'reformed' without adding the word 'Pretended;' to compose a Body, and in this quality, to salute and harangue personages of distinction; to have in their churches elevated benches for the officers of their religion; to adorn their churches with the arms of the King or of the city, and to accompany their magistrates when they entered in the churches, or went out. The preachers were permitted to teach only in their ordinary dwellings, or in several places considered as annexed. They were forbidden to exercise the ministry out of their churches, and longer than three years in the same place; to visit the sick, lest they might hinder them from returning to catholicism. Again the preachers were forbidden to visit the prisoners, to utter in their speeches a single word against the Romish religion; and to solemnise baptisms, marriages, or burials with a splendor honoring their ministry.

"As to the Consistories and Synods, the Court suppressed their power in rendering them less frequent; in imposing upon them Commissioners; in requiring a *Procès Verbal* of their deliberations; and in prohibiting them from inquiring about certain affairs. Moreover, the Court sapped more efficaciously their authority, by depriving them of the collection of charities; of the management and distribution of money; and by transferring to the Catholic hospitals the legacies and donations granted to the Consistories. The credit given by science was retrenched too, at least, as much as it was possible, by forbidding their professors to teach the languages, philosophy, and theology; by destroying their best schools, among which the College of Sédan, whose polite literature flourished a long while, and whence sprang a great many learned men.

"Compelled in the cities to respect the Catholic Rites; to abstain from dealing and working on feast days; compelled to bow to the Holy Sacrament carried to the dying, or to hide themselves; compelled also to resort to a great many other practices hurting their consciences, the Calvinists fled to places where the Lords of their religion admitted them to meetings in their castles. But soon after, the Court deprived them of this resource, by fixing the number and quality of those who should be allowed to assist at these assemblies; and even by denying to many Lords the right of admitting the Protestants—a measure leading certainly to the interdiction of the ministers, to their expulsion as being useless, and consequently to the destruction of their churches. Thus, more than one hundred of their temples had been cast down under various pretexts, before the revocation of the Edict of Nantes.

"Let us by these ruins appreciate the building. However well it was based—how solidly soever it had been elevated, so many strokes had shaken it. It only stood on a feeble prop spared by the Court, but to sap more certainly all the building. This sole stay was the Edict of Nantes which served to authorise, both the restrictions of the privileges of the Calvinists, and the new laws imposed upon them. All the preambles of the aforesaid rules, declared that they were practised according to the Edict of Nantes; but as soon as it was useless to use this artfulness, Louis XVI. revoked it, on the twenty-second of October, by another Edict registered the same day, which Edict included eleven articles as follows:—

"The First Article suppresses all privileges granted to the 'Pretended Reformed' by Henry IV. and Louis XIII.

"The Second and the Third forbid the exercise of their religion all over the Kingdom, and without exception.

"The Fourth binds the ministers to leave France within fifteen days.

"The Fifth and Sixth fix rewards for future converts.

"The Seventh forbids them to hold schools.

"The Eighth compels the fathers, and mothers, and guardians, to educate their children and pupils in the Catholic religion.

"The Ninth and Tenth bestow amnesty and restitution of their property, to emigrants who will return within four months.

"Finally, the Eleventh renews menaces of the punishments decreed formerly against relapses. Notwithstanding, it authorises the Calvinists to remain in their own houses; to enjoy their property; to deal without being disturbed, provided they do not meet to exercise their religion.

"This last concession which granted a shadow of freedom of conscience, was odiously violated by the wild zeal of many public officers. It caused the vexations which were termed Les Dragonnades. The King having, in sending his edict through the provinces, ordered the Commandants, Governors, and Lieutenant-Governors, to use the greatest severity in executing this edict; many of them employed violence, believing that it would be an easier, shorter, and perhaps more efficacious way to succeed, than to follow strictly the royal instructions. Then they commanded soldiers termed, 'Dragons' to accompany the missionaries. These men, instead of seeking the Calvinists in order to lead them to the catechism and to mass, invaded the houses, settled there as in an hostile country, wasted the provisions, stole the furniture, and often gave themselves up to the worst excesses of indecency and cruelty. These persecutions having convinced the 'Reformed,' that the Court intended their general massacre, flocked out of the Kingdom. More than 200,000 of them left France, in spite of the ordinances forbidding emigration under the penalty of the galleys, confiscation of property, and annulling the sales made by the emigrants one year before their departure." (Anquetil—History of France.)

Americans, this is one of the master-pieces of Papal and Jesuitical tolerance. I say, Papal and Jesuitical; for it was chiefly at the instigation of the Pope and of the Jesuits, that the Court of France was so tyrannical and cruel. Louis XIV. kept a flock of mistresses, married, unmarried, confessing, receiving sacrament: who bestowed upon them absolution and communion? The Jesuits with the consent of the Pope. The King confessed and received sacrament, though rolling scandalously in lasciviousness and adultery, and creating rivers of blood: who bestowed upon him absolution and communion? The Jesuits with the consent of the Pope. Who were this cohort of novel missionaries, or rather apostles of Mahomet, escorted by these soldierly thieves, licentious and murderous, who, with drawn sword compelled the Protestants to walk before them as a flock of cattle, when they led them to the Catholic ceremonies against their consciences? The Jesuits with the consent of the Pope. Who depopulated France? The Jesuits with the consent of the Pope. Who ruined so many Protestant families? The Jesuits with the consent of the Pope. Who filled the prisons with Protestants? The Jesuits with the consent of the Pope. Who deprived fathers and mothers of their children? The Jesuits with the consent of the Pope. Who snatched children from their parents to convert them to Romanism, and with such cruelty that the Edict of Turin forbade to seize lads under twelve years of age, and girls under ten? The Jesuits with the consent of the Pope. Who impoverished France by compelling the wealthy, the talented, the artists, the learned men to fly to foreign countries (for undoubtedly the Protestants, though the minority, were the most enlightened and influential in society)? The Jesuits with the consent of the Pope. Who separated families; converted France into an arena of slanders, of denunciations, of persecutions, of murders, of scaffolds? The Jesuits with the consent of the Pope. Who changed that country of generous sentiments, of arts, of letters, of learning, into a land of tyranny, destroying intellectual liberty, martyring the apostles of religious and social freedom whose only crime was to be gifted, learned, honest, conscientious, lovers of mankind, of Christ and his gospel; to be censurers, by their moral and Christian behavior, of the immoral and antichristian behavior of Kings, Emperors, the Great of the world, secular and regular clergy, and mainly the Jesuits and Popes? Who, say I, introduced into France such an incredible transformation? The Jesuits with the consent of the Pope. . . . .

But why stop? Why feel irritated? The revocation of the Edict of Nantes is an insignificant crime among the numberless sins of the Jesuits. Let us continue their terrible history.

Year 1709.—In France Louis XIV. excited by the blind hatred of the Jesuits against the nuns of Port Royal and their defenders, expelled these nuns from that convent, on the twenty-ninth of October—the demolition of which convent he ordered on the year following. The tombs were to be violated: the dead bodies dragged out of the chapel and of the church-yard, to be thrown indiscriminately into a common grave.

The Reverend Father Jesuit Lachaise, confessor of Louis XIV., the deadly enemy of the Protestants, and one of the most influential authors of the revocation of the Edict of Nantes, died. His last words to the King were these: "Sire, I supplicate you to choose a confessor from our society. It is very much attached to your Majesty: but it is very extensive, very numerous, and composed of various characters all fond of the glory of the Order. No body can warrant you safety in the case of their displeasure, for they will not hesitate to commit a crime."

"The King, struck with these words, related them to Maréchal his first surgeon, who, in the first moment of his fright, reported them to Blouin, first *valet de chambre*, and to Boldue first apothecary his intimate friend, who in my youth, narrated to me several anecdotes."—(Various Histories—for the quotation see Memoirs of Duclos, vol 1, p. 134.)

Year 1710.—The Jesuits slandered the Cardinal De Tournon to the Emperor of China, because he had said, talking about their crimes and principles: "If the infernal Spirit had come to China, he could not have been more noxious than the Jesuits." The Emperor being excited by them, killed this Cardinal and banished his Apostolic Vicar.

The Jesuits remained at the Court of this tyrant, enjoying and surrounded with honors and dignities. They still were finally expelled.

The Reverend Father Jesuit Le Tellier replaced the Reverend Father Lachaise in his office of confessor of the King of France. And by what means? We answer in the very words of the Lord De Caylus, Bishop of Auxerre. "On the next day after the death of the Reverend Father Lachaise, the Jesuits hastened to present three of their candidates to Louis XIV. Two of them offered the most brilliant and seducing titles; but the Reverend Father Le Tellier stood back humbly, with downcast eyes, holding his large hat in his united hands, and not uttering a word. This hypocritical countenance being favorable to him, he triumphed."

The same Bishop added: "Father Le Tellier was right in lowering his eyes, for he had in his look something which was ambiguous and crosswise."

The Roman Catholic priest Anquetil himself, detailing in his History of France the intrigues, artfulness, and cruelty of the Reverend Father Jesuit Le Tellier—particularly against the Cardinal de Nouailles—writes, that Le Tellier kindled France;

that he obtained from Louis XIV. the dreadful Bull "Unigenitus . . . ." which the Jesuits, and he at their head, had caused to be issued from Rome, should be registered on the fourteenth of January, 1715. "The Father Le Tellier," writes Anquetil, "applying every one of the articles of this Bull in its severest tenor, 80,000 'lettres de cachet,' viz., orders of incarceration, were signed against the Jansenists, who were persecuted, imprisoned, and partook to some extent of the fate of the Protestants.

"When Louis XIV. died, this ambitious monk, a man without a heart, selfish and tyrannical by nature and principle, was exiled to Amiens. Then France rested a little. Many thousand men, who languished in prison on account of their religious belief, were released from their chains and restored to freedom and to their families. A great many others who, for the same cause, had been banished from France, were allowed to return."

Year 1723.—Peter the Great expelled the Jesuits from Russia.

Year 1731.—The Reverend Father Jesuit John Gérard had been appointed Rector of the Royal Seminary of Marine, at Toulon, France. He seduced a handsome young lady, eighteen years of age, named Catherine Cadiére. Being her confessor, he visited her very often, under the pretext of directing her conscience. Fearing the consequences of his crime he obliged her to take drugs to procure abortion. Then he led her to the convent of Ollioule, a small town in the neighborhood of the city, where he was allowed to see her without a witness. On the request of her parents, the President De Brest ordered this young lady to be concealed in a convent of the Ursulines, where she revealed all the circumstances of the criminal behavior of the Reverend Father Jesuit. Gérard, enraged, answered that she was possessed by the devil, and stirred up the nuns against her. This scandalous affair being brought before the Great Hall of Parliament, Mademoiselle Cadière and her actual confessor, a

Reverend Father Carme, were imprisoned. The debates demonstrated that the Jesuit Gérard was guilty of sorcery, quietism, spiritual incest, procuring abortion, and of subornation of witnesses. This cause was decided on the eleventh of September. (Original papers in the Archives of the Parliament.)

Year 1756.—The avarice, vexations, tyranny, murder, crimes of every kind of the Jesuits in Paraguay, had become so odious that the people arose and expelled them. In spite of all their struggles, this delightful country escaped from their hands.

Year 1757.—In France, the murderer Damiens, brought up, instructed, and confessed by the Jesuits, stabbed Louis XV., intending to kill him. Two Jesuits were hanged with this monster. All France terrified, rose and exclaimed against them.

Year 1758.—On the third of September, two horsemen shot Joseph I., King of Portugal; but his arm only was wounded. The authors of this crime were discovered, and on the eighteenth of January, 1759, the Marquis of Tavora and the Duke of Avegro were torn to pieces alive, their bodies burnt, and the ashes thrown into the Tagus. The Reverend Father Jesuits Malagrida, Mattos, and Alexander, who were declared instigators of this regicide, were imprisoned. After a while, the Marquis of Pombal, Minister of Joseph I., openly charged the Jesuits with this crime, and asked the Pope Clement XIII., to submit to a commission the examination of this affair; but, the Pope wavering, he decreed his famous law of expulsion.

Angry, Clement ordered that the manifesto of Pombal be destroyed by the hand of the executioner. Then, the bold minister answered to this declaration of war by confiscating all the property of the Jesuits in Portugal. He ordered the execution of the Father Malagrida, proved to have participated in the murder of the King; and by another order—on the same day, at the same hour, all the Jesuits living in the kingdom were compelled to embark on board of several ships, which, landing in Italy, left them on that shore. (History of the abolition of the Jesuits, by the Marquis De Saint Priest.)

Year 1760.—The bankruptcy of the Reverend Father Jesuit La Valette, the amount thereof was three millions of francs, disclosed their love of money, their incalculable wealth, their insincerity, their hypocrisy, their quackery, their impious profanation of the gospel of Christ which they perverted (as they still do now) to suit their monstrous principles and teaching, to suit all their infernal wickedness and designs, to suit all their tremendous crimes. Anquetil—though a Roman Catholic priest belonging to the ecclesiastical administration, and consequently being their friend—is still obliged to aver this too palpable fact, and to write as follows:

"For a long while the Jesuits were accused of thinking in their missions, more of their temporal benefit than of the preaching of the gospel. They were accused, too, of concealing under the veil of apostolical zeal their immense commercial operations, and of seducing with money the most influential men, in the Courts, through whom they governed the Catholic Kingdoms. Whatever might have been the use made of the proceeds of their commercial operations, it is certain that they gained a great amount of money. One of their Fathers, named La Valétte, General Visitor and Apostolical Prefect of the missions which were established in Martinique (a French Colony), stored there a great deal of merchandize; loaded ships; held a public bank; and scattered his paper, that had an immense circulation all over France and Europe.

"The ships of this Father Jesuit were crossing the seas with security and richly loaded, when the Englishmen seized many of them which were addressed to the brothers Lionay and Gouffre who held in Marseilles an important bank. Expecting two millions of francs in merchandise, they had accepted bills of exchange for a million and half; and as several of these bills required a prompt payment, they wrote about it to the Father Jesuit De Sacy, General Procuror of the missions, who held in Paris the correspondence of La Valette. De Sacy informed about this affair the Superiors of the Order in Rome; but the General died at the same time, and the election of his successor having required some time, the order of counting money was issued too late. The courier bringing it arrived at Paris on the twenty-second of February, 1756, and the Jesuits had become bankrupt on the nineteenth.

"The Jesuits disclaimed the acts of the Reverend Fathers who had been their agents, believing that it was the best way to stop such scandal which became known everywhere.

"During four years the bankers tried all means to induce the Jesuits to acknowledge their debt, but these Fathers refused it obstinately till they consented to a kind of composition. As they did not fulfill this last engagement, the creditors, who were a great many, laid their claims before the tribunals. The Jesuits obtained letters-patent, by which they were allowed to be summoned only before the Great Hall of the Parliament. It is said that they intended to avoid the juridical decision of this affair: but, contrary to their expectation, the suit took place in 1760.

"The Jesuits made a mistake in exposing their means of defence. All the Order were accused. They pretended at first, that the business of the Father La Valette concerned only their convent of Martinique. Afterwards they said that the Father La Valette ought to be charged alone as a violator of the laws of the church, which forbid the monks to deal, and, thereby, as being culpable only of a personal crime.

"The bankers replied, that in the government of the Order of the Jesuits, all is under the direction of the General; that he is the sole owner and dispenser of the property of the Order; and that La Valette according to the Constitutions of the Order was merely the agent of the General.

"The Jesuits offered to demonstrate, that, according to their Constitutions, their Society considered as a body possesses nothing; that the property belongs to each Convent, or House, or College of the Order, which, consequently, are not security for each other.

"The proposal of the Jesuits was accepted, and, on the eighth of May, 1761, a sentence of the Parliament condemned the General, and with him all the Society to pay the bills of exchange, all the expenses of the suit, the damages and interest.

"The Jesuits were compelled to yield to this judgment. They paid, in six or seven months, more than twelve hundred thousand francs without selling any property of the Order." (Anquetil—History of France, vol. 4, p. 333.)

Year 1762.—On the sixth of August, the Parliament expelled the Jesuits from France, annexing to the decree an extract of their odious doctrines, "which," said they, "are held without interruption by the priests, students, and other members of the Order of the Jesuits, even advocated by them in public thesis and in lectures delivered to youth, from the first organization of that Society until this time, with the approbation of their Theologians, the permission of their Superiors and Generals, and with the applauses of the other members of the said Order. These doctrines destroy, by their consequences, the law of nature, that rule of morals which God himself has inscribed upon the heart of man. Their dogmas, too, break all the bonds of civil society, authorising theft, falsehood, perjury, the most inordinate and criminal impurity, and generally all passions and wickedness; teaching the nefarious principles of secret compensation, equivocation, mental reservation, probabilism, and philosophical sins; extirpating every sentiment of humanity in their sanction of homicide and parricide ; subverting the authority of Governments and the principles of subordination and obedience; inculcating regicide among faithful subjects ; and, in fine, overthrowing the foundations and practice of religion, and substituting in their stead all sorts of superstition, with magic, blasphemy, irreligion, and idolatry."

Year 1766.—The Jesuits stirred up the mob against Squillace, Minister of Spain, who escaped death only by flying far from Madrid. In this rebellion, a monk, holding a crucifix, led the populace who routed the Guard-Vollone. Charles III., terrified, harangued the people, but they did not listen to him. Then he promised the expulsion of his minister, and the Jesuits calmed the rebels. This sedition was called, 'the sedition of the hats.'

The King and his Court suspected a secret conspiracy of the Jesuits : nor where they deceived in this, for the Superior Provincial had organised a plot for removing the King, in order to crown the Infant Don Ludovico, by seizing him four days afterwards during the stations in the churches, and by shutting him in a monastery.

Year 1767.—On the second of April, a royal decree termed 'Fragmatical Sanction,' expelled the Jesuits from Spain and all her colonies.

Then, the Pope Clement XIII., to reinstate the Jesuits in the political world, issued the Bull 'Apostolicam . . . .' confirming them in all their privileges. Having been threatened by Portugal, Spain, and France, he still yielded and resolved to abolish the Society of Jesus. For that purpose, he had ordered a Consistory for the third of February, 1768, when, during the night two days before, he was suddenly seized with all the symptoms of being poisoned, and died with cruel suffering.

At this news, all the world resounded with these words: 'Aqua toffana! Aqua toffana,' viz., 'Poison of the Jesuits!'

We at first sight are astonished that the Jesuits should have killed this Pope, who had, interestedly, it is true, supported and defended them for eleven years against all Europe; but let us recollect that gratitude is a virtue, and as we cannot find a virtuous deed in their political history, we ought not to be surprised at their ingratitude.

Year 1773.—Having poisoned Clement XIII., the Jesuits hoped to crown as Pope the Cardinal Chigi, their creature; but their intrigues were checked. Ganganelly was elected, and on the 21st of July, he (Clement XIV.) issued the memorable Brief: "Dominus ac redemptor," which abolished their order. After having signed this brief, Clement XIV. said: "There is at length this brief of suppression. I do not repent of what I have done. . . . . I adopted this resolution after mature reflection and examination. I thought it was my duty to resolve on this, and, if it were necessary, I would do again the same thing. This supression will bring upon me death." "Ma questa suppressione mi dará la morte." A short time after the following letters were placarded on the walls of his palace: "I. S. S. S. V."—he thus explained their meaning: "In Settembre Sara Sede Vacante"—"In September the Seat will Be Vacant." He had not mistaken; having been poisoned, he suddenly died on the 22d of September, 1774.

Americans, such has been the dreadful history of the Jesuits from their origin to their suppression, including two hundred and twenty-three years.

After the publication of the Bull suppressing the Jesuits, the world was allowed to believe that they had disappeared forever; but the politics of Papacy had brought them on political life; the politics of Papacy had supported them; the politics of Papacy had yielded only to a threatening storm in abolishing them; consequently the politics of Papacy was to bring them to life again; even their death was to be but apparent—a deceitful sleep of a few years.

The Jesuits fled to Russia; and, meeting there, continued to live as a religious body, under the direction of Czerniwicz, whom they elected their Administrator in 1782. At his death they elected as his successor Linkiwicz, in 1785. This Jesuit having died in 1799, they elected Xavier Caren, who was skilful enough to bring about the following event.

From the year 1799 to the year 1814.—The Pope, Pius VI., approved of the reorganization of the Jesuits in Russia; favored efficaciously their development in that country; and gave then to their order his apostolical and solemn sanction. They elected General of the Society, Xavier Caren, their administrator, and began again their political and criminal life.

Knowing that their existence and prospects depended entirely on the will of the Emperor of Russia, they lavished, to win him, the meanest flatteries, and the most seducing protestations of devotedness. He disliked Romanism, but in matters not religious, they promised to him to profess and preach his aristocratical principles, and thus gained his good will and protection.

Though settled in Russia, the Jesuits were dissatisfied, and looked with avidity at the other countries of Europe, where they had not been allowed to have a footing. They felt impatient to invade them, but the word "Jesuits" was used as an epithet for the most wicked men, so much were they hated. The remembrance of their numberless crimes was living in the minds of the people. The kings and emperors were sons of those whom the Jesuits of former times had killed; how were they to overcome these obstacles? They thought that the best way—and the event proved they were right—was to serve the ambition and tyranny of kings and emperors, who, on such a condition, would forget the murder of their ancestors. Then they flattered them, and promised to use all their influence to keep the people under their oppression. Having a swarm of secular emissaries scattered everywhere, they tried to stifle the democratic principles which began to prevail in Europe, and plotted with the French nobility and high clergy who had left France to follow the Bourbons,—that family which, (for many centuries,) had dishonored the throne of France by their ignorange, fanaticism, support of Papacy, tyranny, and cruelty. Afterward the Jesuits went to France, when the allied armies, with their numberless bayonets, had opened to the Bourbons and to them a bloody road.

At this epoch, which was the triumph of tyranny in Europe, (chiefly in France, which fell from that of Napoleon into that of its former oppressors,) the Papacy judged the circumstances ripe enough to raise openly its old standard of domination and despotism.

From the year 1814 to the year 1830.—Speedily the Pope Pius VII. united the rings of the Jesuitical snake, which, for so long a while, had showered poison and death over all the world, and bestowed on him a new political life, issuing on the sixth of August the Bull which established them.

At first, the Jesuits denied their true name, and called themselves "Fathers of the Faith." Under this name, they ran through all the Catholic countries, telling that they were poor and humble missionaries; but, as soon as all was ready, they took again their true name "Jesuits,"—a qualification as much beloved by themselves, as it was generally hated. Seeing that their odious name stirred up the people against them, they hastened to more closely surround kings and emperors, who, it is true, had been heretofore their victims, but who, having stifled, (at least, for a moment,) liberal principles, and sunk Europe again in darkness, superstition, and tyranny, wanted their support.

The Jesuits established colleges in Austria, through all Italy, in Spain, in Savoy, in Piedmont, etc., where they grew up as powerful as formerly; where they still lead government, clergy, and through them the people. Now, let us follow them in France, their favorite field of labor. We say that France is their favorite field of labor, because that country being the most important among the Catholic countries, it is for the Jesuits a mine of money, and for the Pope the most precious diamond of his crown.

A swarm of the Jesuits invaded that kingdom. They crowded together in the capitol, in the cities, in the towns and villages. Supported by the sword, the prisons, and the scaffolds of the Bourbons, they dealt out from their houses, from their confessionals, from the sacred desk, in every way, slanders and hatred against the "Liberals;" stirred up the peasants, who are ignorant, superstitious, fanatical, and inflammable, against their own and true friends, who had sacrificed tranquility and fortune, even exposed their lives, to cast down political and religious tyranny. The Jesuits went so far in their impious quackery and servility towards Louis XVIII., that they compelled the peasants to sing in the churches the canticle of which the burden is "Vive les Bourbons, le Tròne, et la Foi,"—"Long live the Bourbons, the Throne, and the Faith;" as if faith were synonymous with the family of the Bourbons and with the throne. The Jesuits became so powerful, that from Mont Rouge and Saint-Acheuil they ruled clergy and government—clergy, by appointing all bishops—government, by appointing civil and military officers; by distributing charges, employments, gratifications, privileges, favors, and disgraces. And, in what manner? By influencing directly the King, who, knowing full well that his throne would stand only while resting upon them, bore passively their impositions.

What a lamentable sight was France at this mournful epoch! The Jesuits choosing the bishops exclusively from among the admirers and followers of their principles, these bishops taught them to the students, who were numberless; (for, according to the prediction of Napoleon, the barracks had been converted into Romish ecclesiastical schools.) These students being ordained priests, taught in the parishes the same principles; thus, the bishops, the priests, and the mass of the people were soon quite jesuitical. The Jesuits presenting and effecting the appointment of their friends alone to the public offices of the government, hypocrisy, hatred, and inquisition, overflowed France.

It is not all. The churches were crowded with unbelievers, who feigned piety to gain the good will and protection of the Jesuits. These fathers, who did not care for it, confessed, absolved, and gave them the holy communion. Everybody celebrated the praises of the Jesuits, but with the lips only, for they, in reality, were heartily hated. They planted numberless crosses, along the roads, in the fields, in the villages, in the towns, in the streets and squares of the cities—everywhere. They lavished by thousands, Salutes, Benedictions of the Holy Sacrament, Novenas, Missions, Jubilees, Indulgences, Dispensations, and ceremonies of all forms, of the most exciting and incredible inventions. They made the peasants desert their plows and the fields, to assist at all these ceremonies, chiefly, at the processions, which took place many times a week.

Wo to the philosophers or Catholics who were not pleased with these practices! Such were drawn out of their homes by invitations, viz.: by polite but significant words, if they were independent in fortune; and by promises and menaces, if they were poor and dependent for their daily bread. As to religious conviction, as to belief, the Jesuits did not care for them. The forms, the appearances, were all that they required.

Wo to the Protestants who tried proselytism; who dared to talk publicly about their religion; did not approve of the quackery of the Jesuits; did not kneel, and did not adorn their houses when the holy sacrament was carried to the sick, and exposed solemnly in the processions! Wo chiefly to authors who were conscientious and anxious to enlighten the people, and to direct society in another way! Such were declared enemies of the King, of the Jesuits, of God and his Church, and persecuted in every manner.

The Departments of "Foreign Affairs," of the "Interior," of the "Public Instruction," and "Worship," of "Commerce," and of "Public Works,"—all the Ministries, all the numberless Administrations depended upon them, viz.: University, Tribunals, etc., were filled almost exclusively with Jesuits *of the short gown.* Also it was a fashion and a glory to be termed Jesuits *of the short gown.*

In this dark period, the externals of Catholicism shone out in all their splendor, but, certainly the real believers of the Roman Catholic Church have never been there so scarce, and particularly the religion of Christ so low. It was, of course, a condemnable behavior in the French people, still in some degree excusable—the power, intolerance and tyranny of the Jesuits were so dreadful! They so unmercifully deprived the families of their daily bread! They slandered, persecuted so incessantly and so cruelly the Protestants, insulted them so scornfully, exposed them so hatefully to the mockeries of the mob, and excluded them so unjustly and so artfully from the public offices and honors, by the most odious violation of the charter!

Fortunately, highminded and honest men devoted themselves to the holy cause of liberty, of the gospel, and of the public welfare; sacrificed to its triumph all their temporal interests; defied condemnations, fines, incarceration, scaffolds; and began to enlighten the people, to show them the Jesuitical quackery, the artfulness of the contract of association between Royalty and Jesuitism, or rather Papacy. They published newspapers and books, which, in spite of the tyrannical restraints of the government, circulated and penetrated everywhere. The people, opening their eyes, began to leave the Jesuits, and rose up in a threatening attitude. The Jesuits, feeling the soil moving beneath their feet, and their prey escaping them, excited the King Charles X., and his ministers, to issue ordinances against the freedom of the press. This despotical measure, far from stopping the progress of liberal ideas, and of riveting the chains of ignorance, superstition, and servitude, hastened the triumph of *Liberalism*, and of the intellectual emancipation of the people. It caused the Revolution of 1830. In this Revolution the people shed streams of their blood, and died by thousands, to obtain some political rights, which Louis Philippe was soon again to steal from them.

From the year 1830 to the year 1848.—Charles X., the beloved friend and supporter of the Jesuits, having been banished, they turned in fright. Knowing full well what incontestible claims they had to be the objects of the vengeance of the people, they disappeared hastily, left France, and fled to other countries—where their fellows pursued the same work of destruction, but more prudently and more successfully than they had done in France.

A short while after, when the indignation of the people was calmed, they came again, humble and creeping as a serpent in the grass. Seeing that Louis Philippe constituted himself the murderer of liberal ideas, they offered him their services—which services he secretly accepted, with promises of gratitude and reward. And why did Louis Philippe accept these services? Because, being King against the will of the French people, and against his promises of a republican government, and his throne resting on corruption, secret observation, and bayonets, he wanted agents and spies in all the steps of the social scale, which honorable office no one was more able to fulfil than the Jesuits, and the secular clergy under their direction. Truly, as they held the citizens by means of their children, their daughters, and their wives; by the pulpit; by the administration of sacraments; and by the Jesuits *of the short gown*, they might be the strongest supports of his government.

Louis Philippe redeemed faithfully his promises to the Jesuits. Even though the Assembly of Representatives had renewed the decree of their expulsion; though, many times, the Representatives had complained of the *non-execution* of this law; though the Jesuits had not colleges, at least openly, they divided France (as an owner his property) into two provinces, the one in the North—its centre, Paris—the other in the South—its centre, Lyons. They possessed, in all large cities, houses of Professed, or of Missionaries, or of Noviciate. From these points, they influenced, as now, the choice of the civil officers. How were they allowed it? Because, running through all France to preach sermons, novenas, retreats, and missions—having in their houses registered, the amount of all the private fortunes—knowing, from the bishops, from the priests, and devotees, the political and religious opinions of the citizens—knowing, by confession, all political movements, all the differences between individuals, all the intimate secrets of families, they consequently were more able than any one else of the spies, to give exact information to Louis Philippe. From their houses they regulated appointments to the bishoprics, for, being the representatives, the support, and advanced guard of Papacy, (as they style themselves), besides, being in France like the "Wandering Jew," they were able to choose for the bishoprics, the priests most devoted to their principles. As the Government appointed the bishops, they informed the Ambassador of the Pope, in Paris, who secretly presented their candidates to the King, who admitted them always. Hence, who are the Bishops of France? Some, the creatures of political leaders; and the most of them, the friends of the Jesuits, and Jesuits *of the short gown* themselves.

What were and what are now the consequences of all these intrigues? The priests—fashioned by the bishops—held and still hold the doctrines of the Jesuits, are Jesuits *of the short gown*, and lead the population in that way. In France, Jesuitism runs in all the veins and arteries of society, and, if this blood is not purified from all these hostile and deadly elements, the Republic will never grow up: she will fall; for among thirty-five millions of inhabitants, only five millions, and perhaps less, are free of Jesuitism, while all the remainder are led, directly or indirectly, by this Machiavelistic organization. Thus the Jesuits are the majority; by the universal suffrage they send illiberal Representatives to the General Assembly, and Jesuitical laws are passed.

But, to appreciate better what the clergy of France became in the hands of the Jesuits; how they have been fashioned by them; to know what is, in that country, the character of the bishops and priests, and what direction they give to their influence on the people, perhaps it will be useful to produce here an appeal, which I addressed to the priests of France, persuading them to protest publicly and forcibly against the immorality, selfishness, tyranny, and anti-christian principles and behavior of the Bishops of France.

I published this address, in Paris, when, at the proclamation of the Republic, I was, in that capital, one of the editors and publishers of the daily newspaper "La Presse du Peuple,"—"The Press of the People." The Bishops and the Jesuits have never been bold enough to deny positively that what I had written was true. They merely exhausted their usual dictionary of qualifications. I was a rebel, a Beelzebub—they deprived me of all my acquaintances and friends among the clergy, except a few who kept towards me the same feelings, but did not show them, fearing the episcopal and jesuitical vengeance. They misrepresented me among the laymen, and averted from me the members of my family, except my mother, who, thanks to God, keeps for me a maternal love. They marked me as a wild beast, still not attacking my morality, because I fortunately held letters from them, declaring that my standing, both as a man and a priest, had been always honorable. They persecuted me incessantly and with fury; but I repeat it, the Bishops and the Jesuits were never bold enough to deny positively, that what I had written was true. This is the address:

PRIESTS:

Do you see those crowds of people marching under the standard of liberty? They chant the hymn of their deliverance. They suspend their song and look at you. Do you hear them asking, why, far from mingling in their ranks, we fly from them? why their cries of triumph are without echo in our souls? why we look at them as our enemies?

Alas! can we mingle in their ranks? can we partake in their cries of triumph? They have expelled their oppressors, and we still are slaves to the Bishops. Can we look at them as at our friends? The Bishops compel us to be their enemies.

In our infancy, the Bishops told our parents, who were poor, "You have many children; give us one of your sons; with the government money, and that of the faithful, we will educate him gratis. He will be your glory; we will make him happy." Our parents, who were simple as are all men of the people, had faith in their promises, believed that we should be happy, that at a more remote period we should not abjure our families. They gave us to them, but how much were they deceived!

The Bishops, wishing to change us into automatons, said: "Let us mould their intelligence in a small and narrow mould. Let us clip the wings of their reason. Let us stifle sentiment in them, annihilate their will. Still, let us give them an instruction a little higher than that of the people, thus, by them, we shall be able to rule."

They devoted fourteen years to this work of destruction and death; they fashioned us as statues. During the first fourteen years they kept us in their preparatory seminaries; there they began to shape us with the chisel of *ignorance, falsehood,* and *degradation.*

Of ignorance—public opinion, to their shame and our regret, is too well enlightened on this point. Their strifes with the University have exposed them too much for their own interests.

Of falsehood—they painted society to us in dark colors; showed science and history to us under a false light; placed in our hands works written by their creatures or their representatives; forbade us to judge them for ourselves; changed facts; disguised doctrines; sowed in our hearts the tares of contempt and hatred against all teaching which was not from them.

I add, *of degradation*—having stifled in us by ignorance and falsehood all germs of grand ideas, elevated views, and generous sentiments, they caused us to fall into a low egotism. Having bent our will under the pressure of absolute power, we were compelled to believe their word and obey them, without reflection and without reason. What say I? to brutalize ourselves.

Every day, and every time the clock struck, we were compelled to recite vocal prayers. Whether or not the heart participated, they did not care for it. We were forced to assist in long, intricate, and incessant ceremonies—to hear mass every morning—to confess and to receive communion often—to reveal our most secret thoughts—to communicate our most important family affairs—to relate all we had seen and heard—to report our conversations—to denounce our fellow disciples, and to betray our friends. All this was required.

To please them, to be esteemed, to prepare for ourselves what they called a prosperous future in the priesthood, we had to borrow a hypocritical air, to affect a gravity which did not belong to our age, to be always upon our knees at the altar of Mary, to count beads, to murmur prayers, to assume a seraphic countenance in the chapel, above all, to incorporate ourselves in their secret police. Wo to us if our piety was merely internal; if we were too honest to dissemble with an apparent and jesuitical devotion! Then, they declared us unfit for the priesthood—that was to mark us with a hot iron; to expose us to the maledictions of our ignorant and fanatical families, and to send us back into the world as liberated galley-slaves.

Was it not their wish to degrade us? to make us machines or hypocrites? These sculptors of living men have met sometimes with characters too unmanageable, who have tried to shake off the yoke, and break the chains which fettered them. A few months ago a son was returned to his father, not to be reconducted to the paternal roof but to the assizes, and from the bench of the accused to the galleys. He had succeeded, after three attempts, in setting fire to the Preparatory Seminary, where he was unhappy. (Département de L'Aire.)

Priests, have I exaggerated or not? You know that I have not said all; that I cannot say all, for I would trace lineaments too disgusting.

When the Bishops had enfeebled our minds, and tamed our wills; when they judged us malleable and squared enough, they shut us in their Great Seminaries, clothed us with a dress which they called the holy habit, which ought, said they, to sanctify us, (as if the habit constituted the monk.) They deceived us; it was only, because approaching them more closely, we ought to wear their livery.

During four years they buried us in a frightful solitude. There they taught us the theology of the Jesuits; the Jesuitical interpretation of the Bible; the ecclesiastical history written by interested men; the lives of the Princes of the church, which are, to impartial and judicious men, an insulting irony, the history of that which these great men of Romanism were obliged to do.

Finally, they taught us the mystical doctrines contained in a great many ascetic books, which are a tissue of ridiculous lies and puerilities, where it is necessary to glean through many pages, in order to find one truth or one sound idea.

What more did the Bishops teach us in their Great Seminaries? To search and to read successively in a breviary of psalms, homilies, legends, responses, verses, and chapters. What more? To bless holy water, to cross ourselves thirty-nine times a day, to baptize, to marry, to confess, to bury, to preach high-sounding words which are void of sense, to gesticulate, to bend the knee, to handle a censer, to decorate an altar, to fold a dress, to sing psalms, to recite prayers, to say mass, and to ascend the gamut in order to rival the chorister of the village. It would have been preferable had they taught us to read, to write, to cipher, etc., to make us rival the attainments of a school-master.

What more did the Bishops teach us in their Great Seminaries? I was about to forget to mention it. They initiated us into all the secrets of vice; every word which fell from their lips in our course of "*Diaconales*" brought the color to our cheek, and caused our eyes to fall with shame. They then told us: "Let our words not astonish you. You must know all these things in order to question about them the young men, young ladies and wives, whom you shall confess."

That they had no intention of perverting or scandalizing us with such obscene teaching, is all that we could say, to excuse them for such indecent lessons.

Priests, you know that this is the whole stock of science with which the Bishops gratified us, during four years of study and dreadful seclusion.

In what then did they instruct us more particularly? In every thing best calculated to serve their interests, to cause them to attain their ends, to fascinate us, stifle our conscience, and entice us into their snares. They represented to us society as the abode of grief and misfortune—as an arsenal of crimes, a sink of infamy, a laboratory of damnation, a spot of reprobates destined to hell, and as the kingdom of Satan. On the contrary, they painted to us the ecclesiastical profession as the palace of suavities, as the sanctuary of virtue, as the holy ark which floats above the abyss, and carries to the mountain of paradise, after a happy voyage, those who take refuge in the ark.

They said to us in society you will be poor; in the priesthood you will be rich: in society you will remain obscure; in the priesthood you will be admitted to the table of the great: in society the meanness of your extraction will excite contempt; in the priesthood the crowd will uncover their heads, and bow before you: in society you will be without power; in the priesthood you will have authority—you will command in the temple—your preaching will be without control, not one there will speak but yourselves: there your seats will be elevated; before you they will bend the knee, and will burn incense; in society you will be on the road to hell; in the priesthood you will be on the road to heaven. But mark you, added they, that you can enjoy these advantages only on two very express conditions."

"What are they?" we inquired, for the prospect of riches, domination, and honors, above all, of eternal happiness, was very intoxicating to us.

"Behold them," they responded to us.

"The first condition is this: you must never love woman; you must never marry, but remain pure as the angels, though endowed with human senses."

"But," we replied, "God has given us a sentiment of love for woman, which it is not in our power to eradicate; she is our complement; how can we live in isolation, without affection, without family? To do so, we must destroy our senses, and our heart."

"God," said they, "will bestow upon you this strength.—

Moreover, believe us: it is almost impossible to save one's self in marriage—for marriage is the tomb of virtue. In celibacy, chastity is easy."

"What is the second condition?" we asked.

"The second condition," they answered, "is this: you must consider us as your fathers, and obey us."

"We must, then," we replied, "deprive us of our personal freedom."

"Yes," they responded, "but it will be to you a source of happiness and salvation. Obedience will be a sweet bond to you, for our orders will all be paternal."

At first, these conditions seemed hard to us; but feeling not yet the imperious necessity of family affection; not foreseeing isolation in all its austerity; not having our physical nature yet developed, and feeling but feebly its impulse, we accepted the first condition, believing that with some effort we could be able to remain faithful to such an engagement.

Our intelligence being destroyed by the persevering efforts of the Bishops; our will being beaten down during so many years by their teaching, as iron under the hammer, obedience appeared to us easy enough, particularly obedience to men who called themselves our fathers: it then seemed to us that we could be able to promise obedience. However, we still hesitated. Then they began to irritate our desire by smiling pictures, and by their seductive promises. They succeeded in inflaming our imagination—the imagination of young men twenty years old—and would soon have vaporised them in the high furnaces of mysticism—of almost absolute silence—of their exaggerated discourses—of the fanatical works which they placed in our hands—of the corrosive action of endless vocal prayers—of weekly confessions—of daily communions—of continued directions—of a great many practices—in fine, of the complete extinction of all light, of the deprivation of all counsel and all influence of an opposite kind.

We then prostrated ourselves on the pavement of the sanctuary, and promised all that they wished—at that age when youth ought to promise so little, because it knows so little of the world, of which we could know nothing, since we had quitted the breasts of our mothers to imbibe exclusively the poisonous instructions of the Bishops.

It was done, the Bishops had reason to be pleased. They had grafted with a bastard plant our primitive souls, which were rich and noble as they came from the hands of God. They had moulded our will in their own; it was fatally forced to bear its form. Then, they sent us among the people to be their speaking-trumpet for announcing the gospel—the gospel according to their views; and the people know whether or not they are right and disinterested.

We started then, but we were merely automatons. By giving up the dignity of men we had become slaves, not as were the slaves of Rome and Athens—we should be too happy in being slaves on so mild conditions. They turned the wheel, expecting from their masters, according to their deeds, reward or chastisement; but we, priests, trail the fetters. To gain the good will of the Bishops, we must be the most servile among our fellow-slaves. To be whipped morally, it is sufficient that we incline our brows only to the height of our knees. To receive from their hands social death, it is enough that we do not flatter their caprices.

The slaves of Rome and Athens were allowed to love: we may not. They had the affection of their families: we are not allowed it. They were permitted both to think and to feel freely: we are not allowed it, for the Bishops frighten us in the name of God. They mitigated their misfortunes mutually in loving one another as brothers in suffering: we are not permitted to do so: the police is too artfully organized among us; there are too many spies; the Bishops have too well understood, that, to eternalize our slavery they must divide us. If their obedience was displeasing to their masters, they merely endured lashes: if we do not obey the Bishops according to their caprices, they strip us before the people and whip us with the scorpion lashes of suspension and interdiction. Under the whip of their masters they relieved themselves in uttering their grief; in thinking that after this life their sufferings would terminate; we under the Episcopal lashes must be statues, because far from being our fathers according to their promise, they are without mercy; they would double the torture, because the aristocrats and all the army of devotees would laugh at our cries of affliction; because the religious and political despotism being united to support one another, the Bishops possess the right of life and death, they may stifle our complaints. We are not allowed even to look for a relief in thinking that hereafter our griefs will end, because they make us believe, that a knowledge of their will is sufficient to cause God to throw us into hell.

Priests, is it not true that the Bishops compel us to walk like the beasts of burden with the whip of mortal sin and hell? Do they not oblige us under pain of mortal sin and hell to purchase their Rituals? And what are these Rituals? A sort of Ecclesiastical Encyclopedia unsewed, parcelled, and incomplete, of which several volumes are a monstrous repertory of tyrannical prescriptions and ordinances. They bind us even to pay for them very dearly, for, having coercive means for their sale, they have tariffed them at the highest rate.

What tender paternity to compel us to buy, for their benefit, and at an excessive rate, our code of slavery!

Do they not tell us: if you do no accept the employment and dwelling which we assign to you—mortal sin and hell for you! If you go to theatres—mortal sin and hell for you! If you eat or drink in an hotel—mortal sin and hell for you! If you play publicly—mortal sin and hell for you! If you do not recite long prayers—mortal sin and hell for you! Then Christ was mistaken in forbidding them! If you assist at the repasts of baptism, burial, betrothal, or marriage—mortal sin and hell for you! Then Christ sinned in changing water into wine at the nuptials in Cana. Moreover, in drawing the logical consequences of their tyrannical and anti-christian ordinances, Christ should go to h * *, monstrous proposition which we do not dare express.

Priests, is this all? No! You know it too well. It is not the ten thousandth part of the burden which our autocrats impose upon our consciences. They carry their absolutism and the details of oppression so far, that they subject us to such or such a form of hats, under pain of mortal sin and hell, and of shoes, under pain of venial sin and purgatory. Thus we have to fear more the future life than our present servitude.

If at least they might spare us torture, when, submissive and pliable slaves, we obey and suffer silently, our fate would be less cruel; but, no. Potent and haughty, they wish in humbling us to show their greatness. Absolute Kings, they want victims; for autocrats have always usurped sovereignty, with which to satiate their selfishness and cruelty in tyrannizing over their subjects.

Both the spies and bailiffs of the Bishops, knowing the avidity of their masters, slander for the want of rebel priests the dumb and innocent. Then our despots call us to their palaces, and with bitter reproaches and thundering menaces, lash us for disobediences of which we are not guilty—happy again are we if they do not dishonor us before the people, before our colleagues, and in the opinion of all the faithful.

Let us try to justify ourselves, they compel us to be silent. Our sole plank of safety is to aver that we are guilty though we may be innocent, and to ask them for pardon. O, dreadful degradation! And still it is our daily bread! If we beg to know our accusers they refuse to name them: Odious inquisition, which lasts among us, though the people have drowned it in streams of their blood!

Yes, I exclaim with a loud voice: the Bishops are in our days our inquisitors, and they are more unjust and more cruel than those of Spain once were—they, at least, had a phantom of a tribunal.

The African slaves may redeem themselves: their masters are even glad to free them, when worthy of it: we are not permitted freedom. The Bishops forbid us even the consolation of hope. They have changed our slavery into a subterraneous prison, from which we cannot see light. Lest our eyes should discover truth; lest we might be restored to freedom—our consciences having been enlightened—they hinder us from frequenting the high-minded, the learned, the men of progress. They forbid us to read any writings, with greater reason to publish any, without their previous approbation. They forbid to us, under pain of a mortal sin, books which, to a man of good sense, should be instructive, and, like a battery-ram, shaking Episcopal absolutism.

Wo to us if they suspect that we meditate our emancipation; that we no longer believe their words; that the wings of our intellect and reason, which they had clipped, grow, being warmed by the sun of study, of reflection, and correspondence with enlightened men! They cause our libraries and manuscripts to be inspected; give information concerning them to our confessors (whom they know), and question them artfully; forbid us to study; send us to distant and isolated parishes, and, there, surround us as wolves with their spies. If they know that by the strength of our intellectual organization, we have broken and cast off the sepulchral stone of our servitude, thrown far from us the shroud; that we are no longer that dead body—the beauty of which Saint Ignatius extols—that stick worthy of the heavenly admiration, which a Superior holds, carries, lays down, or breaks according to his caprice, then they deliberate.

Should they believe that we are cowardly and harmless, they behead us morally and send us into society, naked, without bread, without reputation, the prey of aristocratic and jesuitical hatred, the derision of the mob, and, above all, the regret of our families, who, having prejudices, suppose themselves to be disgraced.

Should they believe that we are energetic enough to unlock the grave-yard where are buried our fellow-slaves; that our voice will be thundering enough to make them hear these words: 'O, dead! come again to life!' They tell us, 'Mount the steps of our throne, sit at our right hand and partake of our power; afterwards you will reign: but be silent.' Are our souls generous enough, are our consciences strong enough to cast off their offering with contempt, horror, and indignation, they do not behead us morally because they fear dark, shameful, and too true revelations; but by their intrigues they hinder us access to the printing offices open only to the wealthy, and deprive us of all social professions. To complete our misfortunes, the Government which to this day has supported them, does not admit us, to its employments, and though by the most odious violation of the constitution, of reason and natural laws, deny us to be citizens in refusing us the right of marrying, and in declaring that our matrimonial ceremonies performed before a magistrate are illegal and invalid. Our strange fathers, the Bishops, aided by the Jesuits, persecute us to such an extent as to deprive us by their threats and slanders, of our acquaintances, friends, relations, brothers, sisters, fathers, and mothers. What barbarity! They assemble their priests in the Seminaries; there thunder against our defection, curse our names, paint us as Judases, as emissaries of hell . . . . and forbid them, under pain of suspension and interdiction, to read our writings. Is this oppression? Is this tyranny?

People, let me now speak to you. If the Bishops constitute us their slaves, know full well that it is only to oppress you through us. Do not believe that in France you have no longer royalty! You have still eighty-four kings, not elected, but imposed upon you, not constitutional, but absolute, *the Bishops.*

Louis Philippe, that tyrant whom you have expelled, and who has just fled to England to conceal himself and his infamy, had palaces: each Bishop has many of them, purchased for them by the Kings with your money, kept sumptuously and repaired with your money. Louis Philippe had a crown: the Bishops have gold miters. Louis Philippe had a sceptre: the Bishops have gold croziers. Louis Philippe appeared before you with haughty insignia: the Bishops strut before you covered with embroideries, diamonds, silver and gold from the sole of their feet to the crown of their heads. Louis Philippe bound you to salute him 'His Majesty:' the Bishops bind you to call them 'Our Lords.' Louis Philippe had a throne: the Bishops have two; the one in their palaces as autocrats, the other in the churches as Gods.

O, stupid pride! strange blindness! To mimic God by affecting greatness and domination!

Louis Philippe possessed incalculable treasures: the Bishops are loaded with wealth. The amount *De la liste civile* mocked the public misery: the high emoluments of the Bishops insult Christ and the suffering members of his church. Louis Philippe exhausted France by heavy taxes: the Bishops impose upon families enormous exactions, which they dispose of according to their caprices and without control. Louis Philippe had an army with which to support his despotism: the Bishops have numberless legions of girls, lads, men, and women, myriads of Religious Associations and Corporations, and moreover, our sacerdotal army the number of which is *eighty thousand men.* Louis Philippe had a cloud of spies and subaltern agents: the Bishops reckon in their secret police the Fathers Jesuits, the Jesuits with *the short gown,* and several millions of devotees. Louis Philippe, laughing at the public servitude and misery, dated from the *Tuileries* tyrannical ordinances: the Bishops date from their palaces, with magnificent coats of arms, signatures and counter-signatures of their Great officers and Valets, Vicars-general, or Canons, or Secretaries, or Sub-secretaries, 'Mandments' oppressive to the consciences, binding them under pain of mortal sin and hell. Louis Philippe tarnished France in the eyes of nations, ruined her, and hindered the citizens from meeting, from talking, from writing; the Bishops, by their behavior and principles opposed to the gospel, dishonor the Church of Christ, and with their incessant collections and imperious demands of money impoverish families. They do not allow the faithful, not only to act freely, but even they forbid their intellect to think and their hearts to feel.

Yes, people, I must say for our justification and their shame, that the Bishops made us their slaves, only to be through us your absolute kings, your oppressors. In sending us among you they have constituted us—*the enemies of the peace of your consciences—of the tranquility of your families—of your fortunes—and of your freedom.*

1. *Of the peace of your consciences.*—You justly accuse us of preaching from our pulpits, in catechising, and in confessing, an intolerant and fanatical doctrine, evil principles, morals sometimes too severe and disheartening, and of preaching at other times immorality. You accuse us often of representing the gospel as a code of absurd and oppressive laws; as a repertory of menaces, maledictions, anathemas; as a mild code to the rich and hard to the poor; as a code of tyrannical rights for the Great of the world, and of bonds of servitude for the people. You charge us with inculcating wrong in the minds of children,

and confounding their innate ideas of truth and falsehood, of virtue and vice, of justice and injustice, of superstition and religion—but, do not ascribe these things to us; charge only the Bishops, for they have taught us such doctrines, and the most of us believe ourselves to be right in doing so. As to the others who are enlightened, they cannot do differently, because, depending upon the Bishops for their daily bread, they must be blind tools in their hands, and must execute what they are ordered. Thrice wo to them, if they even in a friendly conversation would not approve them instantly! They in this case would declare them prevaricators and rebels; would anathematize them; would expel them from the Ecclesiastical Administrations, and thus would bring on them a social death.

2. *We are enemies of the tranquility of your families.*—People, you accuse us, and justly too, of disturbing your families. Can it be otherwise? The Bishops having said: "You shall not love woman," are we not very liable to entertain unlawful affections, or, which is worse still, to fall into the last degree of brutishness? The proof of it, we pollute monthly your tribunals, your assizes, your culprit's stools, your prisons, and galleys.

The Bishops having said: "You are priests according to the Order of Melchisedech, who had neither father, mother"—which was to say: "You shall not love your family" (for we have been moulded in the Seminaries pretty much as the Jesuits in their houses of noviciate;) "You shall be our children," are we not, to some extent, necessitated to create for ourselves a family, at your own expense, by the mysterious way of the confession?

The Bishops having forbidden us to frequent the enlightened and the learned; to frequent your societies, except to spy your homes, or to ask of you money, lest we might be undeceived; lest we might lose our spirit of servility and selfishness, we are ignorant and rough in our manners. Then, is it not enough to be termed by you, "peasants blacked with ink" (alluding to our standing and dress,) without being deprived of the pleasures of surrounding ourselves with persons of whose hearts and love we with you secretly partake. And are we fond of penetrating into the sanctuary of your firesides; of knowing your domestic business; of being initiated into your secrets; of watching your nuptial couches; of being, without your knowledge, the soul of your families; and of governing yourselves by means of your wives and daughters. Unsatisfied, we desire to extend our sphere of domination. We aspire to rule all interests, sometimes secretly, at other times openly. We counsel testamentary dispositions, stipulations, keep or break associations and alliances, and manage marriages. We succeed in our undertakings almost always, using, according to circumstances, girls, women, and devotees, who constitute our secret police, and whom we direct by the confession.

People, undoubtedly we sow, by our intercourse and intrigues, discord and hatred among your families; but we have so little to do in our parishes that we must look elsewhere for occupation. Moreover, this is a misfortune of secondary consideration; for the Bishops tell us that Christ brought the sword into the world; came to separate brother from sister, son from father. Not only they approve of this spirit of secret observation, but they reward it and compel us, under pain of mortal sin and hell, to visit once a year each family. And, for what purpose? To see for ourselves all that they do; to know their most secret business, and control the behavior of servants, children, mothers, and fathers.

3. *We are enemies of your fortunes.*—Having no families and loving no one, we exercise upon ourselves that particle of feeling which the Bishops could not extract from our hearts. Then we love exclusively ourselves—not our intellectual faculties, for we take too much delight in our habitual saying: "It is preferable to die an old ass than a young learned man," but we love our bodies. And we are joyful before a good dinner; our tables are well served; we are fond of invitations—which induces you to

10*

say, "that we are the heroes of the table; that if any one wishes to meet distinguished gluttons and tipplers, he must dine with the clergymen,"—which causes you to add satirically, "that among us the blade wears out the scabbard."

Whether you may be in want or abundance, rich or poor, provided we satiate our selfishness and the pride of our ministry; whether bread may be wanting on your tables or our tables sumptuously served; whether or not your daughters prostitute themselves to divide with us the money, we do not care. You have children—pay us for their entrance into life, and bestow upon us money. They are admitted for the first time to the communion—bring us money. They marry—bring us money. They die—pay us for the *passport* which we deliver to them, and pay us for the right to weep for them: bring us money with full hands. You wish to free the souls of your kindred which are detained (at least, say we,) in the flames of Purgatory, and for that purpose ask us for prayers and masses; pay us; without money, no prayers, no masses: so much the worse for these souls. You wish us to read a chapter of the gospel over the head of your children—bring us money. You wish us to throw blessed water on your cattle, sheep, goats, pigs, &c., in order to expel from their bodies I do not know what . . . . . probably the devil, to obtain from God that they may be healthy and fruitful—bring us money. You wish us to bless your carriages, wagons, cellars, stables, and houses—bring us money. You wish us to read before mass the passion of Christ, in order to preserve your fields from hail, etc. . . . . . . divide with us your harvest: give us wheat, wine, oil, ... without it, no recitation of the passion; in this case, we do not care for your crops.

Convert our houses which you have purchased with your money, and keep repaired with your money, convert them, say we, into little castles. Fashion our apartments as the ladies' retiring rooms. Besides our emoluments from the Government, give us supplies of money. Raise high steeples with rich domes or elegant spires, in which we may place harmonious bells. Build us splendid and majestic churches. Adorn our sanctuaries with fine marble and handsome carving, with statues and pictures. Purchase us chalices, ostensoriums, ciboriums, and other numerous and valuable altar vases. Purchase us sacerdotal ornaments with silk tissued, silver and gold, shining with embroideries and pearls. Unless you do so, you are not good Christians. Bring us money for all these purposes, and chiefly for our own use. Bring us money, always money. It will be an evident proof that you are zealous for God, since you will show your regard for His churches and His ministers. It will be an evident proof that you are good Catholics.

People, of course we are your exactors, and exhausting you incessantly, we leave you without resources and sometimes without the necessaries of life ; but we grow rich ; we live opulently, and satiate our selfishness. Furthermore, to repair our houses and build majestic churches are sure titles to the good will of the Bishops.

4. *We are enemies of your freedom.*—How could we be friends of your liberty ? The Bishops have taught us in their Seminaries, that love of freedom is a disease in society as in our souls—that political, social, and religious freedom, are as noxious to nations as to private citizens—that they are leading the people to anarchy and individuals to hell—that the Catholic religion being the only true one, the others ought not to be tolerated—that the tribunals of the inquisition were conformable to the will of God in imprisoning, killing, and burning those who were opposed to catholicism—that Kings and Emperors reign and govern in the name of God, so that subjects are bound, not only to endure their yoke, to kiss their chains with humility and resignation, but, also, to obey, respect, honor, and love their tyrants.

They have taught us, that the people are for the Kings and not the Kings for the people—that Republican Government is contrary to the will of God, because it misleads the people, freeing them from authority and increasing their love of liberty, yielding too much to liberal institutions and religious freedom—that according to the views of Divine Providence, society ought to be composed of three classes of men, namely, the Roman Catholic clergy, whose duty is to teach, to direct, to order—the secular power which ought to compel the people by coercive means to execute the sacerdotal will—and the people, who ought to yield without reflection, passively and blindly, to those who lead them by the authority of God.

The Bishops carefully avoided informing us about intellectual improvement, human and social perfectibility, the welfare of the people, and the union of all nations which the gospel is destined to effect. Also, people, what are our political opinions? Generally, aristocratical—and what say I? Properly speaking, we have no political opinions, but that of the Bishops, which is transcendently "Aristocratical and Autocratical," so much so, that they recommend us by secret instructions to support in the elections, with all our influence, chiefly among the peasants, candidates of these opinions.

Yes, people—I repeat it—by sending us among you, the Bishops have constituted us enemies of your freedom, its deadly enemies. How can you expect us to be the apostles of that great maxim of Christ, we who are the meanest slaves, slaves in body, in mind, and heart? How could we preach "Equality" and "Fraternity," we over whom the Bishops are absolute kings and tyrants? We who even envy and denounce one another instead of being brothers? The Bishops, it is true, through fear of your vengeance, tell us to bless your standards and trees of freedom, but beware of them. Do not believe they admire and like your revolution. Keep well in your mind that they hate your Republic. Remember, that, for many centuries, the Bishops have anointed and consecrated the Kings; that, some years ago, they and the Jesuits bade you sing in the churches this impious canticle, "Vive les Bourbons, le trône et la foi." "Long live the Bourbons, the throne, and the faith." The Bishops, it is true, have authorised you to engrave on the front of the churches "Liberty, Equality, Fraternity." But keep in your mind that it was with reluctance; that they would refuse to let you engrave this social trinity in their palaces and the sanctuaries. It would cost too much to acknowledge their crimes, to ask pardon of you, of us priests whom they oppress, and of Christ whose gospel they trample upon.

People, you know now why far from mingling in your ranks we fly from you—why your cries of triumph are without echo in our souls—why we look at you as at our enemies. Spare us, then, your joys and wrath—our chains ask pardon.

Companions in slavery, priests, now at the rushing of nations, after the example of the people, let us ask the baptism of deliverance. Let us recover ourselves. Let us rise as a single man. With the gospel in our hands, and this device on our banner, "Liberty, Equality, Fraternity," let us go to the palaces of the Bishops. Let us tell them:

The measure of your crimes, anti-christian life, and tyranny, has overflown. You, to this day, have led us, as children lead their flocks; but now, we know your childishness, and our rights. We have united and counted ourselves. We say to you: "In the name of Christ, restore us our manly dignity, which, by fourteen years of seductions you extorted from us. Reason, natural law, the gospel, and God annul such concessions! Restore us liberty which you stole from us—freedom of the thought, freedom of sentiment, freedom of word, freedom of action, social freedom, and freedom of conscience! Down with your childish, absurd, and tyrannical ordinances! Down with the retrograde and slavish education and instruction of your Ecclesiastical schools, with your intolerant, immoral, impious, in short, jesuitical principles and teaching! We will be no longer your victims. We will be no longer enemies of liberty, equality, and fraternity among the people, but we will announce to them this symbolical trinity. Down with the pride of your life! Quit your country-houses—they are a worldly pomp, and, having been baptized, you have renounced the pomp of the world! Quit your palaces, that they may be changed into hospitals, to shelter the poor, the sick, the veterans of labor, the widows and orphans—Christ had not even a stone upon which to rest his head! Oh! renounce these palaces! Renounce their magnificent enclosures, where are stationed the equipages of the Great. Renounce their gardens with mighty doors . . . . *mysterious entrances* . . . . their hedges of yoke-elms and thickets, where you spend your leisure moments. Renounce the castles annexed to these palaces, which are occupied neither by the rich, nor mechanics, nor, even by the poor, but by your horses!

"Renounce the carriages from which you extend your pretended paternal hands adorned with diamond rings . . . . *too often tender tokens* . . . . in order to lavish impious indulgences, and to bless the misery of the crowd, whom you bid us to oblige to kneel, when, as a kind of heathen divinity, you pass among them! Renounce these halls with marble pavements; these dazzling lustres with statues marvellously sculptured.

"Shut this portrait-gallery, where each of your predecessors has been impudent enough, to wish after his reign to attract looks and adorations—the odious recollection of whom stirs up horror and indignation!

"Shut this council hall, where our fellow-slaves, united with you to oppress us, open or close their mouths according to your will, always flatter you, and to all your words bow in answering: 'Amen!'

"Shut this hall of interrogation—the witness so often of your lies, inquisitorial accusations, vexations, and tortures—to which you would have kept annexed the prisons of the 'holy office,' had not the people, in demolishing 'La Bastille,' broken their locks!

"Shut this banqueting hall, where by a profusion of rare and delicate meats, of precious and voluptuous wines and liquors, you insult the poor.

"Shut these secretaries' offices, shops of mountebanks, where by means of sums of money, you authorise the people to eat when they are hungry, to use such or such aliments, to marry at such, or such an hour of the day, or of the night; when you declare that money in your hands changes vice into virtue, a sinful action into a lawful one—concubinage into marriage.

"Break your chests, into which the people pour their money still wet with their sweat and tears; and restore them what you stole through your impious and barbarous quackery!

"Quit these caliph sanctuaries, rich wainscots, splendid furniture, soft carpets, effeminate divans . . . . these private rooms . . . . *your voluptuous couches* . . . . !

"Send away these waiting-men and boys who slide along the corridors and galleries, dressed in the court style, who speak to us as Cerberus barked, and serve your pleasures and voluptuousness—relics still beloved of pages and minions, these instruments of the licentiousness of Princes, Kings, and Bishops (as it is proved in the history of Paris by Dulaure), when their senses were wearied with their mistresses!

"No longer a gold cross, heavily adorned with diamonds, shining on your breasts! Jesus Christ died on a wooden cross.

"No longer these worldly and royal insignia, those ornaments which the heathen Pontiffs wore! Christ did not wear them!

"No longer a silk and colored gown! Christ was dressed like the common people.

"No longer soldiers at your doors to guard your sleep and

preserve your treasures! Christ did not require military honors.

"Down with your coinage of money, your impious indulgences and dispensations! Christ did not drink the sweat of the poor and ignorant people. Down with your title of "Our Lord!" Christ was named merely Jesus.

"Down with your titles of Most Illustrious! Christ was humble.

"Down with your armors, liveries, ostentations, and princely magnificence, intended to extort admiration and a sort of idolatry! Christ lost himself among the people, and gained admiration only by his doctrines and virtues.

"Down with your imperious formula: 'We order and command!' Christ loved, exhorted, was not imperious.

"Be our equal, the equal of the people—Christ recommends this to you at least, in saying, "And whosoever of you will be the chiefest, shall be servant of all."

"Be our brothers—brothers of the people—brothers of all Christians—brothers of the unbelievers—brothers of all your fellow-creatures, who, like you, are all sons of God.

"As to us, we lay down all hatred, all vengeances, all remembrance of the past.

"We will live poor; will be virtuous, tolerant, charitable, living examples of the evangelical doctrines which we will announce to the people: in one word, we will follow the examples of Jesus Christ and his apostles—imitate us.

"On these conditions, Bishops, come with us. Let us go to mingle in the ranks of the people. All grouped around the tree of 'Liberty'—all sheltered under its branches as children of the same family, let us swear by Christ, always to love one another—resting our love on his gospel—on God. Let this unanimous shout burst burning out of our breasts: 'Liberty, Equality, Fraternity! Long live the Republic!'

Americans, this is the Address to the clergy of France which cost me so dear, which heaped on my head thundering storms of vengeance and persecutions. But, I repeat it, the Bishops and the Jesuits never dared deny positively, that what I had written was true. They only charged that I was too hard—as if it were possible to write tenderly, softly, on such a subject—a painter represents a city in flames with a red color, the pure color of fire. Thanks to God, this address, in yielding to me the bitterest fruits, has perhaps yielded some benefit to my colleagues—which is to me a source of gladness. But this is not the question.

Americans, since the Jesuits have misled in so anti-christian a manner the Bishops of France, and by means of the Bishops, the priests—since the secular clergy of France are ignorant, not pious, immoral, not zealous, intolerant, in short, not Christian—since in politics they are aristocratical, deadly enemies of democracy and of republicanism—since they rule the elections and keep the mass of the nation in ignorance, fanaticism, and superstition, you naturally infer that such a clergy is the rascality of the Romish secular clergy. Still you are quite mistaken. The French secular clergy is undoubtedly the least ignorant, the least impious, the least immoral, the least indifferent in diffusing the gospel, the least intolerant, the least anti-christian, the least aristocratical, the least inimical to democracy, and of Republican Government, among all the Romish secular clergies of the Catholic world. Judge now, Americans, what the others must be, chiefly those, who, yielding to necessity, proclaim they are republicans, while secretly they are furious against this form of government, and work in the dark to prepare its fall. I would say: 'Experto crede Roberto'—'Believe me, for I know from my own experience."

Let us continue the history of the Jesuits.

From the year 1848 to the year 1850.—In Switzerland the Jesuits were over all the Republic, preaching, confessing, apparently without political views, but intriguing, plotting secretly, publishing, at one time that they did not care for public affairs, and, at another that they were Republicans: aiming at what? To deceive by those fair words and this apparently inoffensive behavior, the Protestants, who, too credulous, began to forget their former mischiefs, admitted them into their parlors and fraternized with them. They held colleges in which they educated a large number of youth, and to which all denominations of believers sent their children. To these colleges flocked together, from all points of France, the nobles and aristocrats, though the teaching of the Jesuits being inferior to that of the French University, they were unable to graduate in France.

All appeared quiet in Switzerland. The Jesuits and other religious societies were looked upon as they are now in the Union. But, in time, they had wrought upon seven Cantons which they ruled conjointly with the secular clergy. Suddenly they fired these people; at first, secretly by spies and emissaries; then, in the confessional; going themselves among families in order to harangue them; mounting to the sacred desk not to preach peace, fraternity, and the word of Christ, but to paint the Protestants as enemies and oppressors (whilst a Protestant born and having his dwelling in a Catholic Canton, was compelled to go to a Protestant Canton for the solemnization of his marriage), to assert in the name of God, that the Catholics dying while fighting to defend their holy religion against them, should gain the crown of martyrdom.

When all was ready—when they had enlisted more than forty thousand men—when they no longer doubted of their success, they called to arms these unfortunate and misled Catholics, and organized them into an army. Thirteen Protestant Cantons being awakened, rise as a single man and rush to arms. A civil and religious war is threatened. The Pope is entreated to pacify the country, by recalling the Jesuits from Switzerland. This prayer is useless, for he is their Superior, their head; they had but obeyed him in stirring up the Catholics, in calling them to arms; even he felt impatient to see them conquerors, to increase his power in Switzerland, to oppress fearlessly the Protestants—as he does directly in Italy, and indirectly, as in the Catholic countries—and after a while to impose upon them by the sword the Romish belief. Consequently, the Pope did not recall the Jesuits, and answered in the customary style and formula of the Papal Court—that he regretted with all his heart, these deplorable events (Rome changed by the Pope into a buther's shop proved lately the sincerity of his feelings)—that he would pray God to withhold his justice and wrath—that he would use all the means in his power for the pacification of Switzerland.

Seeing that the Pope fulfilled none of his promises, though the armies advanced against each other, the Government of the Republic sent to Rome courier after courier, to represent the horror of a war, which was about to be a general massacre: in which fellow-christians and fellow-citizens, acquaintances, friends, kindred, fathers, and sons, were about to kill one another. But all was useless, for the Papal promises had been politic and deceitful. Also he answered—"that he prayed God and had ordered prayers to God—that both he and the General of the Society had deliberated on the recall of the Jesuits—that those Reverend Fathers who are apostles of peace and fraternity, would certainly, and heartily, sacrifice themselves to the general welfare—that since to leave Switzerland was an event calculated to calm this social tempest, and bring safety to the Republic, they would imitate Judas sacrificing his own life for the public salvation!

Whilst barns, cottages, and houses, were the prey of the flames, the armies met; the cannons roared and mowed down entire lines of soldiers. Bloody battles were fought. Many small towns were burned. Freiburg, the general quarter of the Jesuits, the bulwark of the Catholic army, was besieged. In the suburbs and around the city the blood flowed and reddened the waters of the torrents. Several places, chiefly Lucerne, were rather butcher shops than fields of battle. Whilst these dreadful events were going on, where were the secular clergy, the Ligorians, and other Romish religious societies? In the ranks of the Catholic army? No. They had said that their Ecclesiastical and Monacal dress forbade them to carry arms; that their rules and discipline compelled them to avoid the effusion of human blood. Then, where were they? In the military hospitals, attending to the bodies and souls of the wounded and the dying? No. They had referred, as a pretext, to the incompatibility between the calmness and peacefulness of their sacerdotal and monastical life and the tumult of camps—they either hid themselves, or were going secretly to Germany, to Italy, to Rome . . . . intending to come again triumphantly after victory, and to rest secure and safe in case of a defeat.

Where were at least the Jesuits? Fighting, dying, killed? No. They were passing through insultingly the battalions of the Protestant army, escorted, guarded by the French ambassador, who had been ordered to save them by Louis Philippe, King of France, friend of the Pope and of the Jesuits, to whom he was grateful because they gave a powerful support to his tyranny.

What was done in Roman Catholic Europe, whilst the Catholics and Protestants, either assassinated each other in darkness, or killed one another on the field of battle? The Pope, the religious societies, the Bishops and priests prayed and ordered prayers for the triumph of the Catholic army. All over France chiefly, the Jesuits cursed, in their newspapers and from the pulpit, the Protestant army, said masses, confessed, gave communion, ordered novena and retreats, blessed the people with the holy sacrament, and recited public and secret prayers, anxious to call down on the Protestants all the maledictions of heaven, and, on the Catholics, all its blessings. They organized subscriptions of every kind, desirous to send them money, arms, and soldiers. Their money, arms, and soldiers were useless—God did not listen to their wishes and supplications, but blessed the arms of the Protestants: the Catholics, blind and unhappy victims of Jesuitical and Papal fanaticism, ambition, hypocrisy, and cruelty, were completely routed.

At length, this monstrous war reached its end. Thanks to the mercy of the conquerors, human blood ceased to flow; but the supplies of vegetables, wheat, and meat, having been either burned or wasted, entire families died with hunger. The barns, cottages, and houses having been consumed by the flames, and all the mountains, valleys, and plains being buried under a deep snow—for these dreadful events took place in January, which is, in Switzerland, the coldest month of winter—a great many people were frozen to death. The most of the Catholics, having either wasted a considerable amount of money to purchase the ammunition for the war, or lost their dwellings, the most of the citizens of the seven Catholic Cantons were ruined, or, at least, empoverished. In twenty Cantons, the families having met again and having counted themselves, found that either one or several of their members, were dead on the field of battle.

All Switzerland was in mourning. Foreign commercial relations having been interrupted, manufactures were stopped, and the mechanics were without work and bread. The capitalists and rich proprietors having fled to France, money had disappeared. A shower of bankruptcies having ruined many commercial houses, and cast down the internal commerce, business transactions had ceased. As a consequence of so many unhappy events, the provision markets were insufficiently furnished, then a famished crowd wandered here and there, either begging or stealing food, and, withal, clothes with which to shelter them against the deadly cold. More than fifteen thousand families wept over their dead, and looked revengefully at their murderers. The social relations were rare and insincere. The armies fought no longer, but a black hatred, a thirst for vengeance still filled their hearts and swelled daily. The Catholic and Protestant Cantons looked hostilely at one another: and, who can foresee the end of such resentment? God alone.

Fortunately, the Protestants, who, being the majority, are more powerful, knew full well that the Catholics had been misled, had been the victims of the secular clergy, Romish religious societies, of the Jesuits and Pope. They spared their vanquished enemies, and, faithful to the maxims of Christ, forgave the leaders of this disastrous war. They pledged themselves to take efficacious means to prevent its renewal, and to defray the expenses which it had made necessary. Consequently, they shut a great many convents, chiefly those of the Jesuits, their colleges, and expelled these Fathers from Switzerland. They taxed the immense monacal property, sold much of it, and imposed fines upon the richest, the most influential and criminal leaders among the secular clergy.

Americans, allow me to submit to you some reflections on these deplorable and mournful events. Perhaps they are wrong, perhaps right. Whatever they may be, weigh them and judge for yourselves.

Switzerland is formed into a Republic—the United States, too.

Switzerland is a Federal Republic—the United States, too.

Switzerland is divided into twenty-two Cantons independent of each other—the Republic of the United States consists of thirty-one States independent of each other.

The Cantons of Switzerland are united for national security, and governed by a general Diet—the States of the Union are united for general security and governed by a kind of general Diet, a Congress, composed of the Representatives of each State.

Switzerland enjoys liberal institutions—the United States too, even more liberal.

In Switzerland all religions are free—in the United States too, even more free.

In Switzerland, the Protestants are the majority, and the Catholics the minority—this is the case in the United States also.

In Switzerland, the Protestants were not suspicious, were even friendly to all Romish religious societies—in the United States, the Protestants have the same feelings.

In Switzerland these societies preached, confessed, educated youth, the children of all denominations of believers—in the United States they do the same.

In Switzerland these Romish societies were many, and held public schools and colleges—in the United States they are more numerous, and they hold a greater number of public schools and colleges. [As proof of this fact we give the following extract from the *Metropolitan Catholic Almanac of the United States for the year of our Lord* 1850, pages 226—230.]

SUMMARY OF RELIGIOUS ORDERS AND CONGREGATIONS IN THE UNITED STATES.

Priests and Lay-Brothers.

I. "The Society of Jesus embraces—1. The Maryland province, in which there are seventy priests, and about sixty scholastics, who are employed in various institutions and missions; novitiate at Frederick, Md., Georgetown college, D. C., college of the Holy Cross, Worcester, Mass., Washington Seminary and St. John's Literary Institution, Frederick city, Md. They attend about fifty churches or stations in the dioceses of Baltimore, Philadelphia, Boston, Pittsburg, and Richmond. The Maryland province is governed by the Very Rev. Ignatius Brocard, S. J., Provincial.

2. "The Missouri Province, which has seventy-five priests,

fifty-six scholastics, and eighty-three lay-brothers, distributed in the following places, novitiate, near Florissant, Mo., scholasticate near Florissant, Mo., University of St. Louis, St. Xavier college, Cincinnati, St. Joseph's college, Bardstown, Ky., St. Aloysius college, Louisville, Ky. They attend twenty-eight churches in the dioceses of St. Louis, Louisville, Cincinnati, Milwaukie, Chicago, and Oregon city, and sixteen churches or stations in the Indian missions of Missouri and Oregon Territory. This province is governed by Very Rev. John A. Elet, S. J., Provincial.

3. "Twenty-one priests, with several scholastics, attached to a European province, who have charge of St. Joseph's Seminary at Fordham, New York, St. John's college, *ibid.*, and attend several churches in the dioceses of New York, Albany, and Buffalo.

4. "Twenty-two priests, with several scholastics, attached to the Province of Lyons, France, who have charge of St. Charles' college, at Grand Coteau, Louisiana, Jesus School, New Orleans, Louisiana, Springhill College, near Mobile, Alabama, and attend several churches in the dioceses of New Orleans and Mobile.

II. "The Order of St. Dominick numbers about twenty-five priests, who are located chiefly in the three houses at St. Rose's, Kentucky, St. Joseph's, near Somerset, Ohio, and Sinsinawa Mound, Wisconsin. They attend several churches principally in the dioceses of Louisville, Cincinnati, Nashville, and Milwaukee. Very Rev. Joseph Alemany, O. S. D., Provincial.

III. "The Order of St. Benedict has two monasteries, one near Youngstown, Pennsylvania, the other near Carrolltown, Cambria county, Pennsylvania, in which there are seven priests, with nine students of divinity. They attend several congregations in the diocess of Pittsburg. Very Rev. B. Wimmer, O. S. B., Superior.

IV. "The Order of St. Augustine numbers eight priests, who

have charge of St. Augustine's church, Philadelphia, and Villanova College, near that city. Very Rev. J. P. O. Dwyer, O. S. D., Provincial.

V. "The Order of St. Francis counts about twelve priests, who exercise the holy ministry chiefly in the West.

VI. "The Premonstrant Order has a mission in Dane county, diocess of Milwaukee, where there are two priests. Very Rev. A. Inama, Superior.

VII. "The Congregation of the Mission of Lazarists, number about forty priests, who have charge of a Seminary at Philadelphia, a preparatory seminary in Perry county, Missouri, a college at Cape Girardeau, in the same State, a seminary at Lafourche, Louisiana, and are employed in about twenty-two churches in the diocesses of St. Louis, New Orleans, Galveston, and Chicago. Very Rev. Mariano Maller, C. M., Provincial.

VIII. "The Society of St. Sulpitius has twelve priests in the United States, who have charge of St. Mary's seminary and college at Baltimore, and St. Charles' college or preparatory seminary, near Ellicott's Mills, Md. Very Rev. F. L'Homme, Provisional Superior.

IX. "The Congregation of the Most Holy Redeemer, or Redemptorists, number forty-seven priests, who have a seminary and novitiate at Baltimore, Maryland, and serve about fourteen churches and several stations, in the diocesses of Baltimore, Philadelphia, New York, Pittsburg, Detroit, Buffalo, and New Orleans. Very Rev. Bernard J. Hafkenshied, Provincial.

X. "Congregation of the Oblates of Mary.—There are three or four priests of this congregation in the diocess of Galveston.

XI. "The Society of the Holy Cross has five priests, who are chiefly employed at the University of Notre Dame du lac, near Southbend, Indiana. See p. 110. Very Rev. E. Sorin, S. S. C., Superior.

XII. "The Congregation of the Most Precious Blood numbers fifteen priests, with thirty lay-brothers, and five theological students. They are employed in various missions in the dioceses of Cleveland and Cincinnati. Very Rev. Fr. De Sales Brunner, Superior.

XIII. "The Order of Trappists has two monasteries, one near New Haven, Kentucky, the other near Dubuque, Iowa, in which there are seven priests and forty-five religious.*

XIV. "The Brothers of the Christian Schools have charge of three schools and a male orphan asylum, in Baltimore, Md., a pensionate and two day schools in the city of New York, and a school in St. Louis, Mo. The number of pupils in their classes is about 1400.

XV. "The Franciscan Brothers are established at Loretto, Cambria county, Pa.

XVI. "The Brothers of Christian Instruction have charge of a male orphan asylum and two schools, at Mobile, Alabama.

XVII. "The Brothers of St. Patrick have charge of a manual labor school for orphans, near Baltimore, Md., and a day school in the city; they also have a school at Nashville, Tennesse. No. of orphans, twenty-two; of pupils, one hundred and eighty.

XVIII. "The Christian Brothers of the Society of Mary are established at Cincinnati, Ohio.

XIX. "The Brothers of the Holy Cross have a manual labor school at Notre Dame du lac, near Southbend, Ind., and a male orphan asylum at New Orleans. They number thirty-five, including novices.

FEMALE RELIGIOUS SOCIETIES.

I. "The Carmelite Order has a convent at Baltimore, Maryland, where there are twenty-nine sisters, who have charge of a day-school.

* Besides the orders and the congregations above mentioned, it is believed that there are a few clergymen in the United States, belonging to the Carmelites, Eudists, and Priests of Mercy.

"The Congregation of our Lady of Mt. Carmel, have two schools at New Orleans—one for white, the other for colored children, and a school at Vermillionville, La.

II. "The Order of St. Dominick has a convent near Springfield, Ky., with twenty-four sisters, and another at Somerset, Perry Co., O., with the same number. A female academy is conducted at each place.

III. "The Ursuline Order has a convent at New Orleans, with thirty-four religious; one at Cincinnati, O., with nine sisters; one near Fayetteville, O., with seventeen sisters; one at St. Louis, Mo.; and one at Galveston, Texas. An academy for girls is conducted at each of these institutions.

IV. "The Order of the Visitation of the B. V. Mary has a convent at Georgetown, D. C., at Baltimore, and at Frederick, Md., at Philadelphia, Pa., at St. Louis, Mo., and near Mobile, Ala. An academy for young ladies is conducted at each of these places. The number of sisters in all is about 200.

V. "The Sisters of Charity of St. Joseph's have their mother-house in this country, at Emmetsburg, Maryland, but they form one and the same society with that established by St. Vincent of Paul, and whose mother-house is at Paris, France. This union was recently effected. The superior general of the Congregation of the Mission being *ex-officio* superior of the Sisters of Charity, the directors and confessors of the sisters are generally selected from among the priests of that congregation. The Very Rev. Mariano Maller, C. M., provincial of the Lazarists in the United States, has been charged with the direction of the Sisters in this country. We understand that some priests of the above mentioned Congregation are to reside near the mother-house, to watch over the interests of that important institution. There are upwards of three hundred professed sisters in the society, and forty novices. Connected with the mother-house, where there is a flourishing academy for young ladies, are forty missions, in different parts of the United States, embracing principally eighteen female orphan asylums, which contain about 1,060 orphans; twenty-six schools, numbering about 3,400 pupils; and five hospitals, in which from 5 to 6,000 patients were attended during the past year.

VI. "The Sisters of Charity, in the Diocese of New York, have their mother-house at Mt. St. Vincent, near the city of New York. The society has seventy-two members, who have fifteen institutions under their charge, viz.: four academies for young ladies, with 355 pupils; three free schools and several Sunday schools, numbering between three and four thousand children; three orphan asylums, with about 500 orphans, of whom 134 are boys; and one hospital.

VII. "The Sisters of Charity of Nazareth have their mother-house at Nazareth, near Bardstown, Ky. The whole number of sisters is about 140, who have charge of six female academies or schools, numbering from 5 to 600 pupils; two orphan asylums, containing 112 female orphans; one hospital, and one infirmary. One of the schools, with one of the asylums and the hospital, is at Nashville, Tenn.; the other establishments are in Kentucky. Rev. J. Haseltine is ecclesiastical superior of this society.

VIII. "The Sisters Notre Dame have three houses in Ohio, at Cincinnati, Chillicothe, and Dayton, with fifty members, and upwards of 700 pupils in their schools.

Sisters of the same name are also established at Pittsburg, St. Marystown, Pa., at Baltimore, Md., and in the Willamette Valley, Oregon, where they have schools for girls.

IX. "The Sisters of St. Joseph have their novitiate at Carondelet, Mo., where they have also a boarding and day school, a female orphan asylum, and an asylum for the deaf and dumb. Besides these institutions, they have a day school and a male orphan asylum at St. Louis, an academy at Cahokia, Ill.; a male asylum and a hospital at Philadelphia, and a day school at Pottsville, Pa. Their schools number upwards of 300 children, and about 220 orphans, chiefly boys, are supported in the asylums.

X. "The Sisters of Charity of the Good Shepherd have three establishments in this country, viz.: an asylum for female penitents at Louisville, Ky., with about 30 penitents; an asylum for the same object at St. Louis, Mo., and an asylum for widows at Philadelphia, Pa.

XI. "The Ladies of the Sacred Heart have ten establishments in the United States, viz.: at St. Michael's, at Grand Coteau, and at Natchitoches, La.; at McSherrystown, and Holmesburg, Pa.; at St. Louis and St. Charles, Mo.; at Kansas River, Ind. Ter.; and at New York and at Manhattanville, N. Y. In these houses there are about 130 religious and 700 pupils. They also support fifty orphans.

XII. "The Sisters of Loretto have thirteen establishments; eight in the diocese of Louisville, and five in that of St. Louis. The number of Sisters is about 145.

XIII. "The Sisters of Mercy have under their charge an orphan asylum at Pittsburg, with sixty orphans, a hospital, and a pay and free school in the same city; and two academies, one at Loretto, Cambria county, the other near Youngstown, Pa.; two schools and two orphan asylums at Chicago, and one school at Galena, Ill.; also an establishment at New York. There are also Sisters of the same name at Charleston, S. C., and at Savannah, Georgia, 28 in number, and having an academy, with a free school and an orphan asylum in each place. Number of orphans supported by the Sisters of Mercy, about 160; number of female children educated, about 900.

XIV. "The Sisters of Providence have their mother-house at St. Mary's of the Woods, near Terre-Haute, Ind., and have fifty members, who conduct female schools at the above mentioned place, also at Terre-Haute, Madison, Fort Wayne, Jasper, and Vincennes, in the state of Indiana. They have also an orphan asylum at Vincennes. Above 600 children frequent their schools.

"There is a community of colored Sisters of the same name at Baltimore, Md., who have charge of a boarding and day school, and support several orphans.

XV. "The Sisters of Charity of the Blessed Virgin, have two academies for young ladies, one at Dubuque, Iowa, and the other near that city. The number of Sisters, including novices, is thirty-three.

XVI. "The Sisters of the Holy Cross have their novitiate at Bertrand, Michigan, where they have an academy and an orphan asylum. Some of them reside near the University of Notre-Dame-du-Lac. They are thirty-four in number, including novices.

XVII. "The Sisters Pretiosissimi Sanguinis have four communities; one at Minster, in the Diocese of Cincinnati; and three others at Wolf's Creek, Thompson, and Glandorf, in the Diocese of Cleveland. The principal house is at Wolf's Creek. The whole number of Sisters, including novices, is 80. They conduct a school at Minster, Wolf's Creek, and Glendorf, and an orphan asylum at Thompson.

XVIII. "The Sisters of the Immaculate Heart of Mary, have a female academy, etc., at Monroe, Michigan."

Let us not forget, that if the female religious societies cannot move the masses as the religious orders can do, yet they prepare these masses to be moved—being by the charm of their sex very influential over youth, over families. Moreover, as their education in the noviciate, and the principle of obedience to their confessors and directors, (who generally are monks, and if secular priests, elected carefully, and initiated into the mysteries,) are exactly the same as those of the Jesuits, then, though they have not studied theology, and do not know all the mysteries of Jesuitism, they are as dangerous as the Jesuits. Let us pursue our comparison.

In Switzerland, the Romish religious orders, chiefly the Jesuits, led by the Popes, employed several centuries in increasing and centralizing the Catholics into seven Cantons. They used all means. They succeeded principally by circumscribing the marriages of the Catholics within the circle of their fellow believers, or when a Protestant espoused a Catholic, by strictly binding them to raise their children in the belief of Roman Catholicism. In the United States, these societies and secular priests do the same thing, and worse, for circumstances are more favorable.

Their correspondents of Scotland, Ireland, Germany, Belgium, France, of all countries, represent to emigrants the advantages of being in a foreign land near one's fellow-believers and former countrymen, and give them letters of introductions to the Catholics, particularly, to their leaders, who are influential in various States of the Union. Thus, these blind victims of Jesuitical duplicity, come to the several States where the Catholics have begun to centralize themselves.

Likewise, in the Union, the Jesuits, all Romish religious societies, and the secular clergy, urgently advise the Catholics to marry among the Catholics, and if they do not succeed, if a Catholic espouses a Protestant, they strictly compel the Catholics to bring up the children in the Roman Catholic Church.

By such infallible means, and, chiefly, by educating youth, by inculcating on them artfully their own principles, they rapidly and wonderfully accomplish their aim. As proof of it, I extract the following document from the Metropolitan Catholic Almanac for the year of our Lord, 1850, pages 231, 232, 233.

SUMMARY OF CATHOLICITY IN THE UNITED STATES.

DIOCESES.	Churches.	Other Stations.	Clergymen in the Ministry.	Clergymen otherwise employed.	Ecclesiast'l Instit'ns.	Clerical Students.	Male Religious Institutions.	Literary Institutions for Young Men.	Female Religious Institutions.	Female Academies.	Charitable Instit'ns.	Catholic Population.
Baltimore....	67	10	56	46	5	98	6	5	7	7	23	100,000
New Orleans..	60	...	59	15	1	10	3	2	6	7	6	170,000
Louisville....	46	75	55	....	2	5	3	3	4	11	4	35,000
Boston........	63	...	54	9	..	...	....	1	....	1	2	——
Philadelphia..	80	...	82	....	1	24	1	6	6	5	6	165.000
New York....	67	50	83	16	1	34	2	3	3	6	..	200,000
Charleston....	26	60	22	....	1	6	....	1	2	2	6	7,300
Richmond....	14	12	12	....	1	8	....	1	2	3	4	10,000
Cincinnati....	70	25	62	11	2	14	3	1	7	6	6	75,000
St. Louis......	56	25	59	36	4	35	3	2	6	9	8	——
Mobile........	16	18	20	....	1	5	2	1	2	3	3	——
Detroit.......	39	25	27	....	1	7	....	....	....	2	1	75,000
Vincennes....	64	...	36	....	1	9	1	1	1	6	..	45,000
Dubuque......	16	12	17	....	..	...	1	1	1	2	..	7,050
Nashville.....	6	20	9	....	..	...	....	1	1	1	1	3,000
Natchez......	7	14	6	....	..	...	....	....	1	1	1	7,000
Pittsburg.....	65	...	47	....	2	26	2	....	3	5	2	40,000
Little Rock....	7	12	6	....	1	5	....	1	....	1	..	——
Chicago.......	77	32	42	3	1	18	....	1	3	4	8	53,000
Hartford.....	12	...	15	....	..	7	....	....	....	..	..	20,000
Milwaukee...	53	45	45	....	1	8	2	1	1	1	2	65,000
Oregon City, Nesqualy..., Walla Walla, Fort Hall..., Colville....	12	...	20	....	..	...	1	1	1	2	..	——
Albany......	62	30	46	....	..	16	....	....	....	2	4	65,000
Galveston....	16	...	46	....	..	...	....	....	1	1	..	——
Cleveland....	36	40	35	....	2	16	1	....	3	2	6	26,000
Buffalo.......	35	...	41	....	1	9	....	2	2	1	4	65,000
30	1073	505	973	136	29	360	30	34	62	91	97	1,233,350

"From the figures in this table, and from preceding statements, we perceive that there are in the United States, 3 archbishops, 24 bishops, 1081 priests, and 1073 churches. One bishop and 24 priests have died; whence it follows, that during the past year, there has been an accession of 1 bishop and 105 priests. Of the number of priests added to the list, about 52 were ordained in the United States. Of the literary institutions for young men, only 17 are colleges properly so called. Including the number of priests and churches in Upper California and New Mexico, the total would be, of the former, about 1141, of the latter, 1133.

In regard to the Catholic population of the United States, we beg leave to state, that the figures in the above tables were all furnished in the official reports, communicated by the Rt. Rev. Bishops, or others acting under their authority and sanction. These figures show that, in twenty dioceses of the United States, the number of Catholics amounts approximately to 1,233,350. We say, approximately, because if, on the one hand, some of these figures are not furnished as exact expressions of the Catholic population—on the other, they are furnished by those who have the best means of arriving at an accurate opinion, and whose statements are undoubtedly founded on the most reliable data. In regard to the other dioceses from which no definite information has been received in regard to the Catholic population, we do not pretend to offer any thing more than a conjectural estimate, based chiefly on former returns made to us. Supposing, therefore, the number of Catholics in the dioceses of St. Louis, Boston, Mobile, Little Rock, Galveston, and of Oregon Territory, to be 240,000, the total Catholic population in the United States will be 1,473,350: and, inclusive of Upper California and New Mexico, about 1,523,350."

A TABLE

Showing the state of Catholicity in the United States in 1808, (*commenced,*) *and its progress from that time to the present.*

Years:	1808	1830	1840	1841	1842	1843	1844	1845	1846	1847	1848	1849	1850
Dioceses........	1	11	16	16	16	16	21	21	21	26	30	30	30
Bishops..........	2	10	17	17	21	18	17	25	25	26	27	26	27
Priests..............	68	232	482	528	541	561	617	683	737	834	890	1000	1082
Churches..........	80	230	454	512	541	560	611	675	740	812	907	966	1073
Stations..........	..	...	358	394	470	475	461	592	560	577	572	560	....
Ec. Seminaries....	2	9	13	14	17	18	19	22	22	22	22	25	29
Colleges..........	2	8	12	13	13	14	15	15	15	14	16	17	17
Female Acad.....	2	20	47	49	48	40	48	63	63	66	74	86	91

Now, Americans, judge whether or not Romish religious societies, and the Jesuits will be in a few years able to effect in the United States what they did, two years ago, in Switzerland. As to their principles, views, and plans, they are exactly the same. Also, they subject the Catholics who live among you to the same ignorance, superstition, fanaticism, and blind obedience, still as prudently as possible. They teach them not from the pulpit, but in catechising, and chiefly in the confessional,—in the name of God, as his true, and his exclusively true vicegerents in the world, that they are bound to believe and practice what they announce, and to obey what they command.

In the same year 1848, France, Austria, Prussia, Hungary, the Roman States, the Kingdom of both the Sicilies, and several Dukedoms of Italy, cast off the shroud and arose from the tomb in which kings, emperors, and the Romish priesthood had buried them. They protested solemnly against their oppressors, and claimed their rights. But their tyrants answered them by riveting their chains: persecuted, imprisoned, and killed the leaders in the holy cause. Then the people, in accordance with the most sacred of human and divine rights, ran to arms, and defied the numberless soldiers of their tyrants. A general and wonderful battle was about to be fought between the democratic and aristocratic principles; between oppressors and the oppressed; between tyrants and victims; between intellectual, moral, social, and religious tyranny, and intellectual, moral, social, and religious liberty. But, how unhappy were to be the results of these heroical struggles for justice and humanity! How fruitlessly several hundred thousands of its defenders were about to fall under the grape shot or the axes of Kings, Emperors, and Pope!—Under the grape shot or axes of Kings, Emperors, and Pope? What say I? They were to compel, under pain of death, their soldiers, children of the people, to be butchers of their oppressed brothers, who fought for the common deliverance.

Oh, dreadful mystery! How is it possible, that the tyrants, aided by the priesthood, could have blinded the Catholics to such a degree, as to induce them, in the name of God, to support their despotism in killing one another!

In this war, the cities of Austria, Prussia, Italy and Hungary, were to swim in blood. In these countries, the towns were to be burned, and the harvests wasted; innumerable dead bodies were about to cover the fields. Nevertheless, these unfortunate nations were about to fall deeper into the tomb of their former political, social, and religious slavery, until they rise again, and obtain definitively their sacred rights. Alas! when? God only knows.

In this war, France was to expel a King, who, for eighteen years, had dishonored her in the eyes of nations; ruined her agriculture; destroyed her foreign and internal commerce; who held his throne by treason; kept it, and intended to bequeath it to his family, only by corruption; who, sheltered by five hundred thousand bayonets, trampled on her institutions, her rights, her constitution, and exhausted her by an annual budget, the incredible amount of which was 150,000,000 of francs—of which a great part slided into his own hands, into those of his satelites, of his numberless spies, and of more than 160,000 Cardinals,

Archbishops, Bishops, Grand Vicars, Canons, Chaplains, Curates, Vicars, Monks, Nuns, and even Jesuits.

This despot was to be ignominiously banished; the democratic principles to triumph; a republic to be proclaimed; but tyranny was soon after to be perpetual, under the veil of a republican government.

In this war, Rome was to dethrone the Pope, who, impiously, in the name of Christ, tyrannised over the people; though Christ refused to be a king, and fled to the mountains when thousands of men desired to crown him; who said that this kingdom is not of this world; who accepted, it is true, a crown, but a thorny one, which wounded his brow—the only crown worthy of him, of all his disciples, of all apostles of humanity. This autocrat, this tyrant in the right of God, was to be cast down, and the great city to restore its old republic christianized—if I may speak so—by this social trinity, "Liberty, Equality, Fraternity." The oppressed were to breathe a moment; but he was, a short time after, to mount his throne again on bloody steps.

In the meantime, when these mournful events were going on, where were the Jesuits, and what were they doing? They, at first, either left the agitated countries, or effectually concealed themselves, for they knew, full well, that being foes of the people, they had reason to fear their resentment and justice. A few months before, they were noisy in the political world, stirring up the Catholics of Switzerland against the Protestants. Afterwards they were writing in their *averred* and secret press that they did not care for the affairs of the world, denying without shame before the eyes of all Europe, which had been witnesses of their criminal behavior, that they had caused this religious and civil war. They more closely surrounded the kings and emperors, who were their sole hope, because they had been expelled from the main European republic. Now, on the contrary, they were buried in the deepest solemnity, and why ? to secure themselves during the war: either to say to the triumphant Democrats, "Conscious of our wrongs against you, we had left your enemies. From the solitude imposed upon us by our ecclesiastical and monastical duties, we wished success to your arms," or to say to the victorious Kings and Emperors: "We felt very sorry to be bound by our sacerdotal and religious profession, and evangelical horror of blood, not to stir up the Catholics in your holy war against the anarchists; but we entreated God to bless your armies, and he listened to our prayers. Believe that what we say is true. Trust in us, for we have given you for a long time numberless conclusive proofs of our friendly feelings and devotedness."

When the Jesuits saw the King of Naples—whom they confessed, and to whom they administered communion—assassinating by the most infamous treason and cruelty, both in the streets and houses, about fifteen thousand citizens who were inoffensive, and guilty only of being ardent democrats, and wishing a liberal constitution—when they saw him and the King of Prussia stifling democracy, drowning their kingdoms in the blood of its most brave defenders, and the Emperor of Austria heaping the innumerable bodies of heroes on the ruins and ashes of the villages, towns, and cities of Austria, of Italy, and Hungary, then these Fathers commenced clapping hands and congratulating them; celebrating high masses, and singing "Te Deums" of thanksgiving in the churches: promising to perpetuate their power in bringing up youth with aristocratic principles, and in engraving indelibly upon the minds of the people, through the catechism, administration of sacraments, sacred desk and confessional, 'that kings and emperors reign, order and govern in the name of God—that to disobey them, to rebel against them, to cast off their authority, to wish a republican government, or any other form of government determined by the people, are crimes against God, because he has created the people for kings and emperors, and not them for the people.'

We have seen, and still see now, how heartily all these tyrants accepted their proposals. They immediately granted to the Jesuits money, honors, privileges, and colleges; and these worthy fathers occupy now, peaceably and firmly, a seat of distinction near their thrones, and are the strongest supports of their despotism.

However, the Pope, the first head of the Jesuits, was in Gaeta, far from his palaces and beloved throne. He bade them by filial love and their vows of obedience, to stir up the Catholic countries that he might be throned again. Then, these tender and devoted sons of their father, His Holiness, united with the other Romish religious societies, with the bishops and priests. All this crowd of men, devoted body and soul to His Holiness, began to move heaven and earth. From their pulpits they represented the Democrats of Rome as villains, and the Pope as a martyr in the Holy cause of Catholicism—adding, that he was in the most extreme distress and poverty. They collected money to relieve the holy indigent, who, in Gaeta, received, each month, only about *five hundred thousand dollars*, by dispensations, indulgences, privileges, without reckoning what he harvested by his other countless means of winning money—holy indigent, who, evidently, was most needy, and wanted even the necessities of life.

To know approximately the amount of the Jesuitical harvest, among the 731 archbishoprics and bishoprics of the Roman Catholic Church, let us read the following list, which we extract from the *Metropolitan Catholic Almanac, for the Year of our Lord*, 1850, p. 236.

"CONTRIBUTION

"Of the Church in the United States, for the relief of His Holiness, Pius IX.

Archdiocess of Baltimore,	$2,244	48
" St. Louis,	953	65
Diocess of Philadelphia,	2,784	00
" New York,	6,227	41
" Albany,	1,340	00
" Boston and Hartford,	3,412	25
" Pittsburg,	1,100	00
" Cleveland,	200	00
" Richmond,	193	07
" Charleston,	501	69
" Mobile,	317	00
" New Orleans,	2,100	00
" Louisville,	601	57
" Cincinnati,	1,421	28
" Nashville,	62	75
" Dubuque,	200	00
" Milwaukee,	157	00
" Detroit,	374	00
" Chicago,	637	85
" Vincennes,	750	00
" Buffalo,	288	64
" Galveston,	123	60
Total amount,	$23,978	24

Then His Holiness, this martyr in the cause of the religion of Christ—this holy indigent—this being, half God, half man, who stands between heaven and earth to unite them—this being whom mankind and the angels admire, so divine is his power—this being, I say, was relieved; he had at least the necessaries of life, but he wanted to be re-established in his former tyranny. For that purpose, the Jesuits intended, at first, to stir up Ireland, and to enlist there an army of about fifty thousand volunteers. But, England was a Protestant country; how obtain her consent? where find a fleet? Then, they availed themselves of two circumstances.

In France, soon after the proclamation of the Republic, they had appeared again in exclaiming, conjointly with the bishops and priests, that they were Republicans—though they together sent to the National Assembly aristocratical representatives. Knowing full well that to seduce the President was very easy, and that through him they would reach their aim, they surrounded him, saying "that his uncle had bequeathed him his genius and star—that he was the hope of Catholicism and France—that all Europe looked at him and trusted in him to restore social order, to preserve the nations from the Democrats—those anarchists who disturb the world—that they would aid him to reach the imperial throne, but, on condition that he would restore the Pope to his temporal kingdom."

Napoleon, who is as low minded as his uncle was a sublime genius, who is blind enough to flatter himself with ambitious dreams, and thus, leading France straight to a dreadful revolution, and perhaps to anarchy, was flattered by these proposals. He accepted them; was approved by his ministers, who were avowed Jesuits of the short gown; and found an echo in the National Assembly, of which the majority was anti-republican. A decree of war passed. Eight millions of dollars were allowed for the first expenses of the war, and a powerful army was to be sent to Italy, to re-establish the most dreadful and sacrilegious tyranny.

Then the French government presented as strange and as shameful a spectacle, as had ever blotted the page of history, namely:

The French and Roman Republics are proclaimed among the barricades, red with the blood of the democrats, and covered with their dead bodies—they are accepted by the people and ratified by their representatives—the democratic principle generates them—they are born at the same time and from the same mother, freedom. Notwithstanding, the French Republic is to stifle, to kill her sister, who, far from regarding her as her murderer, extends her arms towards her, as being more powerful to protect her cradle and life.

As soon as the French Republic had made all ready for the murder of the Roman Republic, she sent an army against Rome. Then, the French soldiers, though for the most part Republicans in mind and heart, though friends and brothers of the Roman democrats, were compelled by military discipline to go to kill their political friends and brothers, to die themselves by thousands—for what purpose? To cast down a Republic which they admired and loved; to crown again a tyrant whom they abhorred; to dishonor their own country, which they worship—for the glory of which they would have heartily shed every drop of their blood.

The restoration of the Pope to his tyrannical throne, is undoubtedly a very remarkable master-piece of the politics and artfulness of the bishops, but chiefly of the Jesuits, who, now, have acquired the greatest title to the paternal affection of the Papacy. Also, since "His tender Holiness"—trampling on the dead bodies of those whom he called his children and yet has killed—mounted the bloody steps of the throne erected upon their corpses, to tyrannize over his adopted children who deny his paternity, and recognise him only as their oppressor—since that time how happily the Jesuits enjoy themselves near this beloved throne; chiefly in reflecting on their political situation in the world!

Really, they may rejoice. Their riches are countless. Their wealth is almost boundless. They rule all Italy. Spain has been her property for centuries. They are influential in Portugal, demigods in Ireland, Belgium, Savoy, Piedmont, Sardinia, Austria, and her dependencies. They are triumphant in Prussia, and peaceably settled in almost all Germany, and the northern European kingdoms. In France, they hold the majority in the National Assembly, and will likely be permitted, in a short time, to establish their colleges. They are in favor in Russia, and are growing up numerous and influential in England and Scotland. Though expelled from Switzerland, they secretly penetrate there, concealing their religious gown, working in darkness upon the Catholics, and repairing, slowly, but prudently and efficaciously, their losses. The greatest part of Asia, of South and North America, are opened to them, and they have there colleges and missions, (even in California,) by which they gain money and the means of keeping the people in deep ignorance, fanaticism, superstition, and wonderful immorality.

The United States still is to them a wild field—a field covered with thorns, and unprepared to receive the seed of their principles; but they work it so rapidly, so indefatigably, that they succeed beyond all their hopes. Knowing too well that this country is the richest among all; that by its geographical position, by the fertility and boundless extent of its lands, by its foreign and internal commerce, and above all, by its wisely liberal institutions, it is destined to be very soon the head of the world—knowing all this, the Jesuits prepare to locate here their head quarters. And, in what time, under what circumstances will they prepare to locate here their head quarters? When Democracy, in Europe—and it must infallibly happen—shall expel ignorance, fanaticism, superstition, tyranny, and eject the Jesuits who are the supporters and apostles of these evils.

At that time, Americans, you will see, but too late, what is Jesuitism: what monstrous tree will be produced by the Jesuitical seed which you are now so carefully cherishing. You will see, when this Jesuitical tree shall cover all the United States with its numberless branches, whether or not its shade is deadly to morality, to religion, to peace among families and citizens, to the democratic principles, and to your republic.

Yet, this is fated to happen, for they already have not only a footing on your soil, but they are rich, have numerous missions, public schools and colleges, rule a powerful mass of people, and, even though remaining concealed behind the curtain, influence the elections.

From these considerations, we know that the Jesuits rejoice in their political position in all the world; above all, in the prospect of their future condition in the United States.

Americans, such has been the past and contemporary history of the Jesuits; of the formidable society which has played and still plays in the political and religious world—from 1541 until our days—one of the most important and criminal parts related in the authentic archives of history.

The Jesuits have been governed by twenty-three Generals since their origin, namely:

1.	Ignatius Loyola, a Spaniard,	elected in	1541.
2.	James Laynez, a Spaniard,	"	1568.
3.	Francis Borgia, a Spaniard,	"	1568.
4.	Everard Meriurien, a Belgian,	"	1573.
5.	Claudius Aquaviva, an Italian,	"	1581.
6.	Mucius Vitteleschi, an Italian,	"	1615.
7.	Vincenti Caraffa, an Italian,	"	1646.
8.	Francis Piccolomini, an Italian,	"	1649.
9.	Alexander Gothofredi, an Italian	"	1652.
10.	Gowin Nickel, a German,	"	1662.
11.	John Paul Oliva, an Italian,	"	1664.
12.	Charles de Noyelles, a Belgian,	"	1682.
13.	Thyrse Gonzalez, a Spaniard,	"	1697.
14.	Mary Angel Tamburini, an Italian,	"	1706.
15.	Francis Rretz, a German,	"	1730.
16.	Ignatius Visconti, an Italian,	"	1751.
17.	Aloys Centuriono, an Italian,	"	1755.
18.	Laurenzio Riccio, an Italian,	"	1758.

The Society of Jesus was abolished by Clement XIV., under the General Laurenzio Ricci. The Jesuits who then fled to Russia, were governed by three administrators, viz.: Czerniwicz, in 1792, Linkiwicz, in 1785, and Francis Xavier Caren, in 1799.

The Pope having in the same year re-established the Jesuits, Xavier Caren was elected General of the Order.

19.	Francis Xavier Caren, a Russian, elected in		1799.
20.	Gabriel Gruber, a German,	"	1802.
21.	Thadee Broszozowsky, a Pole,	"	1814.
22.	Louis Forti, an Italian,	"	1820.
23.	Roothaan, a Hollander,	"	1829.

Americans, in reaching the end of this writing, I feel very glad to lay down my pen, which I have used in unveiling to you exactly but summarily *the organization and administration of the Jesuits—the means which they use for getting novices—their education in the houses of novitiate—their doctrines and teaching—their past and contemporary history.*

Now, infer the conclusions. Judge for yourselves whether or not the Jesuits are dangerous to your republic—whether or not you ought to beware of them.

THE END.

APPENDIX.

REPLY TO THE SPEECH OF A JESUIT.

TO VERY REV. MR. DE BLIECK, PRESIDENT OF ST. XAVIER COLLEGE.

Very Reverend Father :—

Allow me to address you this letter, in reference to the celebration of Washington's birthday, at St. Xavier College. I heard from a professional gentleman of your faith, who was one of your guests, that you said publicly, before a large assembly, that the work headed, "*Americans warned of Jesuitism,*" (which I published lately, and which circulates now in this city,) *is a tissue of lies,* and that, if a single ch rge therein contained against the Jesuits were *true you would leave your order.*

Rev. Father, to hold such language was to charge me with *falsehood, slander, and humbuggery.* I, therefore, challenge you to prove in a *public discussion,* that what is written in my book is not true. If you accept the challenge, and show that what I wrote is false, I declare on my hand and conscience, that I will publicly retract my error, and burn my work. If, on the contrary, you cannot show it, you will have, in order to redeem your word, to leave your order. If you do not accept the challenge, the public will judge whether you are not obnoxious to the charges yourself. *I wait for your answer.*

Let me now speak to you on the article inserted in the *Cincinnati Enquirer,* (issue of the 27th of February,) in reference to the celebration of Washington's birthday at your College. Reverend Father, are you, and your *fellow Jesuits,* republicans? "Certainly," you answer, "the celebration of Washington's birthday in our College, is an evident proof that we are, even ardent and devoted republicans." Reverend Father, I am very far from suspecting it, for the Pope, who is your superior, is an absolute King; Romanism, which you profess and advocate, is a system of intellectual, moral, and political tyranny; the organization of your Order is anti-republican—even you hate a republican government. The proof of it; your fellow Jesuits disturbed the Republic of Switzerland two years ago; there they stirred up seven Catholic Cantons against thirteen Protestant Cantons; kindled a civil and religious war, and caused thousands of fellow citizens, acquaintances, friends, kindred, and brothers to be killed. Your Order was finally expelled from that country, so criminal had been the behavior of your monks. Rev. Father, you ought to understand why I am very far from suspecting, that you, and your fellow Jesuits, are republicans. You ought to be kind enough to inform me, in what manner a Jesuit reconciles his duties of citizen with his monastic vows. A republican citizen must think for himself, act freely; in one word, be entirely rid of the will of another in the fulfilment of the obligations of citizen. Is a Jesuit permitted it? Not at all; he is expressly forbidden it by his vow of obedience. I read at the pages 285, 287, 295, 296, of the volume 3d, (edition 8th,) of the book entitled "*Practice of the Christian and Religious Perfection*," by the Rev. Father Jesuit Alphonsius Rodriguez, which book is one of the most classical of your novices, and the usual matter of your readings and meditations, I read:—

"A true monk ought to be so dead to the world, that his entrance into religion may be called a civil death; then, let us be as though we were dead. A dead body sees not, answers not, complains not, and feels not. Let us have not eyes to see the deeds of our superiors. Let us be without a word to reply when we are ordered. The dead bodies are ordinarily buried with the oldest and the most worn-out sheets; a monk must be the same for everything."

Again, Saint Ignatius says: "We must yield to our leading by Divine Providence declaring his will by the mouths of our superiors, as a stick which one uses to walk; the stick follows everywhere the one who carries it; it rests where he puts it, and it moves only as the hand which holds it. A monk ought to be the same; he must yield to the leading of his superiors, never move by himself, and follow always the motion of his superior."

"Saint Basilius, treating the same subject, uses another and very proper comparison. A house-builder, says he, uses according to his own will the tools of his art, and it has never been seen that a tool has resisted the hands of a mechanic, and has not bent itself to all his motions. Likewise, a monk ought to be an useful tool, and malleable to his superior.

"We read in the life of Saint Ignatius, that being General of the company, he assured several times, that if the Pope ordered him to embark in any boat whatever, anchored in the harbor of Ostia, near Rome, and to sail on the sea, without mast, without sails, without oars, without rudder, in one word, without the instruments of navigation, even without food, he would obey immediately, and not only without anxiety and repugnancy, but with a great internal satisfaction."

"The following confirms what we said:—'When the Abbot Nisteron entered into religion, he told himself: I profess, now, that I and the ass of the monastery are identical. All which is put upon his back he carries. He bears without resentment the blows of the stick which are inflicted upon him, and the contempt of everybody. He works incessantly, and is satisfied with a pinch of straw granted to him as food. I ought to be in the same disposition of spirit. . . . . ." Other quotations on this subject are unnecessary in this place.

Now, Rev. Father, tell me, if you can, and your fellow Jesuits, being a motionless tool in the hands of your superior, like either a dead body, or a stick, how can you freely fulfil your duties of citizen? Not only is it impossible, but you are bound, at his order, to plot and rebel against the United States, even to leave the country.—Seeing you cannot be both republican citizens, and Jesuits, you must renounce either your Order or your title of citizen; for a slavish citizen is no citizen in the American republic.—"Error!" you exclaim. Then, Rev. Father, show me my error, for otherwise I shall have to conclude, that what the Priests and Jesuits said to me when I was among them is true, viz., that they make republican demonstrations merely to flatter the national pride of the Americans, and that way reach a double end—first, cause Romanism to prevail in the country—second, to change the Constitution when they get the majority, and to give then to the United States a King or an Emperor, through whom the Pope will govern the country, as he does in Austria, Naples, &c.

Again, I shall have to conclude, that you and your fellow Jesuits, celebrated at your College, the birthday of Washington merely from policy; that if you made that demonstration of republicanism, and if it is noised abroad, it is only because knowing that the democratic principles, and the love of a republican government, being deeply rooted in the minds and hearts of the citizens, you have to do so to fill your College with their children, and to grow among them wealthy and influential.

Rev. Father, I now come to your speech, in the report of which my name and the title of my work are not pointed out for political and secret reasons; but which are easily guessed.—The report says, that "you drew a very ludicrous picture of the supposed designs and practices of the Jesuits." You were right—the best way of escaping serious charges is to execute hilarity; chiefly in "the enjoyment of a very handsome dinner," among bottles and glasses, and not to approach the question. Several hundred years have proved, that you Jesuits are the ablest men of the world to slide as an eel out of the hands of your accusers. You ought to know, Rev. Father, what Pascal wrote about it in his Provincial letter—and he, still, was a strong Roman Catholic.

You added, that "the Jesuits are accused of aiming to rule the world, through means of the Confessional," &c. I admire your studied reticences, chiefly your Jesuitical skill in misrepresenting the charges of your opponents, in order to justify your Order and ridicule them. When they accuse the Jesuits of aiming to rule the world, they do not say that it is only through means of the Confessional, but together through preaching, administration of sacraments, public schools, and colleges, through your countless known and unknown means of gaining money, and secret views and plans. Your opponents do not say at all, that your six thousand Priests write and send to your General all the Confessions which they listen to every day—they accuse them merely of violating the sacramental secret of Confession, at least indirectly, in imparting to him the political and important intelligence; therefore, the ridicule of your twelve thousand sheets of paper, which you say your General would have to read every day, returns to you, and together the shame of such an artful supposition.

Moreover, your opponents do not say, that "the governments of England, France, Germany, Spain, the Russian, Ottoman, and Celestial Empires, are all to pass in detail before your General, and their management to be arranged"—from you it is a mere and gratuitous assertion: and when you add that "the absurdity of such conceptions about the Jesuits is the best refutation of them;" you condemn yourself, for those conceptions are your own.

Rev. Father, you added, that your "Order has been accused of a thousand crimes, but (that) in three hundred years not one had ever been verified; that you would challenge the world to bring any thing like judicial proof against the Order, of a single one of these charges, and pledged yourself, that if even one of them were established, that moment you would prove a renegade to the Society."

Rev. Father, listen to me: In 1551, the Jesuits disturbed Germany, by stirring up the Catholics against the Protestants. (See History of Christian Empire by Schrockh, 3, 515. Reflections on the history and constitutions of the Society of Jesuits, by Spitler—History of the Jesuits in Bavaria, by the Chevalier De Lang.) Have not those crimes been "verified?" Is not that historical testimony something like "judicial proof?" against the Order of the aforesaid charge. In 1553, the Jesuits tried to poison Maximilian 2d. (See Pfister, History of Germany—Schneller Œsterr—einfluss, 1, 168—De Hormayr Œsterr Plutarch, 7, 29.) Has not that crime been "verified?" And is not that historical testimony something like "judicial proof against the Order of that charge? In 1554, the Parliament and the Faculty of Theology of France, declared that the Order of the Jesuits is hostile to religion, and to society.—(See Annales—Archives of the Parliament, &c.) Was it without a previous "verification" of the crimes of your ancestors? Are not such decrees sometime like "judicial proof" against the Order of the aforesaid charge? In 1595, the Jesuits attempted the life of Henry IV, King of France; your Rev. Father Guignard was hung after a judicial trial, and all your Order expelled from France. (See the various histories.) Has not that crime been established? Is this not even a "judicial proof" against the Order, of the aforesaid charge? In 1598, the Jesuits were expelled from Holland, and in 1604, from England, Scotland, and Ireland.—(See Annales, and various histories.)—Was it without a previous "verification" of their crimes in those countries? Are not decrees of that sort something like "judicial proof" against the Order, of the crimes of its members? In 1605–6, the Jesuits organized the gunpowder conspiracy; your Rev. Fathers, Jesuits Garnet and Oldercon, were hung and quartered in London, after a solemn trial.—(See the several histories—even the Jesuit Feller.) Has not that crime been "verified?" Is this not even a "judicial proof" against the Order, of the aforesaid charge? The Jesuits were expelled a second time from England, &c.; expelled from Venice, and from several cities of Prussia. —(See Annales, and various histories.) Had such decrees been passed against them without a previous "verification" of their crimes? Are not those decrees something like "judicial proof" against the morality of the Order? In 1618, the Jesuits were expelled from Bohemia and Hungary, and in 1620 from Poland—(See Annales, and the various histories.) Had not their criminality been "verified?" Are not these decrees something like "judicial proof" of the enormities of your forefathers? In 1632, the Jesuits intrigued in the courts of Savoy, Spain, and France. (See History of France, by Anguetil, a Priest, who lived and died in the Romish church.) Have not these crimes been "verified?" Is not the historical testimony of the historians, chiefly of a Priest, something like "judicial proof" against the Order, of the aforesaid charge? In 1710, the Jansenists were persecuted in France, eighty thousand of them were imprisoned. Has it not been "verified" that your Rev. Father, Letellier, was the author of that tyranny and cruelty? The Priest Anquetil himself avers the fact. Is not such testimony something like "judicial proof" against the Order? In 1758, two murderers attempted the life of Joseph I, King of Portugal; your Rev. Father, Malagreida, was hung after trial, as an accomplice of the murderers; all Jesuits were expelled from that kingdom.—(See the various histories, even the Historical Dictionary, by the Jesuit Feller.) Has not that crime been "verified?" Is this not something like "judicial proof" against the Order, of the aforesaid charge? In 1760, your Rev. Father, Lavalette, became bankrupt for three millions of francs; your Order denied he was their agent, and refused to pay their creditors; your General, and with him all your Order, was condemned by the Parliament.—(See History of France, by the Priest Anquetil, vol. 4, p. 333.) Has not that crime been proved? Is not that lawsuit and that sentence something like "judicial proof" against the Order, of the aforesaid charge? In 1762, the Parliament expelled the Jesuits from France, —(See History of France, by Anquetil, &c. &c.) Was such decree of expulsion, (through which they still are forbidden to have colleges in France,) passed without a previous "verification" of their crimes? Is not that decree something like "judicial proof" of the criminality of the Order? In 1848, the Jesuits kindled a civil and religious war in Switzerland; they were checked, and expelled from that republic—all Europe witnessed it. Has not that crime been "verified?" Are not such events something like "judicial proof" against the Order? Now, Rev. Father, it will not do to excite the hilarity of your guests with ludicrous pictures, "in the enjoyment of a very handsome dinner," among bottles and glasses. Although you Jesuits are true squirrels, jumping from one branch to another; or as cats, falling always on your feet, I defy you to escape, for your feet and hands are tied.

If you do not admit that the aforesaid crimes of your ancestors, and of your fellow Jesuits, have been verified, and that there is something like "judicial proof" against your Order, of these charges, I must infer that you do not know the A B C of history. If you deny it, I must infer that you are mostly skeptical or hypocritical; hence, when you boasted that "your Order had been accused of a thousand crimes, but that in three hundred years not one had ever been verified," you spoke, I regret to be obliged to use these words, either as an ignorant or hypocritical man, in which last case your great challenge to the world was a *humbuggery*. Rev. Father, would you say to justify your bold assertion and challenge, that the aforesaid crimes were committed by private members of your Order, but not by the Order itself. Rev. Father, such justification would be too artful and hypocritical to take well, for those crimes were committed to reach political ends; then the Order was responsible. Moreover, suppose that a society of rogues and murderers may be organized and scattered all over the world, might the crimes which they commit in the various countries be attributed only to private members of their society? The idea is absurd.

Rev. Father, I draw now my conclusions. 1st. Not only one, but many of the thousand crimes with which your Order has been charged for three hundred years, have been clearly proved. 2d. "Something like," and more than "judicial proof" against your Order, of a single one of these charges has been brought. 3d. As you pledged yourself that if even one of them were established, that moment you would prove a renegade to the Society—you must, if you are a man of honor, and intend to redeem you word, leave immediately the Order of the Jesuits.

Rev. Father, my position has been such as a Roman Priest, that I *know* whereof I affirm; and you KNOW that I KNOW—hence the *Jesuitism* displayed in *letting me alone.* I am familiar with your "whole workshop," having been let into the secrets of the political intrigue and villany of the Bishops of France many years ago. My pen was sought and fully employed to defend some of the leading men in the church, through the newspapers; and Rev. Father, it was the knowledge of the horrible crimes of such men, and the utter *licentiousness* of Nunneries, that gradually opened my eyes. Having been reared and educated in Catholicism, it took much time and inquiry to make me a freeman—but now I am "FREE INDEED." I wait for an answer.

Your servant,

J. C. PITRAT,

Late a Romish Priest.

A CATALOGUE

OF

BOOKS,

PUBLISHED BY J. S. REDFIELD,

CLINTON HALL, N. Y.

AND FOR SALE BY MOST BOOKSELLERS IN THE UNITED STATES.

THE PICTORIAL BIBLE,

Price Six Dollars.

THE Pictorial Bible, being the Old and New Testaments, according to the authorized version: illustrated with more than one thousand engravings, representing the Historical Events after celebrated pictures: the Landscape Scenes from original drawings or from authentic engravings: and the subjects of Natural History, Costume, and Antiquities, from the best sources. With an elegantly engraved Family Record, and a new and authentic Map of Palestine.

"We have seldom seen a more attractive work, and have no doubt that the cost of the enterprise will be sustained by a large circulation."

N. Y. Evangelist.

"The type is fair and handsome, and the engravings are select and executed remarkably well. They are so numerous and good, as to be in themselves a *commentary*."—*Christian Reflector.*

"Its abundant and beautiful illustrations adapt it for a Family Bible, and will make it highly interesting to the young."—*Christian Register.*

"It is a superb publication."—*Zion's Herald.*

"The engravings are executed in a fine style of the art, and the paper and the type are all that the most fastidious eye could require."—*Hierophant.*

THE PICTORIAL NEW TESTAMENT,

Price One Dollar and Fifty Cents.

THE PICTORIAL NEW TESTAMENT, AND THE BOOK OF PSALMS.

Price Two Dollars.

CHAPMAN ON PERSPECTIVE

BEING PART III. OF THE AMERICAN DRAWING-BOOK.

NOTICES OF THE PRESS.

"The nation may well be proud of this admirable work. In design and execution, the artist has been singularly felicitous; and nothing can surpass the beauty, correctness, and finish of style, in which the publisher has presented it to his countrymen. The book is strictly what it claims to be—a teacher of the art of Drawing. The method is so thorough, comprehensive, and progressive; its rules so wise, exact, and clearly laid down; and its classic illustrations are so skilfully adapted to train the eye and hand, that no pupil who faithfully follows its guidance, can fail to become, at least, a correct draughtsman. We have been especially pleased with the treatise on Perspective, which entirely surpasses anything that we have ever met with upon that difficult branch of art."—*Spirit of the Age.*

"Perspective, is one of the most difficult branches of drawing, and one the least susceptible of verbal explanation. But so clearly are its principles developed in the beautiful letter-press, and so exquisitely are they illustrated by the engravings, that the pupil's way is opened most invitingly to a thorough knowledge of both the elements and application of Perspective."—*Home Journal.*

"It treats of Perspective with a masterly hand. The engravings are superb, and the typography unsurpassed by any book with which we are acquainted. It is an honor to the author and publisher, and a credit to our common country."—*Scientific American.*

"This number is devoted to the explanation of Perspective, and treats that difficult subject with admirable clearness, precision, and completeness. The plates and letter-press of this work are executed with uncommon beauty. It has received the sanction of many of our most eminent artists, and can scarcely be commended too highly."—*N. Y. Tribune.*

"This present number is dedicated to the subject of Perspective—commencing with the elements of Geometry—and is especially valuable to builders, carpenters, and other artisans, being accompanied with beautiful illustrative designs drawn by Chapman, and further simplified by plain and perspicuous directions for the guidance of the student. Indeed, the whole work, from its undeviating simplicity, exhibits the hand of a master. We trust this highly useful and elevated branch of art will hereafter become an integral portion of public education, and as it is more easily attainable, so will it ultimately be considered an indispensable part of elementary instruction. Its cheapness is only rivalled by its excellence, and the artistic beauty of its illustrations is only equalled by the dignified ease and common sense exemplified in the written directions that accompany each lesson.—*Poughkeepsie Telegraph.*"

"The subject of Perspective we should think would interest every mechanic in the country; indeed, after all, this is the class to be the most benefited by sound and thorough instruction in drawing."—*Dispatch.*

"Permit me here to say I regard your Drawing-Book as a treasure. I was a farmer-boy, and it was while daily following the plough, that I became acquainted with the first number of Chapman's Drawing-Book. I found in it just what I desired—a plain, sure road to that excellence in the Art of Arts, that my boyish mind had pictured as being so desirable, the first step toward which I had taken by making rude sketches upon my painted ploughbeam, or using the barn-door as my easel, while with colored rotten-stone I first took lessons from Nature. I am now at college. I have a class at drawing, and find in the several numbers I have obtained, the true road for the teacher also."—*Extract from a letter recently received.*

THE POETICAL WORKS
OF
PERCY BYSSHE SHELLEY.

EDITED BY G. G. FOSTER.

THE FIRST COMPLETE AMERICAN EDITION.

In one volume, 16mo.

"Shelley has a private nook in my affections. He is so unlike all other poets that I can not mate him. He is like his own 'skylark' among birds. He does not keep ever up in the thin air with Byron, like the eagle, nor sing with Keats low and sweetly like the thrush, nor, like the dove sitting always upon her nest, brood with Wordsworth over the affections. He begins to sing when the morning wakes him, and as he grows wild with his own song, he mounts upward,

'And singing ever soars, and soaring ever singeth;'

and it is wonderful how he loses himself, like the delirious bird in the sky, and with a verse which may be well compared for its fine delicacy with her little wings, penetrates its far depths fearlessly and full of joy. There is something very new in this mingled trait of fineness and sublimity. Milton and Byron seem made for the sky. Their broad wings always strike the air with the same solemn majesty. But Shelley, near the ground, is a very 'bird in a bower,' running through his merry compass as if he never dreamed of the upward and invisible heavens. Withal, Shelley's genius is too fiery to be moody. He was a melancholy man, but it was because he was crossed in the daily walk of life, and such anxieties did not touch his imagination. It was above—far, far above them. His poetry was not, like that of other poets, linked with his common interests; and if it 'unbound the serpent of care from his heart,' as doubtless it did, it was by making him forget that it was there. He conceived and wrote in a wizard circle. The illiberal world was the last thing remembered, and its annoying prejudices gall him as they might in the exercise of his social duties, never followed over the fiery limit of his fancy. Never have we seen such pure abstraction from earthliness as in the temper of his poetry. It is the clear, intellectual lymph, unalloyed and unpolluted."—*N. P. Willis.*

NAPOLEON'S MAXIMS OF WAR,

Translated by Col. D'Aguilar.

WITH NOTES.

In one vol., 32mo. Price 50 cents.

"The science of war, in its legitimate sense, is entitled to encouragement, and study, and we recommend that every man of military mind, should possess himself of a copy of 'Napoleon's Maxims.' The work is also one of interest to the general reader, containing, as it does, numerous brief historical facts connected with the most celebrated battles, and men of military renown of almost every age."—*Recruit.*

"It is a work of no little interest to those who wish to understand the principles upon which the greatest captain of the age carried on his operations, and who also desire to understand the errors committed by the inferior intellects brought into the field against him."—*Penn. Inquirer.*

"This work appears in its first American edition, with a recommendation from Gen. Scott, speaking of its utility to military men. That, indeed, is apparent enough; but it has occurred to us that the perusal of the little work, with its full illustrative notes, must be of great advantage also to the general reader, who desires to understand the tactics of the great Emperor. It will be a good companion to Thiers' History, now publishing."—*U. S. Sat. Post.*

W. F. P. NAPIER, C.B., COL. 43D REG., &c.

HISTORY OF THE WAR IN THE PENINSULA, AND IN THE SOUTH OF FRANCE,

FROM THE YEAR 1807 TO 1814.

Complete in one vol., 8vo. Price Three Dollars.

"NAPIER's history is regarded by the critics as one of the best narratives that has recently been written. His style is direct, forcible, and impetuous, carrying the reader along often in spite of himself, through scenes of the most stirring interest and adventures full of excitement. Many of the most distinguished and remarkable men of European history figure in these pages, and are sketched with great distinctness of outline. Napoleon, Wellington, Sir John Moore, Ney, Murat, and others, are the characters of the drama which Napier describes."—*Evening Mirror.*

"WE believe the Literature of War has not received a more valuable augmentation this century than Col. Napier's justly celebrated work. Though a gallant combatant in the field, he is an impartial historian; he exposes the errors committed on each side, refutes many tales of French atrocity and rapine, and does not conceal the revolting scenes of drunkenness, pillage, ravishment, and wanton slaughter, which tarnished the lustre of the British arms in those memorable campaigns. We think no civilian chronicler of the events of this desperate contest has been so just to the adversary of his nation as has this stern warrior."—*Tribune.*

"NAPIER's History, in addition to its superior literary merits and truthful fidelity, presents strong claims upon the attention of all American citizens; because the author is a large-souled philanthropist, and an inflexible enemy to its ecclesiastical tyranny and secular despots; while his pictures of Spain, and his portrait of the rulers in that degraded and wretched country, form a virtual sanction of our Republican institutions, far more powerful than any direct eulogy."—*Post.*

"THE excellency of Napier's History results from the writer's happy talent for impetuous, straight forward, soul-stirring narrative and picturing forth of characters. The military manœuvre, march, and fiery onset, the whole whirlwind vicissitudes of the desperate fight, he describes with dramatic force."—*Merchants' Magazine.*

"THE reader of Napier's History finds many other attractions, besides the narrative of battles, marches, plunder, ravages, sieges, skirmishes, and slaughter—for he learns the dreadful evils of a despotic government—the inherent corruption of the entire system of European monarchies—the popular wretchedness which ever accompanies the combination of a lordly, hierarchical tyranny with the secular authority, and the assurance that the extinction of both are essential to the peace and welfare of mankind. All these lessons are derived from Napier's History, which, in connexion with its literary excellence, and the accuracy of its details, render all other recommendations utterly superfluous. It is a large, neat, and cheap volume."—*L. I. Star.*

EDWARD GIBBON.

HISTORY OF THE DECLINE AND FALL OF THE ROMAN EMPIRE;

A new edition, revised and corrected throughout, preceded by a Preface, and accompanied by Notes, critical and historical, relating principally to the propagation of Christianity. By M. F. GUIZOT, Minister of Public Instruction of France.

In two vols., 8vo. Price Five Dollars.

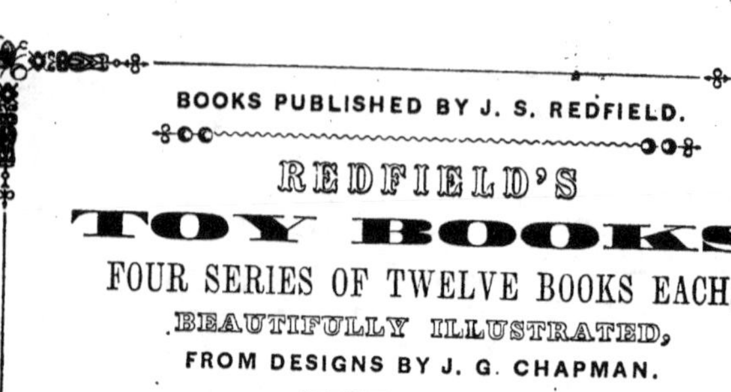

BOOKS PUBLISHED BY J. S. REDFIELD.

REDFIELD'S TOY BOOKS,

FOUR SERIES OF TWELVE BOOKS EACH,

BEAUTIFULLY ILLUSTRATED,

FROM DESIGNS BY J. G. CHAPMAN.

First Series—Price One Cent.

1. Tom Thumb's Picture Alphabet, in Rhyme.
2. Rhymes for the Nursery.
3. Pretty Rhymes about Birds and Animals, for little Boys and Girls.
4. Life on the Farm, in Amusing Rhyme.
5. The Story-Book for Good Little Girls.
6. The Beacon, or Warnings to Thoughtless Boys.
7. The Picture Book, with Stories in Easy Words, for Little Readers.
8. The Little Sketch-Book, or Useful Objects Illustrated.
9. History of Domestic Animals.
10. The Museum of Birds.
11. The Little Keepsake, a Poetic Gift for Children.
12. The Book of the Sea, for the Instruction of Little Sailors.

Second Series—Price Two Cents.

1. The A B C in Verse, for Young Learners.
2. Figures in Verse, and Simple Rhymes, for Little Learners.
3. Riddles for the Nursery.
4. The Child's Story-Book.
5. The Christmas Dream of Little Charles.
6. The Basket of Strawberries.
7. Story for the Fourth of July, an Epitome of American History.
8. The Two Friends, and Kind Little James.
9. The Wagon-Boy, or Trust in Providence.
10. Paulina and Her Pets.
11. Simple Poems for Infant Minds.
12. Little Poems for Little Children.

Third Series—Price Four Cents.

1. The Alphabet in Rhyme.
2. The Multiplication Table in Rhyme, for Young Arithmeticians.
3. The Practical Joke, or the Christmas Story of Uncle Ned.
4. Little George, or Temptation Resisted.
5. The Young Arithmetician, or the Reward of Perseverance.
6. The Traveller's Story, or the Village Bar-Room.
7. The Sagacity and Intelligence of the Horse.
8. The Young Sailor, or the Sea-Life of Tow Bowline.
9. The Selfish Girl, a Tale of Truth.
10. Manual or Finger Alphabet, used by the Deaf and Dumb.
11. The Story-Book in Verse.
12. The Flower-Vase, or Pretty Poems for Good little Children.

Fourth Series—Price Six Cents.

1. The Book of Fables, in Prose and Verse
2. The Little Casket, filled with Pleasant Stories.
3. Home Pastimes, or Enigmas, Charades, Rebuses, Conundrums, etc.
4. The Juvenile Sunday-Book, adapted to the Improvement of the Young.
5. William Seaton and the Butterfly, with its Interesting History.
6. The Young Girl's Book of Healthful Amusements and Exercises.
7. Theodore Carleton, or Perseverance against Ill-Fortune.
8. The Aviary, or Child's Book of Birds.
9. The Jungle, or Child's Book of Wild Animals.
10. Sagacity and Fidelity of the Dog, Illustrated by Interesting Anecdotes.
11. Coverings for the Head and Feet, in all Ages and Countries.
12. Romance of Indian History, or Incidents in the Early Settlements.

www.ingramcontent.com/pod-product-compliance
Lightning Source LLC
LaVergne TN
LVHW010230110826
845151LV00004B/1249

* 9 7 8 1 4 2 5 5 2 5 0 3 3 *